THE CATHOLIC CHURCH AND THE FRENCH NATION 1589–1989

Norman Ravitch

ROUTLEDGE

London and New York

First published 1990
by Routledge
11 New Fetter Lane, London EC4P 4EE
29 West 35th Street, New York, NY 10001

Photoset in 10/12 pt Palatino by
Redwood Press Limited, Melksham, Wiltshire
Printed in Great Britain by
Redwood Press Limited

British Library Cataloguing in Publication Data
Ravitch, Norman
The Catholic Church and the French
Nation, 1589–1989
1. France, Catholic Church, History
I. Title
282'.44

ISBN 0–415–00170–6

Library of Congress Cataloging in Publication Data
Ravitch, Norman
The Catholic Church and the French
Nation, 1589–1989 / by Norman Ravitch.
p. m.
Includes bibliographical references.
1. Catholic Church—France—History.
2. Church and state—France—History.
3. France—Church history. I. Title.
BX1530.R32 1991
282'.44'0903—dc20 90–32307

ISBN 0–415–00170–6

In Loving Memory

NICHOLAS LOUIS RAVITCH
(1973–1989)

"Love bears all things, believes all things, hopes all things, endures all things. Love never ends."

(1 Corinthians 13: 7–8)

Contents

Foreword

This volume is not a comprehensive history of the Roman Catholic Church in France during the last 400 years. For such a history one may go to any number of volumes, written individually or collaboratively; books by such historians as André Latreille, René Rémond, François Lebrun, Adrien Dansette, and Gérard Cholvy. These histories seek to be thorough and relatively encyclopedic, and while they are extremely useful they often tend to obscure significant patterns by overwhelming the reader with sheer detail and making little distinction between central and peripheral developments. Here I have attempted something rather different, a thematic and interpretive synthesis, based on the latest scholarship, of the French Catholic Church's quest for an acceptable role and mission in French national life. I seek to elucidate and explain the struggles of the Church with French political and social forces as it sought to define an appropriate role for itself, while certain political and social forces sought to harness the Church for their own needs. The French Church had once been powerful and was from time to time even perceived as a threat to the autonomy and power of the French monarchy. Under the Bourbon kings it became an instrument of conformity and order, a role which over the last four centuries many have sought to perpetuate despite the great changes in French life and thought. By the late twentieth century religion in France had become privatized and the French Church transformed into an expression of nonconformity in a pluralistic society.[1] From having once had a close association with political and social authority, the Church had become just one of a number of groups and institutions seeking to influence Frenchmen and Frenchwomen and the course of national life. It is hoped that both students of modern France in general and those particularly interested in the confrontations of the Roman Catholic Church with the modern world will find this interpretive history stimulating and informative, for it does seek to contribute to an understanding both of French history and of the Roman Catholic Church.

My interests in French history and Church history are long-standing ones, and the work on this volume has tied together in important ways a number of scholarly and personal concerns. Thus, as I have worked out my own understanding of the course of French history and the history of the Roman Catholic Church, I think I have also clarified and deepened my own position concerning this Church, about its prospects in the modern world and the dilemmas of its current and former adherents, and of its opponents.

I should like to think that the remote genesis of this book had something to do with two years spent in the late 1970s in Grenoble, France, where I encountered both the forces of modern Catholicism and the remnants of an older traditional Catholic culture. Attending mass in the Eglise Saint-Louis, a church in the center of town built in the reign of Louis XIV, meant joining mostly very aged people in a dusty, grimy building whose integral beauty was obscured by centuries of dirt. It meant hearing a so-called Gregorian mass, one in which some Latin was retained in a basically French liturgy, while on the church porch and in the street opposite earnest young men hawked literature from the traditionalist and integrist wing of the Church, literature which proclaimed in apocalyptic tones that the Church had been betrayed by liberals and leftists. In the part of town where I lived, however, two very modern church buildings, Saint-Pierre and Saint-Jean, were the scene of a very different liturgy with younger parishioners and whole families from the *quartier*. These people preferred a leaner, more modern liturgy and an atmosphere in which the emphasis was more on community and social service than on mystical contemplation or obstinate opposition to the course of modern life. But here the occasions of family celebration of such rites of passage as First Communion still attracted a far larger crowd than normal Sunday worship, and those drawn to the Church for such ceremonies, the so-called "seasonal Catholics," seemed far more interested in photographing their young sons and daughters than in worshipping the Lord of Hosts or His Christ. At that time I perhaps understood only dimly the scene before me, the contemporary drama of French Catholicism. This book is the result of seeking to explain it to myself. I hope it will also be useful to others.

I could list any number of people in gratitude for their help, but since the obstacles to this book were as much personal as scholarly, I should like especially to thank those whose affection, concern, and support were the most important for me: John Arul, Kenneth D. Barkin, David K. Glidden, Helen Lee Laird, Jeffrey B. Russell, A. Mark Smith, and Irwin M. Wall. This book is dedicated to my son, Nicholas Louis Ravitch who, despite his residence in Grenoble, certainly would have preferred that I had written a novel.

Norman Ravitch
Riverside, California

I

Towards a royal religion: the establishment of conformity. From the Catholic League through the reign of Louis XIV

Several months before his death in 1715, King Louis XIV decreed that those of his subjects who had once been Protestants or were the children of Protestant parents would henceforth be considered members of the Roman Catholic Church. This curious proclamation was the Sun King's way of affirming that there were no longer in France any recognized dissenters from the Roman Catholic religion of the king. This claim was anything but a generous decision to ignore the "Protestant Problem," for what Louis XIV intended was that any blacksliding into Protestantism by former members of the "Pretended Reformed Religion" would be met with the full severity of the law. The king died in the hope and belief that he had essentially solved France's problem of religious disunity. And outwardly he was correct. At the time of his death in 1715, virtually everyone in France appeared to be conforming to the Catholic Church and its disciplinary requirements, as interpreted by the "Most Christian King" in the kingdom which was styled "the Eldest Daughter of the Church." These sobriquets were designed to emphasize the special place held by the French kingdom and its monarch within Roman Catholic Christendom, a tradition of 700 years' duration by the time of the death of Louis XIV. No other monarchy and no other State in Christendom could boast of such an unbroken spiritual and institutional loyalty.

The concern with Protestantism was but a part, a small part, of a more general concern in the absolute monarchy of Bourbon France. The larger question involved whether or not religion would be a certain support for, or a challenge to, the authority of the monarchy. The small number of Protestants was finally dealt with only after the religion of the vast majority of the population, the Roman Catholic faith, had been made a firm ally of the king and had been intimately intertwined into the fabric of the monarchy and the social order. The Protestants were almost an afterthought in the completion of a task which occupied the kings and ministers of the seventeenth century: to render the Church unable to harm or compromise royal authority, while the State enjoyed all the considerable advantages of its moral authority over the population as a whole. Protestant dissidents could finally be dealt with confidently by the monarchy because the sources of Catholic opposition to royal policy had already been undermined, and a unity of throne and altar had been built with materials designed to last forever. Louis XIV thought he could die assured that the occasional signs of Protestant obstinacy might safely be ignored, for the much more important task of making Catholicism wholly royalist had already been accomplished.

When the king attended daily mass in his royal chapel in the palace of Versailles, he normally knelt and faced the altar while a priest there made the Body and Blood of the Saviour manifest. As he worshipped before the sacrificial mystery on the altar before him, his courtiers, with their backs to God on the altar, faced their king in an attitude of respect and reverence. While the king worshipped his Maker directly, his chief servants appeared to worship Him only indirectly through their reverence for their kneeling monarch. What better sign could there have been of the total appropriation of the Catholic faith by the monarchy? Frenchmen in the royal chapel could well believe with their own eyes what many of their preachers proclaimed, that the king was a god on earth. One served God by serving the king; one displeased God in displeasing the king. The only religion which could be pleasing to God was the religion of the king. Nonconformity thus had no place in the France built by the Bourbon kings and their ministers.

It is true that this scene of the court at prayer, as depicted by La Bruyère, actually reflected conditions early in the reign of the Sun King. Saint-Simon presented a somewhat different picture for the later years of the reign, when a more pious Louis XIV required his courtiers to remain kneeling between the *Sanctus* and the communion of the priest and to be attentive to the liturgy. But the king's later display of piety should not obscure the fact that the earlier practice represented the victory of monarchy over religion, a victory which made the more conspicuous religiosity of the king's old age possible without any undesirable consequences for the fullness of his authority.[1]

ROYALISM OR CATHOLICISM

In 1610 Louis XIII had requested from the Pope and won permission for the observance of the feast of St Louis, king of France, to be made obligatory in the kingdom. This was a liturgical confirmation of the long-standing Catholic character of the French dynasty.[2] The sanctity of Louis IX had given to the Capetian dynasty of France the spiritual legitimacy it required, since the replacement of the first Catholic dynasty, the Frankish Merovingians, by the Carolingians and their subsequent replacement by the Capetians in the late tenth century might have provided an unfortunate example of the mutability of dynasties. The Franks had been the only Germanic tribe within the frontiers of the former Roman Empire never to have been Arian heretics, and Gregory of Tours had regarded them as a people chosen by God to defend true religion in an age of disorder and violence. Popes like St Gregory I in the sixth century and Stephen II in the eighth century had cultivated the support of the Franks and had been willing to flatter the Frankish rulers with recognition of their pre-eminence over all other kings and in the affection of the Roman See.[3] Thus the mutual dependence of the French monarchy and the Roman Catholic Church was a very old one, as old as the acceptance of orthodox Christianity in France and, because of the disintegration of Roman Imperial authority in the west, morally equivalent to a re-establishment of Christianity there. Whatever doubts could have been entertained about the Capetian dynasty and its complete legitimacy were removed by the support of the Church for the Capetians and the benefit derived from the holiness of Louis IX for all his royal descendants. The sanctity of St Louis operated vicariously and effectively through the Salic Law. The idea that the Salic Law – namely, inheritance solely in the direct male line – was the sole determinant of legitimate succession to the French throne implied that a certain line of male rulers had been fore-ordained to rule. This myth, gaining currency particularly in the fifteenth century, had had the virtue of simplicity: one needed to know nothing about law, philosophy, or history to understand that God selected the French king by direct male succession. Such a procedure was believed unique to the French and a sign of God's favor and of their special chosenness. Other peoples might acquire their kings through conquest, marriage, war, or the vicissitudes of fortune, but happy France had a biologically guaranteed line of succession. In the words of Pierre Pithou, a partisan of Henry of Navarre,

> we wish a natural king and head, not an artificial one; a king already made and not one to be made; . . . the king we wish is already made by nature, born in the true garden of the lillies of France, a straight and green shoot from the stock of St. Louis. . . . One can make scepters and crowns, but not the kings to bear them. . . .[4]

Royalist lawyers believed not even the king could alter the provisions of the Salic Law, for it was part of the fundamental law of the realm: the king could no more destroy his own sovereignty than God could violate his own laws.[5]

This Salic Law, which from 987 to 1774 was to give thirty-two kings to France,[6] made the Capetians the longest unbroken dynasty known to Europe. Only the monarchy of Japan with its alleged descent from the Sun Goddess can claim a longer and more sacred legitimacy and unbroken line. The myth of the Salic Law, by removing female inheritance, operated to prevent, it was believed, the French crown from falling into the hands of foreigners. But it naturally could not work automatically to exclude bad Christians from the throne. God evidently provided a biological guarantee of legitimacy for the French monarchy but not a theological or moral guarantee. All the more important was it for each French monarch, then, to take with utter seriousness his obligations to defend true religion and to battle against error. As Claude de Seysell explained in the early sixteenth century:

> When the Christian faith appeared, France was among the first of the distant nations to receive it, and having received it kept it completely and constantly beyond all other realms and peoples without ever nourishing any monster of heresy. . . . The princes and peoples of France always have been more ardent and more prompt than any others to wipe out heretics and infidels and to defend the Roman Catholic church. Even to this day all the nations of Christianity come to learn theology at the University of Paris, as the true fountain whence flows forth the perfect doctrine. There-

> fore, this realm is called the most Christian and the kings most Christian.
>
> So it is essential that whoever is king here make known to the people by example and by present and overt demonstration that he is a zealous observant of the Christian faith and wishes to maintain and augment it to the best of his ability. If the people had another opinion of him, they would hate him and perhaps obey him but ill. Moreover, this people would impute all the troubles that came to the realm to the erroneous creed and imperfect religion of the king.[7]

Claude de Seysell could naturally not foresee that in a half century the Salic Law and religious disunity would bring to the throne of France a man who was biologically but not theologically fit to continue the rule of the God-favored dynasty of the Capetians.

The crisis of the sixteenth-century Reformation was everywhere capable of calling into question the close cooperation of political and religious authority. The Christian religion, we are sometimes in danger of forgetting, always has needed the power of the State to enforce uniformity of worship. St Augustine, in his battle against the Donatists, had held that sinful man needed more than purely spiritual pressure to obey Church law and discipline; he needed also to be coerced by the State. The Donatists had found to their sorrow that they could not ignore the coercive power of the State.[8] The Church had always conceded great privileges to the monarchs and princes in return for their powerful assistance, and despite struggles over the relative authority of Church and State, the Church had become accustomed to a certain dependence on the State. From the perspective not of high politics, where the dramatic struggles over rival authority were played out, but of social life on the local level, Church–State rivalry was essentially absent: the two institutions were seen to be virtually one.[9] Unlike England, the Scandinavian kingdoms, and many of the German states where Protestantism became established and was the firm support of authority, and unlike the Spanish kingdoms and Italian states where heresy was completely eliminated, France alone seemed the theater of perpetual civil war around the issue of religious reform. Thirty years of religious warfare threatened public order and the very survival of the State and monarchy. The conversion of a large minority of Frenchmen to Calvinism – and an important minority, since it included large numbers of the high nobility – raised deadly issues for the French monarchy. For French Catholics a distinction between patriotism and religion was normally inconceivable, since the State had always been the civic expression of the community's religious commitment. In Catholic eyes, converts to Protestantism became doubtful Frenchmen when they abandoned the true faith for heresy. Early in the period of the religious wars no one in France asked whether one should consider religion or monarchy as more important. They were viewed as totally one.[10]

In the midst of the upheaval and cruelties of the French religious wars it became apparent by 1584, with the death of the duc d'Anjou, that the Salic Law would bring to the throne of France a relapsed heretic, Henri de Bourbon, king of Navarre. As distant a blood relation as he was to the ruling monarch, Henry III, and despite his possession of an independent, miniature kingdom in the Pyrenees, Henry of Navarre was the legitimate heir according to the Salic myth and as thoroughly French as anyone could wish. He was no foreigner, but his Protestant faith made him to many Catholics worse than a foreigner. Here was the unexpected crisis: the legal myth designed to provide for an orderly succession of legitimate rulers, one after the other, was bringing to the throne a man who was biologically but not theologically suitable for his high office. The Holy or Catholic League was revived at this critical juncture over this very issue: whether a heretic could succeed to the throne of St Louis. The position of the League had a simple clarity and single-minded purpose, the exclusion of Henry of Navarre from the throne. As Louis Dorléans, a League pamphleteer, claimed, divine law took precedence over even the Salic Law. The practices of the pagan Salian Franks had to give way to a more fundamental law: the king must be a Catholic and defend the true faith. When all the variety of opinions among members of the Catholic League are taken into account, the one consistent thing in all League belief and action was the absolute need for religious unity, for upon religious unity rested the only possibility of national unity. France, if it would continue at all, must continue to be Catholic.

Those influenced by modern ideas of tolerance and secular notions of political authority may find it difficult to take seriously the concerns of the ultra-Catholics of the League in the crisis of the last two decades of the sixteenth century. It would be simple perhaps, especially with the wisdom of hindsight, to view the opposition to Henry of Navarre as an example of bigotry or fanaticism. But those who opposed him while he was still a Calvinist felt justified in fearing that he would harm the Catholic faith of France and even try to establish Calvinism in its place. These fears were not unreasonable in the light of the record of his mother, Jeanne d'Albret, in the kingdom of Navarre where Catholicism had been suppressed, despite assurances to the contrary. All Protestant rulers in the sixteenth century had disestablished the Catholic faith in their realms; indeed, the only true example of real religious toleration in the entire sixteenth century was in Catholic Poland![11]

As an heretic, the son of an heretical mother who had been violent against the Catholic Church, and himself a formerly insincere convert to Catholicism, Henry of Navarre was in perfectly good faith mistrusted by the adherents of the Catholic League. His accession to the throne would throw into total chaos all that they held holy. But the abandonment of the Salic myth was equally intolerable and a fearful step. This was the crisis to which religious disunity had brought the French monarchy at the end of the sixteenth century.

The crisis of the French monarchy was actually a dual one: the struggle over the question of the line of succession was preceded and accompanied by a conflict about the right to depose an evil ruler and the whole question of tyrannicide. After Henry III arranged the murder of the ultra-Catholic leader, the duc de Guise, and of his brother, the Cardinal of Lorraine, and after he rallied to the cause of Henry of Navarre as his heir and successor, the Catholic League in Paris moved to set up its own government and obtained from the Sorbonne theologians the decision that Henry III had lost the legitimate obedience of his subjects. In April 1589, the Paris Theology Faculty struck from the Canon of the mass the traditional words of intercession for the king and replaced them with prayers "pro Christianis nostris Principibus," an act essentially granting spiritual approval for the king's deposition. The murder of the king on 1 August 1589 was the act of a lay brother in the Dominican Order who had been directly influenced by the propaganda and preaching of pro-League churchmen. The League regarded the assassin, Jacques Clément, as a martyr, since it adhered to traditional medieval ideas concerning the right to depose an evil ruler, and it went on to endorse radical theories of popular sovereignty and tyrannicide. On the same basis, the League encouraged the attempt against the life of Henry of Navarre, now Henry IV, in 1594. The would-be assassin on that occasion, Jean Chastel, claimed that the king could be killed because he was an insincere convert to the Catholic faith and had not received papal absolution for his heresy.[12] Thus the question of the royal succession was intimately and fatally tied to the even more difficult question of the relative power of a ruler *vis-à-vis* the Church and the Christian people.

While the traditional teaching of the medieval Church about tyrannicide contained many ambiguities, orthodoxy in this matter was found essentially in the theology of St Thomas Aquinas. His views formed the basis equally of Catholic and Calvinist doctrines on tyrannicide which held that while mere subjects of a king could not rebel against him or kill him, public bodies in certain circumstances might legitimately do so. In addition, it was held possible that certain individuals might receive a special mandate from God to act decisively against evil rulers. The essential agreement between traditional Catholic and Calvinist views guaranteed the wide dissemination of these ideas in a France beset with religious warfare between those very two confessional communities, for among the principal Protestant reformers only Martin Luther had unequivocally condemned all recourse to tyrannicide. French Calvinists, between the Massacre of St Bartholomew's Day in 1572 and the death of the last Catholic heir to the throne in 1584, had under the pressure of their desperation pushed John Calvin's doctrines to extremes, extremes which they quickly abandoned when Henry of Navarre's royal prospects improved, only to be emulated thereupon by the preachers and propagandists of the League who sought equally desperate solutions to their equally desperate plight. League theories went even further than the normative teachings of the medieval theologians, for the Leaguers advanced a radical defense of the right of individuals convinced of their special calling to take the law into their own hands and proposed ideas of popular sovereignty which frightened even many of their own supporters.[13]

The attempts on Henry IV's life, including the successful one in 1610, would be the work of individuals convinced that the king's conversion had been insincere. Certainly someone could in good conscience have doubted Henry's sincerity, since his foreign policy vigorously opposed the House of Habsburg which sought to lead the worldwide Catholic cause against heresy, and Henry extended support to Protestant princes in Germany and even to Moriscos in Spain. The Edict of Nantes, more a unique interim solution to the problem of religious diversity than a true policy of toleration, appeared to ultra-Catholics to be less the work of a ruler sworn to the extirpation of heresy than the duplicity of a crypto-heretic. Finally, Henry IV's devotion to the papacy was considered a sham, since he supported all those seeking to counter Roman authority, whether French Gallicans or English and Venetian opponents of the papacy. While the theology and preaching which could convince ultra-Catholics of the need to eliminate this evil ruler were rather widespread among Catholics, it was the Jesuit Order which got most of the opprobrium for the teaching of tyrannicide. Because of their prominence and also, on occasion, their remarkable ineptitude, the Jesuits were almost uniquely identified with dangerous and radical notions of political revolution and tyrannicide, ideas which actually had been at the core of much Christian political theology for some time. The murder of Henry IV by Ravaillac, the second royal assassination in a single generation, seemed to indicate how dangerous certain religious ideas could be for the maintenance of order and authority. The passions of ultra-Catholics were seen as having thus endangered the monarchy and the nation in two ways from 1584 to 1610: they had called into question the validity and sanctity of the Salic myth which was deemed so vital for the stability of the royal succession, and they had disseminated dangerous notions which would subject kings to churchmen and incite mere subjects to take the law into their own hands. The reaction against the teaching of tyrannicide was so intense that the Jesuits were expelled from the jurisdiction of the Parlement of Paris between 1594 and 1603. The librarian of their Collège de Clermont was hanged for the crime of merely owning a collection of pamphlets approving tyrannicide. If severe or capital punishment for mere belief or advocacy, as opposed to overt criminal action, is a sign of how heinous certain ideas are regarded, this severe punishment clearly indicated the degree of turpitude placed on the theory of tyrannicide.[14] The only comparable examples would be in the law during the French Revolution decreeing the death penalty for advocacy of a "loi agraire" and perhaps also in the prosecution of

American communists in the post-Second World War era for advocacy of the overthrow of the United States government "by force and violence."

French royalists, men who had made their careers, spent their resources, and even risked their lives in the cause of Henry of Navarre's accession to the throne, came to agree with King James I of England that Catholic political theology, along with Calvinism, was the deadly enemy of royal authority. Lawyers, jurists, Parlement magistrates, and royal officials made it their special concern in the early seventeenth century to find ways of making religion the support of royal authority and not a deadly threat to it.[15] During the years of struggle against the Catholic League, these men had been called "Politiques" because they rejected the view of extremists among Catholics and Protestants alike in the Age of the Reformation that political obligation should be one with moral obligation.[16] The "Politiques" were opposed to an ideology which a later century would denigrate with the label of "enthusiasm." But they were also forced to find a religious justification for their support of Henry of Navarre, both for the sake of their and others' tender consciences and to prevent religion from being used with deadly efficacy against them. Their solution was the theory of the "divine right of kings" which utilized the sanction of religion in a way directly opposed to the manner in which the preachers of the League had employed it: it eliminated the role of the Pope and the clergy in disciplining a king and worked towards making him answerable to God alone. The theory of divine right became the means of reappropriating the mantle of religion for the support of monarchy after the dangerous utilization by the Leaguers of the traditional, medieval ideas about resistance to the authority of a sinful or heretical ruler.[17]

The experience of the League, with its threat of social revolution, had demonstrated that the danger in medieval notions of the subordination of secular rulers to the Church lay not only in the excessive power they gave to the spiritual authority, not only in a theocratic threat. There was also a democratic threat, for the Church's suspension of the subjects' obedience to a sinful king could withdraw the final restraint on the revolution of the poor against their betters. The rule of the League in Paris had been at once the experience of theocracy and of radical populism against the political and social hierarchy. Indeed, modern commentators on ideas of the direct or indirect power of the Popes to intervene in secular affairs have emphasized that until modern and secular means of limiting royal power could be devised, the Church's right to intervene remained the only means of preventing despotism and oppression.[18] It was in the theories of the divine right of kings that the answer to both theocracy and democracy was found. Bourbon absolutism was built on this concern and understanding: religion was to be used to support not to endanger royal authority.

A ROYAL CATHOLICISM

Because the theories about the Pope's power to intervene in temporal affairs were blamed for the murder of Henry III and Henry IV, royalists in France, especially the magistrates of the Parlements who were at that time the leaders of the Third Estate, sought to have clearly recognized the principle that the authority of the king was absolutely independent of all ecclesiastical sanction. Although the Gallicans and even the Sorbonne theologians officially as late as 1663 continued to hold that the Pope had the power to discipline a king, they nevertheless insisted that his excommunication had to be confirmed by a General Council of the Church, and the first half of the seventeenth century saw a radical evolution towards the clear view that the king could not be deposed at all, even in the case of an ecclesiastical condemnation for heresy. While magistrates, theologians, and churchmen all generally agreed that regicide was intolerable, churchmen normally hesitated to abandon entirely the right of the Church to relieve subjects from obedience to an heretical ruler. They rejected the view of the Third Estate at the Estates General of 1614–15 that the only remedy for an un-Catholic or an evil king was prayer and resignation.

The position of the French Third Estate was essentially the position also underlying the Oath of Allegiance demanded of Englishmen by James I, an Erastian position subversive of the traditional rights of the Church. But while the French monarchy at that time sided with the clergy and the nobility to reject the Third Estate's espousal of the absolute independence of the secular authority, in fact the Erastian position of the Third Estate none the less quickly gained ground. Since the three orders were deeply divided among themselves on this and many other issues, the crown was able to function in its customary way as an arbiter between them. On the inflammatory matter of the extreme demands of the Third Estate, everyone was forced to rely for pacification on the good offices of the crown: the nuncio and the Pope, as well as the nobility and the clergy. By 1625 the French bishops were already accepting the view, later to be made notorious by Bossuet, that there was no earthly recourse against an evil king. Bossuet would draw from the legal tradition of his own family and from the experience of disorder during the Fronde the lesson that no disorder could be worse than rebellion. His teaching about the independence of the king can be found not only in his *Politique tirée de l'Ecriture Sainte* but also, more importantly, in the Four Gallican Articles of 1682 which, while they appeared to favor bishops and councils over Popes, in fact also proclaimed the divine right of kings as totally free from the disciplinary power of the Church.

The Four Gallican Articles represented a coming together of several long-standing traditions of the Gallican Church. It is no longer believed by historians of this period that the Articles were really imposed upon an unwilling clergy. Certainly Bossuet was, in his leading role at the Assembly of the Clergy of 1682, expressing his true views about the relation of the monarchy to the Roman See; he was not simply trying to please an aggressive king in the prime of life. Even Article I, the least traditionally Gallican of the Four Articles, had the almost unanimous support of the Assembly of the Clergy, for no one there wanted, in the reign of an apparently completely orthodox king, to contemplate the possibility of an heretical monarch.[19] Bossuet had also been very careful not to include in the Gallican Articles the idea, later to be so beloved of eighteenth-century Gallicans and Jansenists, that an individual Catholic could appeal a papal decision to a future General Council whenever his individual conscience demanded it. Thus the Gallican Articles served to protect royal authority equally against Popes, Councils, and individual consciences.[20]

THE MONARCHY AND JANSENISM

The year 1709 was a very bad one for the France of Louis XIV. After almost a decade of war against a British-led coalition determined to prevent Louis XIV from achieving European hegemony by exploiting the accession of the Bourbons to the throne of Spain and its vast empire, France was on the verge of being brought to its knees. Along with serious military defeats, famine and financial bankruptcy seemed likely to force the proud Sun King to seek an ignominious peace with his princely enemies, who included virtually all the rulers of Europe. As if to assert that he still had power in the midst of the evident decline of his strength, or perhaps out of sheer vindictiveness, Louis took time and trouble to pursue and finish off an old enemy within France itself, the Jansenists of Port-Royal-des-Champs. He suppressed the convent, symbol of so much opposition to his religious policy, and had the police forcibly remove the remaining nuns to other religious houses around the country. The remains of those nuns and *solitaires* buried at Port-Royal who had enjoyed some degree of social standing were unceremoniously disinterred and removed elsewhere, while the rest of the dead were thrown into a common grave. Thus the living and the dead among the Jansenists were the king's final victims. In 1711 all the buildings were levelled to the ground, and Port-Royal was all but forgotten for 100 years until the age of Revolution and Romanticism made it a place of pilgrimage on behalf of liberty and individualism. This extraordinary act of hatred could only mean that Louis XIV had indeed persuaded himself that Jansenism had been a deadly enemy to the authority he exercised and to the absolute, administrative monarchy he had brought to an unequalled level of perfection. An understanding of the opposition to Jansenism on the part of the kings and the chief ministers of the seventeenth century is central in appreciating the degree to which religion was made an integral part of the royalist establishment and ideology. Louis' vindictive acts of 1709 and 1711, in the midst of what one might consider more immediate problems, could only mean that the war against religious dissidents was as important to him as his many wars against the princes and states of Europe. Sainte-Beuve described the planning and execution of the final destruction of the Jansenist convent as having been undertaken as carefully and deliberately as if it were "the equal of a coup d'Etat," and this against twenty-two nuns and lay sisters of whom the youngest was 50 years old and several of the oldest over 80.[21] What led Louis XIV to such extraordinary measures and what did Port-Royal and Jansenism really mean to him?

Suspicion of and hostility to Jansenism on the part of the kings and chief ministers of the seventeenth century had become something of a tradition by the time of Louis XIV's assumption of the direction of royal affairs. He apparently had learned from Cardinal Mazarin, along with the basic workings of the monarchy and the need to raise the throne above all factions and classes, a healthy concern about those members of the élite who doggedly defended the theological views of Cornelius Jansen and the Abbé de Saint-Cyran, the founders of Jansenism. Mazarin in his day had inherited suspicion of the Jansenists from Cardinal Richelieu, as he had learned so many other things from his predecessor. There are unfortunately all too many pitfalls in a modern attempt to understand the nature of Jansenism, the threat to authority which some perceived to see in it, and the motives of kings and ministers in opposing the movement. In its narrowest concerns Jansenism would appear to have been, at its core, theological and moral, with tangential, if any, relevance to political affairs. In addition, in the course of time and as a reaction to opposition and persecution, it was capable of many twists and turns. This was certainly true in the eighteenth century when it came to seem significantly more political than religious, but even in the seventeenth century there were different kinds of Jansenists and different sorts of Jansenisms. Finally, all modern attempts to distinguish between political and religious motives are perhaps bound to fail or, what is worse, to distort, for the idea that religion has nothing properly to do with politics and with social concerns is a modern idea which stems from the privatization of religion, itself the result of modern secularism and something utterly alien to the years before the nineteenth century. Still, historians seek to know whether a particular policy of Richelieu or Mazarin concerning Jansenists was religious or political in nature. Jansenism and both its supporters and opponents have for more than 300 years excited the curiosity and passions of historians, theologians, and literary scholars, without anything like an adequate consensus about its importance in French life emerging. Yet an attempt must be made to integrate the policy of the French monarchy in the seventeenth century towards Jansenism into our understanding of the creation and strengthening of royal Catholicism. Opposition to Jansenism in fact became a central part of the absolute monarchy's program for the domestication of religion and its appropriation by the throne.

There are facts about Jansenism which can be at once true and yet misleading. One particularly misleading fact is the evident alliance, at first tactical and finally virtually indissolubly conjugal, between the Jansenists and the magistrates of the Parlement of Paris: an alliance between Jansenism and Gallicanism. Members of the *noblesse de robe* and of the subordinate legal profession were indeed early among the leading supporters of the Jansenists, and in the face of royal opposition and persecution perhaps only the Parlement of Paris could and did give the Jansenists any meaningful institutional support. Both Saint-Beuve in the nineteenth century and Lucien Goldmann, a mid-twentieth-century Marxist literary historian, insisted that Jansenism was the form of spirituality expressive of the needs and interests of a certain upper-bourgeois élite, a social connection which could not be ignored or underestimated, despite all the evident difficulties in evaluating it definitively.[22] Yet the connection of the Jansenists with the Gallican magistrates of the Parlement of Paris obscures the true origins of Jansenism: it was part of the *dévot* movement of the Catholic Reformation in France of which the Catholic League of the late sixteenth century was the earliest manifestation. Jansenism in its origins was not tied to the Erastianism of the *politique* magistrates at all but was, instead, part of the attempt to battle against Protestant heresy by means of a thorough reform of French Catholicism, with full acceptance of the decrees of the Council of Trent and the conversion of the élite. Both Cornelius Jansen and the Abbé de Saint-Cyran came from home regions where religious rivalry between Catholics and Calvinists was very real, and their revival of a certain Augustinianism was their Catholic answer to the intellectual, theological, and disciplinary thrust of Calvinism. In a sense, they so resented the Protestant appropriation of Pauline and Augustinian theology that they were determined to struggle to make this theology dominant in the Catholic Church which had given it birth and to exclude the alternate theological approaches introduced by the Jesuits, with whom they bitterly disagreed over the way of meeting the need of reform and the Protestant challenge.

There were several kinds of Gallicanism in the France of the sixteenth and seventeenth centuries, depending on whether the traditional theories of the autonomy of the French Catholic Church were being interpreted by kings and their ministers, by bishops and other high ecclesiastics, by Sorbonne theologians, by learned parish priests, or by the magistrates of the Parlements. All forms of Gallicanism involved some degree of wariness about the intentions of the Roman See and considerable pride in the place of France among the Catholic states of Christendom. In the midst of the religious wars, when the dilemma of a Protestant heir to the throne of St Louis had first arisen to trouble consciences, Henry, duc de Guise, had daringly attacked Gallicanism as the particular aberration of the Capetian dynasty and promised that if he were made king, he would fully restore the French Church to full Roman obedience. In turn, the Leaguers who followed him made it very well known that they favored full acceptance and implementation in France of the decrees of the Council of Trent. In 1593 the Estates General of the League, which assembled in order to elect a king in the place of Henry of Navarre, voted to accept the Council of Trent in its entirety; that is, to accept not only its theological decrees (not a problem in France) but also its decisions about discipline and reform. Gallicans believed that acceptance of these disciplinary decrees would destroy the Gallican liberties of the French Church and make it more defenseless against Roman encroachments. The Church and clergy tried unsuccessfully under Henry IV and Louis XIII to have the decrees of Trent accepted in France, but the opposition of the Gallicans was always effective in thwarting their desires. The assassination of Henry III and Henry IV persuaded the magistrates of the Parlement of Paris and other Gallican circles that Rome placed in serious jeopardy the national independence of the French State and the security of the monarch by its support for teaching about the superiority of the spiritual power over secular rulers. The French clergy was finally reduced in 1615 to having its own Assembly formally receive the Tridentine decrees, for nothing positive could be expected from the Parlement of Paris or the Estates General. While reform of the French Church was certainly not opposed by the Gallicans, they wished the reform to be undertaken without subservience to the decrees of Trent and the Roman See which had closely supervised the deliberations of that Council.[23] Although the Abbé de Saint-Cyran was later to express some reservations about the Council of Trent,[24] he and Cornelius Jansen shared fully the desire of the French clergy to further the goals of the Catholic Reformation. Their position was that of the *dévots*, not that of the Gallicans.

Saint-Cyran can even be said to have become the effective head of the *dévot* party in the 1630s because of his connections and friendship with the leading figures of the French Catholic Reformation. The *dévot* party was viewed by influential members of the magistracy and by other royal officials as the direct heirs of the Catholic League and, as such, the partisans of Spain, Rome, and other opponents of the French State. They were tarred with the brush of regicide, for their preference for religious belief and sentiment over dynastic–national objectives was held the cause of the murder of two kings and the devastation of the religious wars. Although Richelieu had himself first entered court circles through the patronage of the *dévot* party, his political development went in the opposite direction from theirs: where they emphasized the struggle against Protestantism in Europe and accepted the leadership of the Catholic Habsburgs, thus favoring an alliance with the dynastic enemies of France in opposition to religious heresy, Richelieu came to place French dynastic interests first. He behaved like a true heir of the *politique* tradition, developing his conception of *raison d'état* within the framework of *politique* political theory which taught that French and European religious disunity, however unfortunate a fact, required politics to be conducted apart from theological considerations. He also held traditional Gallican views about the religious qualities and goals of the French monarchy which necessitated rejection of the claims of the House of Habsburg to leadership of the Catholic cause, claims which even some Popes had feared and, when able to do so, had rejected. Richelieu seems to have believed sincerely that a Christian monarch and his ministers could pursue *raison d'état* without thereby necessarily separating politics from morality, but the clearly practical result of such attempts can be seen in retrospect to have been the secularization of politics.[25]

Richelieu believed that he had good reason to fear the particular subordination of politics and dynastic interest to international Catholic interests which the political program of the *dévot* party required. If successful, such a policy would have opened France up to the dangers of foreign and civil war, as during the religious wars of the previous century, and would have placed France in subordination to the House of Habsburg, whose territories surrounded France on virtually every frontier. In addition, the king's mother and brother and many members of the highest nobility were eager to recover their power and would not hesitate to exploit an ultra-Catholic program towards this end. Perhaps the most famous example of Richelieu's sensitivity to the use of religion against royal policy was his demand in 1637 that Louis XIII dismiss his confessor, the Jesuit Father Nicolas Caussin.

Although a Jesuit, Caussin was no lax moral theologian. He had believed it his duty to show the king that some of his official policies were morally questionable. Caussin used the confessional to arouse the king's scruples over his split with his family and his pursuit of war against Catholic Spain on the side of Protestant allies in Germany, and he had done this by taking the more spiritually demanding theological position that a penitent sinner required *contrition* before absolution could be given. Richelieu had himself written a work of moral theology holding that the less demanding *attrition* was sufficient, a position consistent with the Council of Trent, although the Council had been as unable to settle this question definitively as it had been to deal with the question of free will and predestination which lay at the heart of the disputes between Augustinians and Jesuits. Thus the more rigorous moral position, one that appealed to Saint-Cyran and his followers, had serious political consequences. In Richelieu's mind the theological and the political were thus inextricably joined: the rigorist position held by those soon to be called Jansenists was directly connected to the ultra-Catholic political policies which he regarded as disastrous for the power and survival of the French crown.

Richelieu's perceived need to defend the doctrine of attrition for political as well as religious reasons came only two years after Cornelius Jansen had published a bitter attack on Richelieu's foreign policy, the *Mars Gallicus*, in which he had supported the primacy of religious values and the interests of international Catholicism over purely secular French concerns. Jansen had in fact rejected typical French apprehensions about the Habsburgs' own misuse of religion for their own purely dynastic purposes and had threatened those who fought against the "Catholic" side in the Thirty Years War with eternal damnation. For Jansen, who at the time of his death held the bishopric of Ypres in the Spanish Netherlands, the Thirty Years War was a war of religion, while for Richelieu it was evidently a dynastic war, or what modern historians might prefer to call a modern war between nation states "in-the-making." Jansen's views were undiplomatic enough and rigid enough to embarrass his friend, Saint-Cyran, but Richelieu definitely held Saint-Cyran responsible for this attack upon his cherished conception of *raison d'état*. Jansen had stated the basic issues between ultra-Catholicism and royal Erastianism very well indeed, and Richelieu came quickly to believe that he had in Saint-Cyran, a man he had once admired and whose cooperation he had once sought, a dangerous opponent – a potential center around which could assemble all the opponents of his ambitions for the independence and greatness of the French monarchy. This seems clearly the most important reason leading Richelieu to have Saint-Cyran imprisoned in 1638.[26]

Historians have argued ever since that event about why Saint-Cyran was imprisoned. Some have argued on behalf of theological motives, without convincing those who view Richelieu as essentially worldly that he really would have found harm in abstruse theological doctrines. Others have emphasized political motives exclusively, without being able to show that Saint-Cyran posed any sort of threat to Richelieu's power. One respected authority on Jansenism writes that "unfortunately for the historian, there is far more evidence to account for Richelieu's personal hostility towards Saint-Cyran than there is to show that such hostility existed; the antipathy itself has been argued *a posteriori* from the fact of Saint-Cyran's imprisonment. . . ."[27] In Lucien Goldmann's Marxist interpretation, what Richelieu feared most in Saint-Cyran and his followers was their advocacy of withdrawal from the world, which if followed by the élite would pose great dangers for the absolute monarchy that was being constructed. Goldmann's search for the social roots and significance of Jansenism is stimulating and exciting, but his contention that Richelieu primarily feared the consequences of Saint-Cyran's asceticism remains pure speculation.[28] It was also the height of irony that the monarchy would push the Jansenists into various forms of resistance to the crown; the Jansenists would thereby finally become known and notorious for anything but passivity and withdrawal. But when the incidents involving Father Caussin and the publication of the *Mars Gallicus* are carefully considered, Richelieu's position, if necessarily understood somewhat on the basis of circumstantial evidence, seems clear enough: Saint-Cyran and his devoted followers, those soon enough to be called Jansenists, were the heirs of those ultra-Catholics who had brought France virtually to the point of dissolution through the initiatives of the Catholic League, and they were potentially just as dangerous in Richelieu's day, when the Habsburgs were again involved in a war in which a "Catholic" victory would mean serious defeat for the independence of the

French monarchy and State, and the dangers of aristocratic uprisings still haunted those trying to build up the power of the monarchy. This understanding of Richelieu's action against Saint-Cyran and of his suspicion of the Jansenists seems the most convincing that modern historians can suggest. Ronald Knox's charming conclusion that in Saint-Cyran Richelieu "smelt the heresiarch" is unfortunately just pious piffle.[29]

Cardinal Mazarin viewed the problem of Jansenism in the same way as his predecessor. Whatever differences there were between his policy and that of Richelieu stemmed most likely from Mazarin's status as a layman: he had none of Richelieu's interest in theological questions. Mazarin also observed the beginnings of what would be the characteristic traits of the Jansenists, their dogged refusal to conform to royal or papal policy and their continual appeal to individual conscience and public opinion. This was why he could regard them as *frondeur* in spirit even if they had not actually participated in the Fronde rebellion of the magistrates and the nobility. It was enough that for reasons of their own they, along with the lower clergy in Paris, supported the cause of his chief adversary, the Cardinal de Retz. The Jansenists' recourse to the defense of spiritual individualism and the lower clergy's support for *Richérisme*, an ecclesiological position giving greater authority and prestige to the ordinary priests and less to the episcopate, emphasized for Mazarin the dangers to social hierarchy and royal absolutism in all dissident religious parties and positions. Mazarin was also fully Richelieu's heir in his pursuit of *raison d'état*. His foreign policy, particularly the alliance with Oliver Cromwell and the war with Spain, offended Catholic opinion and tarnished his reputation in Rome. As much as Richelieu he needed to prevent religion from being used to undermine his political objectives. It is not clear whether he truly feared the Jansenists or merely pretended concern in a cynical manipulation of the Jansenist problem in order to placate Pope Alexander VII. Once the Roman authorities understood that the French were occupied with the disciples of Jansen and Saint-Cyran, they were eager to seize the opportunity to discipline the excessively independent Gallican Church and happy to have Roman authority recognized and relied upon by the French crown. Mazarin may have been more Machiavellian than even Richelieu in the whole Jansenist matter, but the clear conclusion remains none the less that Mazarin passed on Richelieu's attitude towards the Jansenists essentially unchanged to his young charge, Louis XIV.[30]

Whatever Mazarin conveyed to the young Louis XIV about the dangers of Jansenist religious dissidence was necessarily devoid of any theological content: Mazarin had no interest in such arcane debates and Louis no deep understanding of the religion he professed. The king had been taught only a few basic prayers by his devout Spanish mother, and while in daily attendance at mass in the royal chapel at Versailles he characteristically recited the rosary because he could not follow the liturgy very well. The king's religious knowledge was thus roughly on the level of that of a peasant. But he did know that religion could be a powerful pretext for disobedience and therefore could be dangerous in the hands of those who placed their own understanding or conscience above the king. His most profound fear was disunity, which generally led to disorder and insecurity. There was evidence enough in his childhood and in French history in the half century before his birth about the perils of disunity and disobedience and of the encouragement which religious parties could give to those seeking upheaval. Louis learned a single, simple-minded but powerful, lesson directly from Mazarin and indirectly from Richelieu's ministry, and he adopted a rigidly hostile attitude towards any potential source of opposition to royal authority, religious or secular. He sensed the dangers to his authority and to his objectives in the individualism and insubordination of the Jansenist party. Even when Jansenists resisted Roman authority, in tandem with his own opposition to Roman encroachments, Louis still blamed them for their lack of proper obedience despite their support for his own policies. And the good relations which the Jansenists had with his most bitter papal enemy, Innocent XI, undoubtedly hardened his suspicion of their positions and tactics, something which his Jesuit confessor, in turn, could easily have exploited against the Jansenists. It mattered less to Louis that the Jansenists had certain positions, sometimes hostile and sometimes favorable to Rome; what mattered most was their refusal to obey, their cultivation of support in certain influential social circles, and their temerity in seeking vindication in the court of public opinion.[31] The final destruction of Port-Royal-des-Champs was, thus, no accident or side show. It was symbolic of what Louis and his ministers strove to accomplish throughout his entire reign: the domestication of religion and the drawing of its teeth.

THE MONARCHY AND THE PROTESTANTS

Parallel to the tragic history of Jansenism is the farcical history of the suppression of Quietism, equally the work of Louis XIV's hyper-sensitivity to the misuse of religious appeals. Where Jansenism, in no sense a mass movement, had been essentially confined to a certain upper-bourgeois élite and to clerics, the sympathy for the mystical teachings of Madame Guyon, given the label *Quietism* in order to classify yet another heresy, was confined to a few aristocrats at Versailles. That it should have aroused the ageing Bossuet, in his final days, to the dishonorable persecution of a harmless woman and, worse, to a bitter dispute with Fénelon who, with Bossuet himself, was the glory of the Gallican Church, shows perhaps how terribly pervasive was the fixed view of Louis XIV that any religious enthusiasm posed a deadly threat to his regime. Bossuet's orthodoxy was impervious to all mystical appeals, and he could only suspect the worst from a doctrine like Quietism which seemed like all uncontrolled mysticism to call into question the need for ecclesiastical structure and discipline. But Bossuet also suspected that Fénelon and the few aristocrats who were attracted with him to Madame Guyon were partisans of a reform of the absolute monarchy and were forging spiritual weapons against it. Called by Louis XIV under Bossuet's influence to act against Quietism as it had already acted against Jansenism, Rome, knowing that Fénelon was totally orthodox, chose to satisfy the French crown with little more than a gentle admonition for Fénelon. Madame Guyon and her few devotees paid the price of imprisonment and persecution already exacted from much more dangerous opponents of the king's political and religious sensibilities, and Bossuet ended his career as a caricature of the consummate Gallican churchman. After the regime's confrontation for three-quarters of a century with Jansenism, it was in no condition to assess the real importance and potential danger from Madame Guyon's doctrines. It could only act with total suppression.[32]

The Jansenists and Quietists had no legions, and fear of their beliefs and activities was largely theoretical and ideological. The situation of the French Huguenots was rather different. They had in the sixteenth century brought to Valois France the disasters of civil war and had called into being their counterparts on the other political–religious extreme, the Catholic League. It was the military power of the Huguenots and the regime's fear of their ability to undermine royal authority which led to the Edict of Nantes in 1598, a recognition of the free exercise of the Reformed Religion in certain specified places in the kingdom. The fate of the Huguenots – persecution, exile, forced conversion, and the execution of their clergy – has won them the normal sympathy for the underdog and the victim of oppression, not least because of the importance of Protestantism and Free Thought in the historical profession, particularly in English-speaking countries. It is all the more important, therefore, to emphasize that the rights given them by the Edict of Nantes were unusual and had been granted only out of necessity. The religious and political rights they enjoyed through seven or eight decades of the seventeenth century were not expressions of a laudable or progressive theory of toleration. While the provisions of the Edict were in force, France experienced an anomalous religious situation, one found elsewhere only in Poland. The French Huguenots simply enjoyed religious rights based on their military ability to defend themselves against the crown. The French clergy and the papacy deplored this permissive attitude towards heretics, as did much of the French population, and foreign Protestants certainly were not in favor of granting anything similar to their own Catholic minorities. Henry IV had resorted to the Edict of Nantes out of the need for the pacification of his country, and he took analogous measures of appeasement to return former leaders of the League to monarchic loyalty. All these policies were at the same time signs of royal weakness and measures designed in the long run to restore royal power.

The provisions of the Edict of Nantes giving the Huguenots the right to maintain a certain number of fortified places recognized that they already controlled these fortresses and would have to be guaranteed their right to hold them. The Edict gave them nothing militarily that they did not already have, but this form of security was ultimately bound to fail. No government could accept the existence of a "state within a state," certainly not a monarchy like that of the French. For the Huguenots to rely on their military forces meant that their existence rested on the maintenance of the feudal spirit. In this way the Huguenots were fatally linked to the cause of aristocratic dissidence and revolt, and no one understood and expressed this more openly than Cardinal Richelieu when he made one of his principal goals in the creation of a strong monarchy the destruction of the "Huguenot Party."[33] It is not really necessary to try to determine whether Richelieu also opposed the Huguenots on religious grounds, for one of the foremost Catholic objections to Calvinism was political – namely, that Calvinism undermined authority. French history seemed to teach this lesson well enough, and the history of Calvinism elsewhere provided additional proof. In addition, during Richelieu's ministry, the Huguenots had not hesitated to cooperate with the English and even with the Spanish in time of war. Richelieu's successful destruction of their military power by the 1629 Peace of Alais meant that the Huguenots would henceforth have to depend solely on royal grace and would be allowed to die a slow death.[34] Having lost their last rebellion, the Huguenots opted for security in an expression of ultra-royalism, eager at every opportunity to prove their inoffensiveness to those in authority. For this reason they avoided any involvement in the Fronde, and only in the revolt of the Ormée in Bordeaux could their loyalty be to any degree faulted.[35] The more vulnerable the disarmed and hated Huguenots became, the more they believed themselves forced to rely on the good will of the regime, despite what increasingly became official hostility, disdain, and "dry" persecution. One is forced to make comparisons with the classic behavior of Jews in hostile environments who relied on governments to protect them from popular animosity because the governing class appeared to be slightly more mildly hostile than the population as a whole.

Like the Presbyterians during the period of the English Civil War whom they admired, the Huguenots stuck to a belief or delusion that they could eventually convert the king and the ruling class to their particular form of church government. They were, like the Presbyterians, opposed to the doctrines of regicide and only half-heartedly in favor of the rebellion which led to the execution of Charles I,[36] and they probably did not realize how much the English Revolution had compromised them in the eyes of their Catholic countrymen, for the English seemed to be living through the same disorder and anarchy that the French had experienced in their earlier religious wars, and all because of the dangerous doctrines of Calvinism.[37] The Huguenots seem to have misread Richelieu, going so far as to ask in 1631 that their ministers be permitted to address the king without kneeling, a privilege enjoyed by the Catholic clergy and one which the Huguenot ministers had lost. Richelieu finally granted them this favor, one which could only have encouraged them in false hopes, as if the regime regarded them with the same collaborative benevolence as it did the Catholic clergy.[38] The Cardinal was perfectly willing to lull them into a false sense of security, and they were perfectly willing to be anesthetized. Flattering, benevolent words for the Huguenots were appropriate when using them as a counterweight to the *dévot* party which desired an ultra-Catholic foreign policy and when trying to satisfy foreign Protestant allies. Mazarin's policy towards them was consistent with that of Richelieu: flattery when useful, as during the conclusion of an alliance with Cromwell; but refusal to extend any rights not specifically granted by a narrow interpretation of the Edict of Nantes.[39] There is here a clear line from Richelieu to Mazarin to Louis XIV, as in the case of Jansenism. Louis learned from his mentor, and from the mentor of his mentor, a single-minded and simple-minded lesson: the eventual reduction of dissidents to obedience through total conformity to the religion of the king.[40]

Louis XIV's desire to bring the Huguenots to full obedience was a general objective but one not directly implemented during the first twenty years of his personal rule. In this period it was rather the Catholic clergy which seized every available opportunity, particularly at meetings of its General Assembly, to urge the king to fulfill his coronation promise to eliminate heresy in the kingdom. Catholic complaints about the Huguenots increased in the early 1680s largely because of the fierce anti-Catholic agitation in England in connection with the movement to exclude James, the Catholic Duke of York, from the throne. The importance of anti-Catholicism in English political and constitutional development in the seventeenth century should not be underestimated,[41] nor should the influence of English and French events upon one another be ignored.[42] Attempts to blame particular individuals for the sudden hardening of policy towards the Huguenots, or to point the finger of blame at the growing piety or bigotry of the king himself, are probably misguided. Reasons of foreign policy were uppermost in the mind of Louis XIV: during the height of his troubles with Pope Innocent XI he desired to be seen as ultra-orthodox, and when William of Orange arose to become the chief opponent of French expansionism in Europe, Louis feared that this Calvinist prince might pose too strong a temptation for the loyalty of his own Calvinist subjects. Although there was in place before 1684 no long-standing plan for the Revocation of the Edict of Nantes, this very quickly became the perceived means of solving a number of foreign problems and crowning the king's military and diplomatic achievements with the glory of having eliminated religious heresy.[43] It was clearly only a matter of time before the Huguenot question would be dealt with in a decisive way, and the requirements of foreign policy actually dictated the timing of the Revocation.

The crowning irony of having the Huguenots pay the price of Louis XIV's diplomatic goals was that the assault on the Huguenots may have precipitated the Glorious Revolution in Britain, which did more to undermine Louis' foreign objectives than any other single action he took.[44] It brought his most determined enemy, William of Orange, to rule over Britain where he could more effectively coordinate the diplomatic, military, and financial struggle against the hegemonic ambitions of France. Set against this, the suppression of domestic religious dissent seems not only mean-spirited but self-defeating. As Louis lay dying in the summer of 1715 he could persuade himself that he had strengthened France by bringing it religious unity. He had destroyed Port-Royal and had forced upon his clergy acceptance of *Unigenitus*, a papal bull condemning a series of Jansenist and Gallican propositions. He had exiled the clergy of the Reformed Religion and encouraged conversion to the Catholic Church by large numbers of Huguenots through a combination of bribery, cajolery, and terror. Little did he know, however, that the issues of Jansenism and Gallicanism would embitter the relations between churchmen and magistrates throughout most of the eighteenth century, and that in the wilds of Languedoc a remnant of the Calvinist clergy was regrouping to conduct the first synod of the "Church of the Desert."[45] The conformity he had sought was only superficially accomplished – and at a very high price indeed – but it was the reality with which France entered the Age of the Enlightenment. The Catholic Church in France had been assigned a clear role by the absolute monarchy of Louis XIV: the spiritual administration of the State. Along with the monarchy's intendants, judges, tax collectors, and military personnel, the clergy was there to serve the needs of the State and monarchy.

II

"A Frenchman without being a Catholic": Catholicism and citizenship in the eighteenth century

Upon hearing the news of the so-called "Edict of Toleration" promulgated in 1787 by the reformist government of Louis XVI, the Protestant pastor of Sainte-Foy joyfully explained that "henceforth one can be a Frenchman without being a Catholic."[1] Just a few years later during the French Revolution, some of the priests who accepted the reforms of the Civil Constitution of the Clergy claimed that they had done so because they were "citizens before being priests."[2] Indeed, those priests supporting the Revolution did view themselves, first, as citizens of a regenerated France and only, second, as clerical functionaries, while those clerics opposed to the Church reforms of the Revolution clung to an older conception of their primary identity, namely as members of an ecclesiastical hierarchy.[3] Thus for both Protestants and Catholics the era of Reform and Revolution raised and sought to address difficult questions about the relationship of religion to citizenship.

THE CONFESSIONAL STATE

In eighteenth-century France a number of important struggles over religious and civil obligations took place which the policies of the seventeenth-century monarchs had sought to solve but had actually only exacerbated. These struggles had previously received so much attention from traditional political and ecclesiastical historians that more recent students of the period have preferred to ignore or have undervalued their importance. A recent revisionist critic of modern historiographical trends in English history warns us appropriately of the danger of such historical anachronism. Arguing for the need for true historical sympathy, J. C. D. Clark suggests that many modern historians may be constitutionally ill-equipped for assessing religious issues:

> The political values of eighteenth-century England were those appropriate to a society Christian, monarchical, aristocratic, rural, traditional and poor; but those of historians of the 1960s and 1970s were drawn from a society indifferent to religion; hostile alike to authority and to social rank; urban; "plural"; and affluent.[4]

One particular concept for which modern students of history may have difficulty generating any sympathetic understanding is that of the eighteenth-century *confessional state*. Yet it was this particular religious–political arrangement which created the climate in which the issues of religion and citizenship arose in their most troublesome form. The characteristics of the confessional state in eighteenth-century France resulted from the policies and failures of the long reign of Louis XIV. In seeking to have religion play a reliable role in the administration of the French people, the monarchy created many of the dilemmas which the intellectual Enlightenment and the political Revolution were called upon to solve.

The confessional state had two essential characteristics: the identification of civil status or civil rights with conformity to the creed and practices of an established religion; and the restriction of public office and the practice of certain professions to those conforming to it. There was present in societies with such arrangements neither the modern practice of religious liberty nor the medieval unity of life and faith. The confessional state was thus the product of the religious diversity created by the sixteenth-century Reformation and the result of the failure in many lands to restore the religious unity of the medieval Christian past. In some post-Reformation countries religious unity had been successfully re-established: among Catholics, in Spain, Portugal, and in most Italian states, where religious dissidence had been prevented or totally suppressed; among Protestants, notably in the Scandinavian kingdoms where no religious dissenters of any importance could be found. But everywhere else in Europe religious unity had not been restored, usually because the use of force had failed and it would have required unacceptable levels of violence to renew the struggle in a religiously divided Europe, with all the dangers of invasion and anarchy during combined civil and foreign war; a wholly impossible recourse for all but a dwindling number of fanatical true believers.

Where there was no religious unity, there was still an established Church and a variety of disabilities for nonconformists. Sometimes nonconformists received a certain legal recognition, as in Britain after 1688 where some kinds of Protestant dissenters had legal recognition while Catholics and non-believers had to rely on the increasing disinclination of the authorities to enforce the harsh laws on the books against them.[5] In the German states after the Peace of Westphalia the right of the sovereign princes to change the religion of their subjects was sufficiently restricted by treaty so that some degree of liberty of conscience for minority Lutherans, Catholics, or Calvinists was recognized, rights respected more by some rulers than by others. Some princes were relatively tolerant, like the Electors of Brandenburg, while others like the Archbishop of Salzburg in 1731 and the Habsburg princes before Joseph II tended rather towards the enforcement of religious unity whenever possible. Only in France under the Edict of Nantes (1598 to 1685) and in Poland from the last quarter of the sixteenth century to the middle of the seventeenth century was there legislated a type of legal toleration which allowed persons of different confessions to enjoy true civil status and to hold public office. In France, a strict and intentionally ungenerous interpretation of the Edict of Nantes from the time of Richelieu and Mazarin slowly transformed France from a condition of legal toleration into a narrow confessional state. Louis XIV had not, of course, intended to create a confessional state. He had intended to restore religious unity and indivisibility, but his eighteenth-century successors had slowly been forced to give up the fiction that there were no Protestants in France and had tacitly acquiesced, first by sporadic enforcement and then by non-enforcement of existing anti-Protestant legislation, in the existence of a large number of Protestant dissidents without access to civil rights, to certain professions, or to public recognition.

The confessional state could in practice be more or less tolerant, since it did not necessarily deny the right to dissent from the establishment cult but only the right of dissidents to enjoy civil rights. Some absolute monarchs even favored official toleration for religious dissidents since such a policy could further their goal of the subordination of the established Church to the State.[6] In eighteenth-century France, except for Lutherans in Alsace whose status had been established by international law, and Jews who were essentially resident aliens, everyone else was legally considered a member of the Roman Catholic Church. But in fact there were several important groups of dissidents whose status caused much controversy and called into question the nature of authority and citizenship: open or crypto-Protestants of Calvinist heritage; Catholic dissidents adhering to various "Jansenist" positions which had been condemned both by Rome and by the French government; and hardy non-believers, those who produced and some of those who consumed the scandalous works of the Enlightenment. None of these dissidents, unlike their homologues in Britain, enjoyed any legal recognition, but some of them could expect considerable unofficial support and protection. Many of the Parlements defended and protected the "Jansenist" dissidents with remarkable success, while the *philosophes* came to enjoy the favor and protection of men in high places and needed less and less to fear the censorious fulminations of bishops and Parlements. Protestants were the most vulnerable of all the dissidents, as well as the most numerous, but even they came to enjoy a degree of security which derived from the growth of liberal sentiment within the élite and from the recognition of the importance of their financial and economic role in French life. Thus the confessional state could not totally ignore the realities of life and thought in the eighteenth century. The Catholic Church and its clergy had been given by the monarchs and ministers of the Old Regime a definite role in French life. The eighteenth century was partially to challenge this role and to suggest an updated version, a revision which can be seen to have been at once revolutionary and also far from inconsistent with a long-standing historical pattern.

THE SACRAMENTS, RELIGIOUS OR CIVIL

In 1754, in the midst of acrimonious conflict between Paris's Parlement and its archbishop concerning the refusal of sacraments to alleged Jansenist dissidents, a bizarre scheme was proposed to satisfy the Parlementary magistrates' concern about secular independence from the Church while mollifying the embattled churchmen at the same time. This scheme, in what appears the offspring of Machiavellian politics and Enlightenment irony, would have conceded to the Parlements the essential control over the dispensing of the sacraments, while the clergy would have been bought off with a renewed persecution of the Protestants against whom the harsh laws of the realm had for some time been enforced only intermittently. Although nothing ever came of this plan it had the merit of raising the central issue of the confessional state. The author of a brochure entitled *Le Conciliateur ou Lettres d'un ecclésiastique à un magistrat sur les affaires présentes* was once believed to have been Turgot, later famous as a reformist intendant and minister, but more probably he was Loménie de Brienne, a future archbishop and also a reformist minister of Louis XVI. The author attacked this suggested "solution" to the controversy about the refusal of sacraments with the sage observation that all the troubles stemmed from the regrettable fact that citizenship in France was defined by the reception of the Catholic sacraments. "I should wish," he remarked, "that it were not the sacrament of baptism, nor that of marriage, which determined the status of citizens."[7]

It was, however, indeed the reception of the sacraments which alone gave legal recognition to subjects of the "Most Christian" king of France. Modern notions about the separation of Church and State, the rights of conscience, and the integrity of religious feeling and belief as private matters all interfere massively with an understanding of the role of religion in a confessional state. We must not only avoid a modern and secular frame of reference in trying to understand the role of religion in pre-Revolutionary France, we must also beware of equally distorting Protestant biases or references.[8] An additional bias to be avoided is that of modern post-Vatican II Roman Catholicism which, in seeking to purify the Church of the inauthentic accretions of the centuries, can also destroy one's capacity for sympathetic understanding of the past. The Catholic sacraments always, in fact, contained both a "sign of mystery" and a meaning of "oath" or "initiation." Thus the sacraments had a socially binding meaning along with a more interior and mystical meaning concerning divine grace. Bernard Plongeron reminds us that baptism and confirmation marked the entrance of a person into the life of the community; that the sacrament of penance reconciled the sinner to God *and* to his fellows and enabled him to participate in the reception of Holy Communion which was a community sacrament; that ordination gave special powers to a small but indispensable group of men in the social hierarchy, while marriage for a much larger number of men and women served as the very foundation of the social order. The sacraments, then, could never be considered wholly apart from their political and social meaning, although these meanings certainly did not exhaust the significance of the sacraments.

The case of the sacrament of marriage was unique in that it was the only sacrament which was first based on nature itself; the theologians always had had some difficulty in defending it as a sacrament or at least in explaining what its recognition by Christ and the Church had really added to its natural attributes.[9] Thus the average Frenchman or Frenchwoman and the average Catholic were one and the same. He or she was born into the community by baptism, established his or her social position through marriage, performed his or her Easter duty with the other members of the parish community, and departed this life with the last sacrament and burial in consecrated ground. In practice, if not in theory, there was no separation between the communitarian and the spiritual meaning and content of the Catholic sacraments. Protestant controversies, the Tridentine Catholic responses to these controversies, and liberal, secular disdain for the intermingling of the mundane and the divine all distort the issue by obscuring the actually experienced meaning of religion in pre-modern Europe.[10]

Louis XIV had needed to believe that he could restore the religious unity of France by administrative action, and the encouragement of important elements among the Catholic clergy, when added to certain diplomatic imperatives, had led to the Revocation of the Edict of Nantes, removing whatever rights of citizenship remained to Protestants. To abrogate these rights and to pretend that all Frenchmen and Frenchwomen were henceforth Catholics meant that the external marks of Catholicity were required of former Protestants, as they were of all Catholics, in order for them to be regarded as subjects of the king and citizens under the law. There was a certain resemblance here to the forcible conversion of the Jews in fifteenth-century Spain, but with an important difference. The Spanish Jews had been given the choice of conversion or expulsion by the Catholic kings of Castile and Aragon, and those accepting conversion, however sincerely or not, had been turned over to the mercies of the Inquisition to enforce true conformity to the Catholic faith.

However much the Spanish rulers might have initially erred in encouraging insincere conversions, with the establishment of the Inquisition they determined that the New Christians were not to be allowed a merely perfunctory adherence to their new faith, since that would have meant the condoning of sacrilege. It was indeed sacrilege to force the reception of the sacraments upon people who only feigned belief. The Inquisition, whatever its horrors for the modern spirit, did seek the true conversion, albeit by terror, of the New Christians. And in a certain sense it succeeded, for the number of heretics burned by the Inquisition was great only at the beginning of the period of the assimilation of the New Christians. Eventually, most of the New Christians, by fair means or foul, did become conforming Catholics, no less sincere and no less conformist than the Old Christians.

In France after 1685 there was no expulsion of Protestants; indeed, they were forbidden to emigrate at all. And the amount of force which would have been necessary to make them into real Catholics, something equivalent to that once employed by the Spanish Inquisition, was never contemplated. Consequently, the fiction that all Frenchmen were Catholics meant that those who wished their civil status to be recognized had, except for sincere converts to the Catholic faith, to commit sacrilege as the price of citizenship. The only other recourse was to live in violation of the law. More specifically, to baptize children in a Protestant rite, to marry before a Protestant minister or without any religious sanction at all, to fail to make the annual Easter duty – all this was in violation of French law. Thus ex-Protestants had the choice, in the absence of true conversion, of profaning the sacraments or breaking the law. The authorities behaved far less brutally towards them than had the Spanish Inquisition towards the crypto-Jews, but the Spanish persecution had been more logical and it ultimately had succeeded. In the eyes of the French Catholic Church the sacraments dispensed to Protestants without faith were reduced to a simple secular meaning. If the Protestants suffered social and economic discrimination and varying degrees of harassment throughout the eighteenth century, and occasionally, as in the Calas and Sirven cases, murderous persecution, the Catholic sacraments suffered a type of secularization which discredited religion and reduced the established Church to an instrument of political and social oppression. For most Protestants, whether conformists or not, and for many Catholics in the social and intellectual élite, the façade of French Catholic spiritual unity came to be seen as an abomination and the capstone of an entire structure of tyranny.

The harsh laws against the Protestants notwithstanding, the French government at various levels was forced to recognize that Protestants had not disappeared and could not be repressed. Even though the law decreed the death penalty for Protestant ministers found in France, the government within a generation after the death of Louis XIV came to value the tacit cooperation of these same ministers in ensuring the loyalty of the Protestant populations, especially during times of war and distress. During the Paris bread riots of 1775, when circular letters were sent out to all *curés* urging them to encourage calm among their parishioners, the same letters were sent to Protestant pastors; in effect, the outlawed ministers were being treated like unofficial civil servants. In Toulouse in 1739, well before the notorious Calas Affair would convince some that Catholic bigotry was still virulent, the Parlement of Toulouse had in a legal dispute actually recognized the legality of a Protestant marriage.[11] The apparent intolerance of the Toulouse magistrates towards the Protestants during the Calas Affair in 1762 would be more the result of their identification of Protestants with rebellion and disobedience than a real concern with the religious issues between the two confessions. The magistrates viewed the Protestants much as they viewed the Jesuits whose order they were in the process of dissolving and expelling: religious deviance was a problem of public order and poor citizenship, and it was on this basis that they prosecuted those found guilty in the Calas Affair. When the magistrates in Toulouse came to the conclusion that Protestants could be citizens too and that their rights and property could enjoy the protection of the law, tolerance on principle replaced the earlier view, one of indifference intermittently punctuated by persecution and brutality.[12]

From the 1750s on the view was increasingly expressed that the Protestants needed to be given a civil status in France. The Protestants would have accepted the need for marriage before a Catholic priest if the priest were recognized in this process as merely an officer of the crown.[13] But the Catholic clergy which, with some notable but all too few exceptions, had not in the days of the Revocation scrupled to force Protestants to Holy Communion against their will, now began to have qualms about giving the sacrament of marriage to these nominal Catholics. Curiously taking a stand on the one sacrament which everyone recognized had a prior validity in natural law, namely marriage, the *curés* insisted that those known in the community to be former Protestants must undergo a probationary period of regular Church attendance, followed by a written abjuration of heresy, before they could receive the sacrament of marriage. Such a period of probation could be several months in length or even as long as one year. The government rejected such rigorism and insisted that the *curés* be more accommodating with the "former" Protestants. When the Catholic clergy refused essentially to cooperate with the government's wishes – thus asserting a different interpretation of the requirements of the confessional state – the government began to relax enforcement of anti-Protestant legislation even further and seriously to contemplate other solutions. As early as 1754 Turgot proposed the creation of a special civil status for Protestants which would take their civil recognition out of the hands of the Catholic clergy entirely.[14]

From 1750 to the beginning of the reign of Louis XVI, there were published about 100 *mémoires* with the specific recommendation that the Protestants be given a civil status.[15] This new direction culminated in the 1787 Edict of Toleration which, despite its name, granted not the toleration of non-Catholic religion but rather some of the concrete privileges of citizenship to Protestants: they might henceforth live in France and practice a profession; they might contract marriage legally before a magistrate; they could have their births registered before a judge; and they could receive dignified burial. In short, the Protestants received official recognition as citizens, second-class citizens perhaps, and they were given less perhaps than the Edict of Nantes had once granted their ancestors. But in the climate of opinion in the few years before the Revolution of 1789 they came to be viewed in a uniquely new way. They were now citizens. Those provisions of the Edict which conceded a certain role to the Catholic clergy in the registration of the civil status of Protestants were rejected by the Catholic Church, with the result that the status of the Protestants was totally laicized, since by the terms of the Edict the Protestant pastors had not been given any role to play in the granting of a civil status to their flock. The opposition to the Edict of 1787 by the Catholic clergy and by some of the magistrates of the Parlements was considerable, for they essentially objected to the concept of a civil status for non-Catholics and to the utilization of Catholic ecclesiastical personnel and facilities for the accommodation of secular concerns.[16] The entanglements of the confessional state were here rapidly coming apart.

The problems which the large number of French Protestants created for the confessional state unknowingly bequeathed by Louis XIV were replicated by the case of that other group of religious dissidents whom the Sun King had also sought and failed to integrate into a desired conformity, namely the so-called Jansenists. The destruction of the community and site of Port-Royal-des-Champs in 1711 had not ended the Jansenist question, for in his zeal to achieve total obedience from disputatious clerics and rebellious laymen Louis XIV had appealed to a papacy all too eager to accommodate the king in his anti-Jansenist ardor. The Bull *Unigenitus* of 1713 was so ill-conceived a condemnation of a variety of propositions, some Jansenist, some Gallican, some important, some trivial, and some even totally orthodox, that it single-handedly created a strong party out of those opposed to royal and papal policy on a number of questions; a party which could drape itself in the honorable and traditional mantle of Gallicanism, signifying the defense of the autonomy of the French Church from undue Roman intervention and the exaltation of the French monarchy above all ecclesiastical interference. To diehard Jansenists whose moral and theological concerns were, in fact, increasingly uncongenial to the secular élites of eighteenth-century France, union with the defenders of Gallicanism in the Parlements and the legal profession offered a new lease on life. Henceforth, an aggressive Gallicano-Jansenist party challenged the Jesuits and their supporters at every turn, sought to have the monarchy allow a greater constitutional role to the Parlements, and ultimately crowned their considerable efforts with an almost unattainable success, the total suppression in France of the Society of Jesus in 1762.

The great struggle between the Parlements and the episcopate over the dispensing of the sacraments to those who refused to accept and obey the Bull *Unigenitus* raised again the question of who in the confessional state was to control the sacraments and, therefore, the whole matter of citizenship. While the clergy had been willing for two generations after the Revocation of the Edict of Nantes to force ex-Protestants to the Catholic sacraments, this ill-conceived policy raised disturbing issues of profanation and sacrilege. By the middle of the century, however, the clergy turned its attention to those Gallicans and Jansenists who were still refusing to recognize *Unigenitus* and sought in many individual dioceses and parishes to withhold the sacraments from those notorious opponents of the Bull. The "orthodox" party's suspicion about the orthodoxy of opponents of the Bull led to an attempt to treat them, in effect, like heretics. But to deprive them of the sacraments also meant to assimilate them essentially to the status of the crypto-Protestants: a group without civil rights or civil status.

The Gallicano-Jansenists were too well-connected and too important to accept an equivalent of the second-class status enjoyed by the Protestants. The two sides in the disputes between supporters of the Jesuits and defenders of the Gallicano-Jansenists had rarely shown any mutual forbearance; each used every weapon in its arsenal and pursued a war to the death. It was to the Parlements, most especially to the Parlement of Paris, that those persecuted by the sacramental policy of the "orthodox" party appealed, and the Parlements were able to use their sharply honed skills effectively in defense of those whose civil status was in danger of being compromised. The Church might very well claim to control the inner meaning of the sacraments through the power of the priesthood, and the Parlementary magistrates as good Catholics did not challenge this. But the refusal of sacraments to those allegedly disobedient to the Church was an external act which had to be overseen by the secular authorities; otherwise the Church would be permitted to exercise a despotic power over French citizens. Refusal of sacraments to any individual stigmatized him officially as a "public sinner," something which fell under the jurisdiction of the courts of the realm. It was central to royal political ideology and to Gallicanism that the kings and their servants should control the external manifestations of religion.[17] The Jansenists in the eighteenth century placed their only hope for survival and victory in the ability of the secular authorities to curb the undue ambitions of a Church increasingly inclined to accept Roman direction and to pursue dangerous paths of domination. Thus the bishops, individually and collectively, asserted one particular interpretation of the relationship of the sacraments to the status of citizenship, while the Parlements and their Gallicano-Jansenist clientele developed a different understanding of this connection.

In 1755 Le Franc de Pompignan, Bishop of Le Puy, made the incredible assertion before the General Assembly of the Clergy meeting in Paris that the sacraments "'do not belong to society . . . Citizens have no right to them by virtue of birth.'"[18] He had apparently come face to face with the realization that if all Frenchmen and Frenchwomen were Catholics required by the law to receive the sacraments of the Church, then indeed since the sacraments conveyed citizenship, citizens could demand their right to receive the sacraments. If the Church insisted on its own rules for the reception of the sacraments, it would be asserting its power to determine citizenship. Correspondingly, if the Parlements asserted, as they did, that the secular authority had the right to defend the individual citizen from being deprived of the sacraments, they in turn were asserting a certain supervision over the Church's right to determine the conditions for the reception of the sacraments. Each party was seeking a supervisory role over the other.

In the tangled web of the confessional state, when religion and political and social status were intertwined, which authorities indeed were competent to regulate disputes over the issues of "sacramental" citizenship? As the clergy was unwilling that Protestants be given civil status without their conformity to the laws of the Church, they were also unwilling that nonconformist Catholics take their civil status for granted. It is hard to know what the churchmen really proposed doing with the Protestants and the Gallicano-Jansenist opponents of *Unigenitus*. Probably they did not think beyond a certain deepening of discrimination in order to encourage conformity and, eventually, true conversion to the official cult. They knew that force had not worked to any appreciable degree for the conversion of the Protestants. They probably thought that the much smaller number of opponents of the Bull could be intimidated into conformity. In any case, those who favored the Church's strict control of the sacraments were undermining the foundations of the confessional state without knowing what they were proposing in its place, for the re-establishment of total conformity of life and faith was, at best, an illusion. To create a class of people deprived of the sacraments was to create a class of quasi-citizens whose status was independent of the sacraments. The Parisian magistrates, who from 1757 on did in fact win control over the dispensing of the sacraments in the parishes of Paris,[19] were actually asserting that citizenship had little to do with theological conformity to the Church and were gropingly moving towards a laicized conception of citizenship. In both cases, the confessional state was being undermined by still unclear principles of secularism. The policy of the royal government all through this dispute was confused and vacillating, but the government of Louis XV permitted the magistrates ultimately to gain the upper hand.[20] Whichever version of the confessional state achieved dominance, it was not the Church that emerged victorious. What R. R. Palmer has written concerning Protestants applies to Catholic dissidents as well, namely that toleration was more the result of the growth of the State than of intellectual advances:

> The state had so far replaced the church as the chief authority in society, had so centered allegiance, hopes, and values upon itself, and had so improved its administrative technique and its means of dealing with individuals however numerous or remote, that the rival administrative machinery of the church was no longer useful to it, and the religious views of private persons became irrelevant to practical politics.[21]

To say that secularizing forces were undermining the foundation of the confessional state does not entirely make clear what secularization signified. Those using terms like secularization, laicization, or de-Christianization mean to indicate varying degrees of hostility or indifference to certain aspects of religion and a wide range of motivations and interests. Perhaps one of the best definitions of secularization comes from a leading historian of the Enlightenment, Peter Gay. For him, secularization involved "a subtle shift of attention; religious institutions and religious explanations of events were slowly being displaced from the center of life to its periphery."[22] This particular definition avoids the pitfall of equating secularization with total or clear hostility to religion, for it emphasizes instead a gradual process having many causes and taking many different forms, but one which results finally in the marginalization of religious concerns and religious culture. The process of developing a secular conception of French citizenship constituted just such a gradual reduction of the exclusively religious definition of political and social status. The Enlightenment, at first slowly and thereafter with accelerated effect, strove to reform the intellectual and moral understanding of eighteenth-century man by pushing traditional religious insights and concerns away from the center and from the public arena towards the periphery, namely towards the private concerns of the individual.

THE IMPORTANCE OF VOLTAIRE

There are many reasons for a student of the Enlightenment to place the figure of Voltaire at the center of his investigation. This is even more true for the student of Catholic France. Voltaire, by his experience, his concerns, his aspirations, and his fears – as well as his undoubted genius – occupies a central position in any discussion of the secularization of French life and thought in the eighteenth century. The conflicts between Jesuits and Jansenists were extremely important in the growth of his particular attitude towards religious controversy. His passionate rejection of religious intolerance made him an important voice in the advocacy of civil rights for French Protestants. And his philosophical and historical commitments singled out certain central features of historic Christianity as primary targets of his life-long crusade for Enlightenment. He serves as an excellent example of how a member of the social and intellectual élite rejected the tutelage of the Catholic clergy and became the prototype of the emancipated bourgeois. It was in "Voltairean" man that the French Church first encountered its most implacable foe.

Voltaire's entire career may be summarized by the three individuals whom he singled out directly or indirectly as the targets most worthy of his assault. Jacques Bossuet, Bishop of Meaux, represented for Voltaire the ideologist of a Bible-centered philosophy of history which sought to place all human culture under the Judaeo-Christian interpretation of the nature and destiny of man. Voltaire wrote his own world history, the *Essai sur les moeurs,* to refute the biblical view of the meaning of history which had found in Bossuet its classic expression. Blaise Pascal represented the pessimism and irrationalism of Christian theology and philosophy and the Christian denial of the autonomy and goodness of man and the natural world. Pascal had praised Christianity for being the only religion "against nature." Voltaire understood clearly that if Pascal were right in his basic concerns and insights, then the Catholic Church and all that went with it were not only defensible but absolutely necessary. Finally, the figure of Gottfried Wilhelm Leibniz, as satirized in *Candide*, represented the rationalistic philosopher whose predilection for abstraction and deductive reasoning clashed with Voltaire's commitment to a pragmatic, empirical pursuit of the science of man and nature. In his opposition to Bossuet, Pascal, and Leibniz Voltaire developed his genius and his lasting influence. It was no accident that two of his three main targets were Christian heroes of the flowering of the French Catholic Reformation, for it was the transformation of Catholic France that Voltaire made his paramount objective, indeed his fixed vocation.

There is not complete agreement among Voltaire scholars about how he developed his passionate anti-clericalism. His upbringing among the Jansenist bourgeoisie of Paris and subsequent education by the Jesuits at the Collège Louis-le-Grand apparently made him antagonistic towards both of these rival expressions of the Catholic Reformation. From a Jansenist upbringing he seems to have developed not only a strong reaction against austerity and Christian traditionalism, but also to have accepted something of the Jansenists' tendency to equate religion with severe moralism, their disinterest in mysticism, their opposition to certain forms of "baroque" piety, and their use of satire and invective against opponents. From the Jesuits he absorbed a rationalistic attitude towards religion. Without retaining from his family background any particular sympathy for the Jansenists, he did know at close hand how fiercely the Jesuits and other anti-Jansenists in the Church pursued Jansenist dissidents, and his appreciation of the intellectual attainments of the Jesuits was always tempered considerably by his revulsion at their role as persecutors.[23] He came, thus, to be extremely wary of both parties within the French Church and developed a passionate fear and loathing of persecution, an anticlericalism so passionate that on each anniversary of the Massacre of St Bartholomew's Day he took to his bed with a fever, a morbid reaction to the memory of the murderous hatred of which Christians were all too capable.[24]

In his *Le Siècle de Louis XIV*, Voltaire painted an unfavorable picture of the Jansenist movement, disputed Pascal's brilliant attack on the Jesuits, and praised some of the Popes for their efforts to pacify the religious fanaticism which Jansenism provoked, but he reserved his greatest disdain for the Jesuits who, in his view, had persuaded Louis XIV that his religious obligations required the persecution of the opponents of the Bull *Unigenitus*. His satire concealed the passionate nature of his anti-clericalism. When he charmingly asked which was more singular, that uneducated nuns should be required to sign some statement about a Latin book they had never read (Jansen's *Augustinus*), or that they should refuse obstinately to take direction from their ecclesiastical superiors, he was seeking to do more than amuse his readers. He was employing the tools of common sense and satire to express without "enthusiasm" his enthusiastic hatred of theological disputes which, when allied to power, inevitably led to persecution.[25]

Much has been made of the alleged cynicism of Voltaire's attitude towards religion, namely that despite his hatred of Christianity he believed religion necessary for the maintenance of the social order. His own encouragement of religion on his estate at Ferney, where he went so far as to build a church and lead his peasants to Sunday mass, was more than cynicism and patronizing élitism. The notion that God was necessary for the preservation of the social order was a traditional argument derived from the social nature of religion. Voltaire, like the bourgeois he was, disliked speculative approaches to God. He preferred to approach religious questions through appeals to utility and morality, an attitude which had already flourished among the bourgeoisie of the Catholic Reformation.[26] And Voltaire's attitude was not all that different from that of the monarchy and its chief servants. Indeed as churchmen from the 1760s on defended the Catholic faith against attacks from the *philosophes*, they also began increasingly to use arguments about social utility. The famous "Avertissement du clergé de France ... sur les dangers de l'incrédulité" of 1770 proclaimed the necessary role of religion in the defense of order and the preservation of authority. The crisis of the French Revolution would only increase the resort to arguments of order and social utility, whether by Gallicans or Ultramontanists, by Catholics favorable to the French Revolution or by those violently opposed to it.[27] The characteristic Voltairean attitude – "if there were no God, He would have to be invented" – was actually a widely held position among Catholics as well as non-believers. It is possible that Voltaire may have looked forward to a time when the masses would be educated enough to be able to perform their social duties without the need for an established religion,[28] but in the short run religion was deemed to be absolutely necessary. It only needed to be purged of its persecutory proclivities and made rational and social. Peter Gay notes that the only work of Jean-Jacques Rousseau to receive Voltaire's enthusiastic approval was the "Creed of the Priest of Savoy" from the *Emile,* for in that work a natural and social religion was magnificently proclaimed.[29] The attitude of Voltaire and Rousseau towards natural religion and their hostility to Christian intolerance were to be enthusiastically taken up by the eighteenth-century élite which was ready to throw off ecclesiastical tutelage and to think for itself.

THE BOURGEOISIE

Any consideration of the eighteenth-century élite's relationship to the Catholic Church involves a number of problems. Much historical work in this field has labored under what R. R. Palmer called the "heavy burden of German *Historismus.*"[30] More generally, a number of influential sociological theories have been employed to explain the growth of the modern élite, the bourgeoisie, and the relationship of economic and social developments to intellectual and religious change. No sooner does one consider conflicts between the social teachings of Christianity and modern economic theory and practice than one is challenged to agree or disagree with the theories of Max Weber concerning Protestantism and the "spirit of capitalism." Let one even casually imply that the bourgeoisie had an important role in the eighteenth-century Enlightenment, and in the outbreak and development of the French Revolution, and one is assumed straightaway to be in thralldom to a rigid Marxism which not only distorts the past but also somehow supports and sanctions particular positions in the Cold War of our own time. On the other hand, a rigid, conscientious avoidance of all sociological insight and any reference to Weber, Troeltsch, Sombart, Marx, or Engels would greatly impoverish our understanding and reduce historical writing to a mindless narrative. The élite of seventeenth- and eighteenth-century France consisted of several different groups from the nobility and the upper reaches of the bourgeoisie. One can identify tendencies towards the consolidation of these groups into a modern class of "notables" and also, in a contrary direction, towards the creation of a rigid demarcation between nobility and bourgeoisie, but there is little doubt that the modern, post-revolutionary élite of France may appropriately be termed the "bourgeoisie." Consequently, it seems legitimate to use the terms bourgeois and bourgeoisie as the embodiment of established culture and values in the modern period. Bourgeois and bourgeoisie are, in a discussion of modern France, indispensable terms, whatever the ideological baggage with which some may be burdened. And to begin with, we need particularly to understand what sort of a Catholic Christian the bourgeois Frenchman of the eighteenth century was.

The disciples of Marx and Weber alike seem to agree that Protestantism much more than Catholicism was a form of Christianity congenial to the needs and interests of the bourgeoisie. They assume that Catholicism remained, either in fact or in "spirit," most congenial to the social and economic values of feudal society and to the two great landed classes of that society, the nobility and the peasantry. Whether, as for the Weberians, a change in religious understanding in the direction of a worldly asceticism led to a spirit favorable to capitalistic economic enterprise, or whether, as for the Marxists, the enterprising bourgeoisie reformed a feudal Catholicism according to its needs and invented Protestantism, Catholicism allegedly was and remained a religion unable to satisfy the non-feudal strata of society. The Catholic bourgeoisie of France, thus, was allegedly bound to come into conflict with a Church that had essentially no place for it.[31] The alienation of the bourgeoisie in the eighteenth century is thus interpreted as a latter-day Reformation or as an additional stage in the emancipation of the bourgeoisie. If the French bourgeoisie had failed to win its rights earlier by not establishing evangelical religion in France, the next stage of its development according to this view was necessarily a more secular movement, the Enlightenment.[32] Such a view makes the French bourgeoisie seem somewhat backward in comparison with its counterparts in Protestant Europe, particularly in Britain and the Dutch Republic, but it also seems to account for the comparatively greater virulence of its anti-clericalism and even hostility to all religion. The alienation of the French bourgeoisie from the Church becomes so inevitable as to cease needing explanation at all.

Emphasis on the feudal, aristocratic social ethic of Catholicism can be excessive because it ignores the fact that the medieval town was particularly receptive to Christian ethics; indeed,

Christianity had been from the start an urban religion. The early medieval towns welcomed an ethic of egalitarianism and charity which corresponded to townsmen's love of peace and opposition to the extreme social distinctions of the feudal countryside. The medieval Catholic social ideal did emphasize values which promoted conservatism and collectivism perhaps more than individualism, but the close ties between Christian and urban values lasted for many centuries.[33] Individualism and acquisitive instincts were held in check by the social control exercised by the medieval Church. In time, intellectual change, economic opportunity, and political developments undermined the ability of the Church to police the strivings of the individual Christian, and supernatural limits came to have less effect in restraining the freedom of the individual and his activities.[34] If the Protestant Reformation is seen as the creation of a religion more suitable for the urban bourgeoisie, the same can be said for the Catholic Reformation.

Recent scholarship has shifted one focus of Reformation studies away from concentration on the differences and conflicts between Catholicism and the Protestant churches to an understanding of how both Reformations worked in parallel directions towards a more disciplined, a more ascetic, and a more urban Christianity, one which can be seen as more relevant to an educated, urban élite. With such a perspective, it becomes less important to see how Calvinism, for example, allegedly satisfied the bourgeoisie more than Catholicism than to recognize that the Catholic reformers, in the spirit of the Council of Trent, aimed at the creation of a godly society as much as did Calvin. Indeed, there were many parallels between the moral ethic preached and enforced in the Geneva of Calvin and the Milan of St Charles Borromeo. The Reformation involved the separation of the élite from popular culture and popular religion, the pursuit of rationality, decorum, sobriety, diligence, and order, and the emphasis on self-mastery and self-control as primary Christian values. For all reformers, the primary targets were the undisciplined features of medieval Catholicism.[35] The disciplining of unruly medieval man was justified ideologically both by the doctrines of Predestination and Election and by the theology of salvation through disciplined Good Works, and both seem equally to have encouraged élite striving in all social and economic callings. The disciplined life which the churches encouraged worked to create the new wealth which, in turn, became a problem for Christian ethics and helped to give the élite a sense of its own power and importance.[36] One historian has gone so far as to claim that bourgeois class consciousness arose partly in opposition to the superstitious beliefs of the populace, that the religious differences between élite and populace were perhaps more important than differences in wealth.[37] The Catholic Reformation, to the extent that it succeeded in imposing an urban, simplified, and orderly Catholicism upon the masses, also sustained the rationalizing tendencies of the French bourgeoisie which enthusiastically cooperated with it during the seventeenth century.

The emancipation of the French élite from the tutelage of the clergy explains the growth of anti-clericalism which could but did not necessarily have to become hostility to religion *per se*, and which essentially signified the unwillingness of the élite to continue an uncritical acceptance of the leadership of the clergy. When the marquis d'Argenson was describing the growing anti-clericalism in mid-eighteenth-century Paris, he declared: "'We know as much as the priests about the attributes of God.'"[38] Indeed, the élite increasingly challenged the right and the competence of the clergy to guide its spiritual and moral life in the same way it had in the past and was still guiding the lives of the masses. Anti-clericalism was a stage in the self-awareness and self-assertion of the élite, particularly of the bourgeoisie which needed to demonstrate that it was not "of the People." Criticism of the clergy was a necessary step in the development of its autonomy.[39] The noble and bourgeois élite earlier had participated with enthusiasm in the work of the Catholic Reformation, a process which introduced rational order into religious belief and practice parallel to the rational order of the élite's social and economic life. The Catholic reformers as much as the Protestant ones worked for what Weber called the "disenchantment" of the world.[40] The baroque piety favored by the spirit of the Council of Trent may in Protestant eyes have seemed far from evangelical simplicity, but compared with the spontaneity and communitarian expressions of piety in the Middle Ages, it was a considerably "slimmed down" form of religious expression. The Catholic virtue of charity was over the course of several centuries transformed into *bienfaisance* or beneficence,[41] a difference of considerable importance, perhaps best explained as the difference between the meaning of *charity* when used by St Paul or St Francis and the meaning assigned to it in modern *charitable* institutions. It was, as we might say today, the difference between Love and Welfare. The destitute ceased being viewed as images of Christ and became instead persons in economic difficulty, sometimes through no fault of their own (the deserving poor) and sometimes through sin and vice (the undeserving poor). The Catholic Reformation made catechetical teaching increasingly a matter of morality: in the list of chief virtues, moral purity and political and social obedience beat out charity, humility, faith, and devotion. In the words of a leading historian of seventeenth- and eighteenth-century religion in France, "the evangelical ferment was transformed into [moral] book-keeping."[42]

The very success of the Tridentine Reformation in reforming French Catholicism along lines desired by the social élite was in fact the cause, in turn, of a certain alienation of the élite from the clergy. The élite, particularly the bourgeoisie, could see itself as pre-eminently Christian since the Tridentine reforms corresponded so closely to its moral and cultural values. The Church seemed to have narrowed the expression of religious faith and to have given approval to the values and prejudices of the bourgeoisie. Becoming more self-confident and self-assured, the bourgeoisie came in time to find the conservatism and traditionalism of the clergy confining and anachronistic, particularly when customary clerical attitudes and practices clashed with the ambitions of an increasingly wealthy, enterprising, and ambitious bourgeoisie, and when the bourgeoisie identified abuses in the existing social order which the moralizing clergy tended on principle to defend. The clergy's very devotion to good works and duty in the parishes made them very close to Voltaire's *bon curé* and Rousseau's "priest of Savoy," even though the clergy of course had not in its seminaries read the works of the *philosophes*. These seminaries had succeeded admirably in creating the best educated clergy in French history, but the education they dispensed diverged significantly from lay culture, and the educated clergy which emerged was more cut off culturally from the lay élite which increasingly contested its leadership.[43]

While the sentimental conception of the priest as *bon curé* was applauded by the lay élite, it itself expected to be more than the mere recipient of priestly attention. It wished to play a more active role. The Tridentine reforms had set apart the clergy for leadership and correspondingly demanded passive obedience from the laity. This brought the clergy into conflict, first with the lay élite which believed it deserved a more elevated role, and then with elements of the populace itself which came to resent the firm control over social customs and daily life which the clergy sought to exercise.[44] The bourgeois, once so traditional and pious that he preferred the more intransigent "Jansenist" theologians to those who sought to make concessions to the modern spirit, came, in the words of Bernard Groethuysen, finally to find the concessions which the Jesuits were willing to make inadequate, "and he wanted to believe even less." From this perspective, the bourgeoisie was "not merely a class that has generally lost its faith, but rather one whose practice and whose thought, whatever its formal religious belief, are *fundamentally* irreligious in a critical area, and totally alien to the category of the sacred."[45] In the last analysis, it was a true belief in Providence that the bourgeoisie lacked, the confidence of the nobility, at least in former times, and the populace that divine intervention was a real possibility in human affairs.[46] And it was largely the course of the Catholic Reformation which paradoxically encouraged the bourgeoisie to lose confidence in the reality of Providence. What the "enlightened" and the bourgeois, and even many of the Tridentine clergy, contemptuously called *superstition* was what the people regarded as the presence of the divine in their midst.

Once one sees the ways in which the Tridentine reforms reinforced certain moral tendencies among the Catholic bourgeoisie, it should be possible to realize that the attempt on the part of some eighteenth-century churchmen, usually Jesuits, to keep abreast of modern life and thought was necessarily more than merely a way of meeting the challenge of the Enlightenment. Peter Gay is probably mistaken in seeing this search for "relevance" as a "treason of the clerks."[47] Only an ultra-Jansenist interpretation of the Catholic tradition could lead one to conclude that all Catholic humanism and modernism were necessarily detached from the traditional teachings of the Church. Jesuit humanism moved in the same direction as much of secular thought, and it was the destruction of the Society of Jesus which greatly weakened those within the Church skilled in speaking to the élite in a modern, yet orthodox, idiom.[48] The fact that the Church failed to persuade the élite that its teachings were compatible with modern life and thought may conceal the actual energy it heroically expended in the attempt, and one is tempted with Gay to regard these efforts as paltry and misguided. Yet it was the Jansenist emphasis on the incompatibility of Christianity with modern life which the bourgeoisie most strongly rejected, and despite the influence of the Jansenists' resistance to royal despotism on the political education of the bourgeoisie, the theological concerns of the Jansenists tended to make them increasingly irrelevant in the struggle between the Church and the Enlightenment.[49]

What also contributed importantly to the failure of the Church to keep the allegiance of the bourgeoisie was the politics of the Church, its defense of its privileges and its continued opposition to religious tolerance.[50] The Jesuits had, despite their humanism and modernism, pursued the Jansenists with intolerant fury, and the Jansenists, in turn, saw no virtue in tolerance. In 1765 the Jansenist *Nouvelles Ecclésiastiques* attacked d'Alembert's advocacy of religious toleration in these acerbic terms:

> "When will that happy time arrive, when we will see mosques in one street of Paris, synagogues in another, here some Protestant temples, there some pagodas, when we will make our Capital into a Pantheon where every race will find its temple, and every idol its altar? It is by this confusion of cults that religious troubles will be banished; it is from this chaos that peace will be born."[51]

Rejecting this traditional Catholic position against religious freedom with abhorrence, the bourgeoisie held with Voltaire that it was the intolerance and persecutory zeal of the Church which most needed to be opposed. With him, the bourgeoisie praised only the beneficient pastor who eschewed theological controversy for morality and social meliorism.[52]

One attempt at reconciling the élite with the Church was through the so-called "Catholic Enlightenment," a product of theological reflection which sought to extend and revise the Tridentine reforms in the light of modern developments. Hostile generally to the Roman Curia and to the Jesuits, Catholic reformers won support from reforming princes and their ministers in several eighteenth-century Catholic states: Spain, Portugal, the Habsburg lands in Germany, and Habsburg and Bourbon principalities in Italy. These reformers sought, with the power of the State, to correct abuses in the Church by continuing the simplification of worship and the utilization of ecclesiastical wealth for educational and other social purposes. They also ventured on the dangerous ground of exalting the role of laymen and parish priests over the hierarchical domination of the upper clergy, and advocated experimentation with vernacular liturgies.[53] The only example of anything analogous in France was the reform of monasticism in the 1760s, for the French monarchy was too exhausted by decades of religious controversy to seek reform within the Church. Turgot was perhaps the only minister in France who held ideas similar to those of the Catholic Enlightenment, and his ministry lasted only briefly. He had wished to revise the coronation oath to be taken by Louis XVI to eliminate all reference to the extirpation of heresy, and he advocated toleration and the legalization of Protestant marriage.[54] The failure of efforts to reform the monarchy and the increasing intransigence of the French Church weakened the prestige of both. The Catholic Enlightenment, seen from a modern perspective as an early *aggiornamento*, had its greatest impact outside of France, but it involved the kind of modern Catholicism which in France might have contributed towards lessening the alienation of the élite from the Church and from Christian faith. Hardly touched by the Catholic Enlightenment but significantly influenced instead by the *secular* Enlightenment, the French élite entered the revolutionary era with perhaps unrealistic expectations about what new role the Church could be given in a new age. And the clergy for its part was hardly well prepared for the challenges ahead.

THE CHURCH AND THE REVOLUTION

Many are familiar with the great confrontation between the French Revolution and the Roman Catholic Church. Little needs to be repeated about the schism between Catholics accepting the Revolution and those following the decrees of the Roman Pontiff, the suppression and persecution of Catholicism during the Reign of Terror, and the separation of Church and State in 1795 which lasted until Napoleon Bonaparte's Concordat with Pope Pius VII. It was during these years that the calendar was reformed to replace the birth of the Saviour with the proclamation of the French Republic as the fixed point of chronological reference. A new world was born, a world of mass politics and mass mobilization on behalf of the nation-state. What is less well known and appreciated, however, is that the makers of the Revolution intended for the Church something rather different. They intended certainly to reform the abuses of the Catholic Church as they dismantled the "Old Regime" of which it was so integral a part, but they sought first to offer the Church and the clergy a new role. If the monarchy had succeeded in transforming the Church into the spiritual arm of its administration, the revolutionaries intended no less to harness religious feeling and traditional Catholic faith for the support of the new France they were creating. And no more than the monarchs of the seventeenth and eighteenth centuries and their chief ministers did they intend to permit the clergy to pursue its own private agenda to the detriment of the welfare of the State. The continuities between the purposes, methods, and problems of the leaders of the Old Regime and those of the New must not be ignored or understated. If we have learned anything from the theories of Alexis de Tocqueville and Karl Marx we should expect that those "revolutionary" changes that most endure are those for which "history" has well and carefully prepared. All the contradictions and problems of the confessional state were not solved by the Revolution, for indeed the confessional state was not so much abolished as transformed into the modern nation-state where formal religious bodies play a lesser role but tests of ideological orthodoxy often continue to be imposed for the granting or refusal of civil and political rights.

The clergy and the lay élite entered the revolutionary period with very different notions about the roles they wished the Church to play in the regeneration of France and different conceptions of regeneration itself. With the encouragement of Louis XVI's government the election of clerical deputies to the Estates General was heavily weighted in favor of the lower clergy. From its *cahiers de doléances* and its pamphlets published during 1787–9 it was apparent that the clergy identified the abuses in Church and State with aristocratic domination and shared much with the bourgeois Third Estate. However, the reformist clergy differed with laymen in one crucial respect: where the clergy sought the reform of France through its re-Christianization under the leadership of a "purified and revivified Church," the Third Estate sought regeneration through the establishment of liberty and equality.[55] This was the beginning of a misunderstanding about *liberty* that is still with us. The clergy had indeed to a great extent already joined with the lay élite in eschewing theology in favor of emphasizing the social utility of religion, but its concept of civilization was still *Christian*, still based on the notion that Christianity perfected the social order.[56] The lay élite intended that the Church continue, as under the absolute monarchy, to be integrated into State service, with the clergy taking direction from the secular authorities. Indeed, the only feature of the Civil Constitution of the Clergy which really went significantly beyond Gallican tradition was the provision that the *curés* be elected by active citizens. Thus the selection of clergy was placed in the electoral hands of the bourgeoisie, a clear indication of who was to lead and who to serve.[57] Enough of the clergy was either persuaded of the good will of the revolutionary laymen or felt sufficiently pressured into acquiescence for about 52 to 55 per cent of the parish clergy to take the oath to the Civil Constitution required of ecclesiastical functionaries. The failure of the National Assembly to declare Catholicism the official cult and its unwillingness to deny full citizenship to Protestants had upset but not alienated the "patriotic" clergy. Even after papal condemnation of the Civil Constitution became widely known, between the spring of 1791 and the autumn of 1792, retractions of the oath still left the percentage of conformists above the level of 45 per cent of the working clergy. Most of the massive retraction of the oath came later during the Reign of Terror and was based on much more than mere Roman disapproval.[58] Thus the priests and the bourgeois revolutionaries made considerable efforts to keep up their cooperation. Even the most emancipated bourgeois had to agree with Rivarol: "When one has made this world unbearable for men, one surely must promise them another one."[59] Cooperation between clergy and bourgeoisie did not last, and the ensuing breach between them would require at least a half-century or more to be healed, another example of what some historians call the "*dérapage*" of the Revolution, its "skidding off the track."

What pushed the religious policy of the early revolutionaries "off the track" was unquestionably the unexpected violence of anti-clericalism and anti-Catholicism among elements of the middle and lower classes. Those legislating the Civil Constitution of the Clergy and establishing the loyalty oath which split the Church into "patriots" and "non-jurors" had expected their essentially Gallican reforms to encounter little difficulty. That Pope Pius VI should refuse to accept reform of the Gallican Church and that many Frenchmen and Frenchwomen, clerical and lay alike, should treat papal opinions with serious respect were unexpected and intolerable to many of the revolutionaries. Most had anticipated that Rome would accept from the National Assembly what it had accepted from the Old Regime: the right of the Gallican Church to regulate its own affairs. The rhetorically violent Hébert was incredulous about Louis XVI's concern with papal opposition:

> "What is the power of the Pope for enlightened men today? Is he still to terrorize the nations in the century in which we live? Are the decrees of the National Assembly less respectable than the decisions of the Council of Louis XV? Should he [the king] not already see that the damn priests seek to stir up schism in the kingdom in order to ignite civil war and renew the horrors of the League."[60]

This unexpected opposition to the ecclesiastical reorganization by the National Assembly was assumed by the revolutionaries to be part of a general aristocratic and royal conspiracy to stop the Revolution in its tracks, and all the latent hostility to the Church which had been suppressed and concealed under the Old Regime was now free to surface. Those long outraged by the intolerance of the Church, by the forced conformity of Protestants, Jansenists, and Free-Thinkers, by the Tridentine pretensions of the clergy to regulate closely the daily lives of the laity, and by the cultural and social conservatism of the Church were at last free to express their animus and to indulge their conspiratorial fantasies with impunity. The strength of anti-clericalism and anti-Catholicism among various strata of the French population demonstrates how mixed were the successes of the Catholic Reformation in France. The conformity of the Old Regime evidently concealed a considerable degree of de-Christianization and secularization among the French people. The Revolution allowed, indeed encouraged, this alienation to come above ground. The murderers of priests and nuns, the desecrators of churches and cemeteries, and the inventors of new cults and new festivals cannot have been created overnight. They were necessarily long in the making.

The inability of the officially recognized "Constitutional" Church to win or keep the allegiance of a majority of practising Catholics meant that it could not serve as the intended means of harnessing religious faith and feeling in the cause of the Revolution. Between the violent hostility to religion which grew on the Left and the increasing identification of papal Catholicism with Counter-Revolution on the Right, the Constitutional Church lost its very *raison d'être* even before it was officially disestablished early in 1795. Among those sympathetic to the attempt to keep the alliance between patriots and patriotic clergy alive, like the Cercle Social of the Abbé Claude Fauchet, the Abbé Adrien Lamourette, and Nicolas de Bonneville, two rival conceptions of the role of religion in the revolutionary age arose. Some like Fauchet insisted that since the cult of the Fatherland was in a number of ways akin to apostolic Christianity, Christian worship actually furthered the goals of the Revolution. Others like Bonneville with regret found Christianity increasingly unsuitable for patriotic purposes and sought to have it superseded by a civic and philosophical religion.[61] Fauchet and Lamourette understood that in the pluralistic environment created by the Revolution the Church could no longer demand exclusive rights, but they were loath to abandon the connection between Church and State which the Constitutional Church had all too briefly enjoyed.[62] Fauchet, in fact, sought to win the support of the bourgeoisie for the Church by emphasizing that Christian faith was essentially one of unity and brotherhood – in other words, that it was akin to the revolutionary *fraternité* or nationalism which was emerging as the emotional foundation of the Revolution. The Abbé Fauchet was groping towards a religion of nationalism and equality; what he considered sincerely as the flowering of Catholicism actually came to be the two great rivals of Christianity in the west from that day to the present, namely nationalism and socialism.[63]

The revolutionaries preferred to abandon the Constitutional Church in favor of their own patriotic cults which, whatever their names, were all founded on deism and patriotism. Deism reached its public form in the movement of Theophilanthropy which under the Directory received unofficial governmental approval for a time, while patriotism was enshrined in the *Décadi* ceremonies.[64] The revolutionaries were convinced that one could not separate religious and political authority. Where in the modern world democrats expect the gradual regeneration of man through education, during the French Revolution a religious cult was deemed necessary. The revolutionaries were indeed the firm disciples of Rousseau's "Priest of Savoy."[65] Sharing Rousseau's theoretical doubts in *The Social Contract* about the utility of

Christianity, in practice they first had shared his relative conservatism in considering Christianity as a desirable social institution where it had already for a long time been established. For Rousseau, "the stability and order of the State seemed . . . more important than any question of particular religious 'truths.'"[66] Rousseau's position could be quite illiberal for, as Maxime Leroy reminds us, "there cannot be religious freedom in a State where, as Rousseau proposed it, the Sovereign (yesterday the king or a coterie, today the people or a faction) is declared master of the religious symbol," for only "good religions" would be permitted by the State.[67] Some of the persecution of Catholicism during the Revolution was influenced by certain interpretations of Rousseau, as was paradoxically also the final decision of Napoleon Bonaparte to restore Catholicism. The religious element in citizenship thus remained a dilemma and a challenge.

Napoleon's decision to restore Roman Catholicism to France, although under tight secular supervision, was unquestionably based for the most part on his consideration of the harm which religious conflict inflicted on civic peace. He had seen the role of outraged religious feeling in keeping alive in the Vendée the bitter rebellion against the revolutionary Republic and had, during the Italian campaign, renewed his childhood appreciation of the hold of the Catholic faith on traditional populations. He was determined, as he seized power and sought means of making it firm, that religion would not be used against his authority and the stability and welfare of France. Religion, he said, had to be taken out of the control of *émigré* bishops in the pay of England. His own education in the ancient classics and in the newer classics of the French Enlightenment had made him, at least in religious matters, a disciple of Voltaire and Rousseau. Napoleon believed with Voltaire that religion could only be justified by its utility, and he said with characteristic aplomb that he saw in Christianity less the mystery of the Incarnation than the mystery of the Social Order. He viewed the clergy, once integrated into his system, as his spiritual administrators.[68] With the Rousseau of the conservative, non-utopian writings, Napoleon believed that it was better to make a traditional religion serviceable than to indulge in the dubious quest for substitute cults. He summarized his amalgamation of the lessons of the Enlightenment in the public version of his address to the Milanese clergy on 5 June 1800:

> I too am a philosopher, and I know that in no society can a man be honest and just if he does not know whence he comes and where he is going. Reason is not sufficient to give him this light, without which every man is obliged to journey in the dark. The Catholic Religion alone, with its infallibility, confronts man with his beginning and his end.
>
> No society can exist without morality. There can be no sound morality where religion does not exist. . . .[69]

Thus the revolutionary experience led Napoleon to modify the teachings of the *philosophes* with the practical evidence of the dangers of religious upheaval. The result was the restoration of Catholicism through the Concordat with Rome, a restoration, however, which continued many important accomplishments of the Revolution: Catholicism was not given dominant, exclusive status in France; the clergy was not reconstituted as an Estate, nor was it given independent landed wealth; freedom of religion was proclaimed; and the State insisted on the lay status of marriage and divorce.[70] Thus, the confessional state was not restored. Protestants received a status comparable to that of Catholics, with their clergy also salaried by the State. And Jews, although their cult was not financially supported by the State at that time, had official sanction of their religious organization, thus for the first time receiving more than a grudging grant of citizenship. Except for the newly independent American republic, nowhere else in the west did men enjoy such a degree of religious liberty as in Napoleonic France. Napoleon revealed himself to be a new Henry IV. Like the first Bourbon king of France, Napoleon had been forced to adopt the religion of the vast majority of his subjects in order to stabilize his authority. And like Henry IV, he sought the means of making the restored Catholic faith an important buttress of authority, but one deprived of the power to subvert secular government. Napoleon had his bishops and priests swear an oath not to the constitution nor to the laws of the State, but to the existing government itself, requiring also their promise to inform the authorities of all plots against the regime. The Imperial Catechism of 1806 taught not only traditional obedience to constituted authority; it also placed at the core of the subject's religious obligation total loyalty to the civil authority. Contrary to the normative position of Catholic theology in generally enjoining obedience to authority without "particularizing" obedience to a designated regime, the Imperial Catechism actually made specific loyalty to Napoleon the essence of the religious obligation of the French subject and citizen.[71]

Napoleon's religious settlement thus was at once the triumph of popular religion and a way of stifling religion as a "vehicle of protest." It also dealt the death blow to those tendencies of the Catholic Enlightenment which were suggesting the development of a new Catholic ecclesiology in which the clergy would operate in a less hierarchical structure and the laity would play a more active role in the Church.[72] Napoleon abandoned the confessional state but not the advantages of a religion preaching hierarchy, order, and obedience. One might fruitfully compare his post-revolutionary view of religion with that of Edmund Burke. Burke had before the revolutionary upheaval favored considerable toleration of religious dissent, but the French Revolution convinced him that only the confessional state could prevent chaos. In a 1792 speech to the House of Commons he said:

> "In a Christian commonwealth the Church and the state are one and the same thing, being different integral parts of the same whole. . . . Religion is so far, in my opinion, from being out of the province or the duty of a Christian magistrate, that it is, and it ought to be, not only his care, but the principal thing in his care; because it is one of the great bonds of human society, and its object the supreme good, the ultimate end and object of man himself."[73]

Napoleon was unquestionably authoritarian, but a comparison with the views of Edmund Burke makes clear that he was not a conservative. He never restored the Old Regime connection between citizenship and formal adherence to an established Church. And while his religious settlement contained both liberal and conservative elements, his struggle against the Pope during the period from 1809 to 1815 helped to convince many Catholics that a government based on revolutionary principles, or like Napoleon's regime, one based even *partly* on revolution, would always place the Catholic faith in danger. This served to encourage the alliance of the Church and much of its faithful with the Bourbon legitimists, a position which amounted to an abandonment of any attempt to play a new role in French life.[74] The authoritarianism of Napoleonic France, and its restoration of a Catholicism without renewal, helped to convince both Catholics and anti-clericals that the Church could not and should not play in modern France a role different from the one it had played under the Old Regime.

The Revolution, thus, offered the Church a role in which, under the direction of the lay élite, it would serve the spiritual needs of the people and the civic and social needs of the regime. The Church was not theologically, intellectually, or socially ready to meet this challenge and to seize the opportunities offered by a pluralistic society. Nor was the lay élite of liberal nobles and bourgeois sufficiently sympathetic towards the dilemmas of a clergy suspended between the old and the new. Napoleon for his own purposes worked on behalf of healing and reconciliation, but his considerable accomplishments made it all too easy for the clergy to return with relief to something like a *status quo ante*. The very gratitude of the Catholic clergy for the restoration of religion made them constitutionally unable to avoid widening the breach still further between those seeking change and those determined to restore the Old Regime and the old ways at the first opportunity. Religion was indeed restored under Napoleon, but the clergy was placed in a condition of abject servitude towards the government, one unparalleled in French history. Under Napoleon, and also under his legitimist and Orléanist successors, the clergy felt all of the constraints imposed upon it from the beginning of the Bourbon monarchy, while it enjoyed nothing of the autonomy, the wealth, or the status it had still retained up to 1789.

III

Prophecy or order: the nineteenth-century Church in search of a role

The history of the French Catholic Church in the nineteenth century has conventionally been cast in terms of the Whig interpretation of history, even as recently as the Second Vatican Council of the 1960s. The fortunes of the Church through years of revolution and frequent changes of political regime have therefore been described, whether by liberals or conservatives, radicals or reactionaries, as the confrontation of the Church and its clergy and faithful laity with the legacy of the French Revolution. In this interpretive framework, liberal Catholic heroes are pictured as battling mightily, if often with only modest success, on behalf of the accommodation of the Church to modern political, social, and intellectual realities. Their more successful opponents within the Church, whether called traditionalists, intransigents, or integrists, are seen as resisting acceptance of the revolutionary heritage and delaying any modernization of the Church and its teachings for more than a century; these opponents of modernization are also viewed generally as committed to the restoration of aristocratic and monarchic political structures and against the rising tide of democracy and mass politics. Much of the history of nineteenth-century Europe has been written in this Whiggish manner, and the story of the Catholic Church's evident resistance to modernity has been fitted fairly comfortably into this pattern. This pattern or paradigm was itself, in the first place, the product of the great controversy about the course and meaning of the French Revolution and its aftershocks, and it seemed especially appropriate in understanding the course of the "bourgeois" nineteenth century.

In the particular story of the French Catholic Church, liberal historians, whether Catholic or not, generally have identified several protagonists who sought Catholic accommodation with the course of modern history, men like Lamennais, Lacordaire, Montalembert, and Dupanloup who in one way or another were frustrated by the malice or ignorance of those more powerful Catholic leaders who objected to any such accommodation. The opponents of liberal Catholic efforts are best represented and symbolized by Louis Veuillot, the vitriolic editor of the Ultramontanist newspaper *L'Univers*, and by Pope Pius IX whose policy after 1848 seemed resolutely designed to defy all compromise with modern civilization. These men and their followers were generally able successfully to limit the effectiveness of liberal Catholic initiatives. The interpretations of reactionary or conservative historians have also been beholden to Whiggish notions of the inevitable movement of history, and the heroes of the liberals were, in turn, the villains of the conservatives, and the opponents of liberalism their own heroes. Many conservative historians seemed readily to accept the inevitability of a liberal victory because their thought often was infused with an apocalyptic spirit that expected the continuing victory of a Satanically directed modernity until the intervention of Divine Providence. Thus, most historians were fairly well agreed on the general outline of French Church history after the French Revolution. And the interpretive framework they favored was far from erroneous; it did after all explain the course of French Catholicism coherently, with thematic consistency, intellectual stimulation, and political relevance.

It is possible, however, to seek an alternative interpretive framework; one which ignores the obvious struggles of liberal Catholics against conservatives in favor of illuminating a rather different confrontation, one between Catholics who essentially wished to explain and, thereby, to maintain the world as it was and those who wished in some profound sense to change it. Such a confrontation juxtaposed two groups, the partisans of what may be called "bourgeois" Catholicism – a Catholicism of order, a Voltairean Catholicism – against advocates of a prophetic Catholicism, one most appropriately identified with the career of the Abbé Lamennais. A prominent historian of medieval Christianity, Jeffrey Burton Russell, once described the major themes of medieval Church history in terms of "prophecy and order," a set of boundaries which may also have some relevance for other periods of Church history. One is also reminded of an often quoted phrase from Karl Marx's *Theses on Feuerbach*: "The philosophers have only *interpreted* the world differently, the point is, to *change* it."[1] There were some Catholics who, like Marx, wanted to change the world radically.

It seems possible to use these insights fruitfully by re-staging the drama of nineteenth-century French Catholicism, this time as a struggle between those desiring to have the Church support the status quo and those with a more utopian vision of what the Church should be in the world of the nineteenth century. In such a framework, liberals, radicals, conservatives, and reactionaries disappear for a time, which may be all to the good. And what is illuminated here, instead, is the perennial concern of the Roman Catholic Church with constituting or reconstituting a Catholic social order. This was a concern which was and could be expressed in both traditionalist and modernist terms, just as the Catholicism of order could be liberal or conservative depending on what the given political and social order to be defended essentially represented. In this perspective, the Church and its leaders can be judged more according to their own standards and insights and less according to the external standards developed by writers and thinkers with little or no sympathy for the dilemmas and concerns of Catholics in the modern world.

The one modern historian who more than any other has recast the interpretive framework of French Catholic history is Emile Poulat who, in numerous works, but especially in his *Eglise contre bourgeoisie. Introduction au devenir du catholicisme actuel*, has offered a convincing critique of Whiggish interpretations of French Catholicism and demonstrated in striking fashion that the Catholic Church's uniquely consistent position has been one of opposition to modern, secular society because of its own commitment to a society which should reflect eternal truth.[2] Thus, Poulat has seen the Catholic Church's attitude towards modern life as integrally *utopian*, something obscured by Whiggish insights and expectations. With Marx and the Marxists, the Church's deepest desire was and is to *change* the world and not merely to *interpret* it. Alongside its conservative concern for order and stability there has existed a profoundly prophetic and utopian vision. This vision goes far towards explaining important affinities between reactionary and progressive Catholic initiatives, and it demonstrates why the Catholic Church could on some occasions become deeply committed to reactionary policies which under the right circumstances could also be radically transformed into something quite different. Poulat's restructuring of the interpretation of modern French Catholic history is an invaluable and indispensable tool for probing the French Church's quest for an appropriate role in French national life after the great Revolution. Such a restructured conception of modern French Catholic history may or may not depict the Church more sympathetically, but it is likely to reveal the Church in a more institutionally authentic light.

BOURGEOIS CATHOLICISM

To speak of *bourgeois* Catholicism or a Catholicism of order, and to associate it with the name of Voltaire, may seem surprising or contradictory. Much of the nineteenth-century French élite, particularly in the first half of the century, was of course Voltairean without being in the least Catholic, and almost all Catholics, however else they might differ, had no trouble in identifying the spirit of Voltaire as the greatest obstacle to a restoration of Catholic influence in France. Yet as was suggested earlier, Voltaire's anti-clericalism must be distinguished from hostility *tout court* to all religion. Theodore Zeldin has aptly reminded us that the social and moral goals of the bourgeois anti-clericals and the Catholic clergy did not always differ as profoundly as they imagined, for it was politics more than ethics that divided Frenchmen into anti-clericals and Catholics; a division which could obscure important affinities and make strange political bedfellows.[3]

The position given to the French Catholic Church and its clergy by the Napoleonic settlement was pre-eminently a role of service to the State, essentially a restoration of the subservient position of the Church under Louis XIV but without enjoyment of the prestige or the exclusivity of the confessional state. In the words of one perceptive historian of the fortunes of the Gallican establishment in the early nineteenth century, the French Catholic clergy belonged "in effect to the most oversupervised and underpaid branch of the French civil service."[4] Like Gallicanism under the pre-revolutionary Bourbons, Gallicanism in the nineteenth century was a political and religious position which placed the Church squarely under the control and in the service of the French State. As such, it was a force for order, for conformity, and, even in the view of the largely Voltairean élite, one indispensable for the masses, "the great majority of Frenchmen" which the Concordat of 1801 identified as Catholic. It was this emphasis on the Church as a useful social institution, firmly under State tutelage, barred from pursuing its own agenda, and permitted no interference with or coercive power over the *private* religious views of individuals, which constituted what may be called a *bourgeois* Catholicism of order. It was upheld by a tacit alliance of Gallicans, bureaucrats, and Voltairean bourgeois who for different reasons could not conceive of France without a Catholic establishment, and who would not tolerate either a clerical independence based on "a free church in a free state" as desired by liberal Catholics, or clerical domination in the spirit of the Council of Trent or medieval Christendom. Such had been essentially the position of Napoleon as he sought to restore religion after the revolutionary upheavals, but with the proper political and social balance and control. Between 1801 and 1905 the Catholic Church was not separated from the French State, and all the struggles over clericalism and anti-clericalism necessarily remained a "family affair" among Frenchmen who were largely committed to the maintenance of the Concordat. It was in this context that Voltairean scoffers, however much they might indulge in clerical baiting, could still desire to secure the advantages of a religious establishment and recommend Catholic faith and discipline to their servants, their employees, their wives and daughters, eventually even to their sons and themselves. Catholicism was to be public in its defense of order and private in its non-interference with the interior life of the élite.

The importance of Gallicanism among those adhering to a Catholicism of order can be underestimated. Historians of the Church have rightly impressed us with the causes of the revival of Ultramontanism in the nineteenth century. The French Revolution and its territorial advances certainly did destroy the princely resistance to papal aggrandizement by overthrowing the Bourbons in France, Spain, and Italy, and by secularizing the great ecclesiastical principalities in the Rhineland. Napoleon's recourse to Pius VII in reconstituting the French Church also did concede to the Roman See a degree of power to make and unmake bishops which Catholic monarchs had successfully resisted for centuries. And the ideology of the unity of Christendom which papal power might seem to symbolize did have strong appeal in an age of conservatism and romanticism following the upheavals of the Revolution and Napoleon. Yet it would be a mistake to think that the rise of Ultramontanism and the corresponding decline of Gallicanism were rapid or complete. Despite the Concordat's apparent abandonment of many a Gallican principle, the Organic Articles which Napoleon unilaterally had appended to the religious settlement with Rome allowed the Gallicans to administer the Church in the spirit of the monarchs, ministers, and Parlements of the Old Regime. The monarchs, bureaucrats, politicians, and bishops of France until as late as 1870 believed that the State could and should control the external manifestations of religion. It was the lower clergy which had no defense against episcopal domination, and the younger clerics influenced by the utopian ideas of Lamennais, who found papal authority attractive and whose views ultimately would triumph; but for much of the nineteenth century those ruling the French Church and State were committed Gallicans.

Politically, Gallicanism could be legitimist, as under the Bourbon Restoration, or it could be liberal, as under subsequent Orléanist and Bonapartist regimes. It could even be republican, but it necessarily remained very much an "establishmentarian" position and adhered consistently to a vision of the Catholic Church as a force for order and stability after a period of crisis. If under the Bourbon Restoration many of the clerics appointed to episcopal office came from the ranks of the nobility and were chosen to further the aims of the legitimists, under the July Monarchy the bishops were increasingly recruited more broadly from the middle classes. Many had been educated in secular schools and some had even followed bourgeois careers before entering the clergy. They were men of some learning and administrative experience, capable of sympathetic dealings and ties with local élites. They were expected to be conciliators, not fanatics, conservatives rather than reactionaries, and to concern themselves more with the good order of the Church and its close association with local élites than with the concerns or welfare of the masses.[5] As the politicians of the Orléanist regime praised the *juste milieu*, the Gallican episcopate practised a moderate Gallicanism and a muffled clericalism which indeed seemed the ecclesiastical equivalent of political moderation. Gallicanism in the nineteenth century meant conformity and accommodation. And the regimes of the nineteenth century were as capable as the monarchs and ministers of the Old Regime of using a Gallican anti-clericalism when necessary to discipline the clergy and keep the Church firmly under the tutelage of the State.

THE IMPORTANCE OF LAMENNAIS

In interpreting the dilemmas of the French Church in the post-revolutionary era, in the light of what came before the Revolution and what would emerge in the twentieth century, no figure is more central than the Breton priest and later apostate, Hugues-Félicité Robert de Lamennais. To appreciate his critical importance to an understanding of the course of nineteenth-century French Catholicism, one must cease regarding him conventionally as a liberal Catholic who fought valiantly against reaction and ended his life as an independent radical outside of the Church which had categorically rejected him. As solely a liberal Catholic, Lamennais is more pathetic than interesting, and liberal Catholicism itself is in fact of marginal importance in the story of French Catholicism, something exaggerated by Whiggish historians. It is rather as the prophet of a truly utopian Catholicism that Lamennais' own stature is really grasped and his importance for the Church assessed. For it was only as a man too far ahead of his time who would leave an ambiguous legacy for his inadequate disciples that he was a failure. In fact, no one in Catholic France saw more clearly than he the actual situation of the Church in modern times. Harold Laski, despite his secularist biases, may have perceived better than most commentators that Lamennais' importance lay in the fact that he heroically straddled two ages: "'He stood at the parting between two worlds. He strove to arrest the onset of forces he was at the last driven to recognize as irresistible.'"[6] Or to put it differently, Lamennais was able to suggest a way of finding in Catholicism the means of amalgamating at one and the same time the traditionalism of the ageing victims of the Revolution, the romanticism of post-revolutionary youth, and the utopian strivings which saw in socialism the fulfillment of the millennial aspirations of Christian civilization.[7]

Lamennais truly understood that the task of a relevant Roman Catholic Christianity was to remake the world and not merely to defend the existing order. If he had any spiritual ancestors, they are more likely to be found in the ranks of the enthusiasts of the Catholic League and the *dévot* and Jansenist opponents of Richelieu and Louis XIV than among the ecclesiastical politicians of pre-revolutionary Bourbon France. Lamennais in an earlier century would no more have stomached a Protestant king or acquiesced in a Franco-Protestant alliance against the House of Habsburg than he could have discerned the construction of a Catholic social order in the policies of Charles X or Louis-Philippe. He was condemned finally for audacity by the frightened Popes of the nineteenth century, and his perfervid commitment to Ultramontanism was stultified by the evident absence in his own day of Popes of the stature of the great medieval pontiffs who had made emperors and kings tremble. His contemporaries trembled instead at his own temerity, and Popes took refuge behind bulls and curial pronouncements. Lamennais died alone and was buried in unhallowed ground because few dared to join him in taking the risk of probing the place and prospects of the Catholic Church in the modern age.

Lamennais's impassioned defense of papal authority and his bitter denunciation of Gallicanism early in his career unfortunately serve to blur his true importance in assessing the dilemma of French Catholicism in the post-revolutionary age. The growth and development of Ultramontanism would, by the middle of the nineteenth century, come to be identified with intransigent Catholic opposition not only to modern politics but to virtually all of modern civilization. If one takes seriously the condemnations of Pius IX's *Syllabus of Errors* of 1864, one might rashly misjudge the nature of Lamennais's Ultramontanism and also the true reasons for his final defection from the papal cause. His opposition to Gallicanism may appear quaint, irrelevant, and illiberal, despite the fact that in the early nineteenth century Gallicanism, whatever its later identification with liberalizing and modernizing tendencies, was a continuation of a royal French tradition which had worked to make the French Church the servant of the State and monarchy. Gallicanism could properly be seen, as Lamennais saw it, as a reactionary force. His purposes, and his favorite causes as well as his special aversions, need to be taken seriously and seen through his own eyes in order to assess his prophetic importance for French Catholicism in the nineteenth century. To dwell upon what may seem inconsistencies or apparently radical changes of opinion in his declining years can only obscure what seems, after a century of scholarship, indeed clear enough.

Hugues-Félicité Robert de Lamennais was born in 1782 and came to manhood just as Napoleon was establishing the foundations of his regime, the Augustan creation of a military monarchy behind the trappings of republican institutions and virtues. Perhaps nothing had a more lasting effect on the young Lamennais than the experience, both direct and indirect, of Napoleonic tyranny. The year 1809 was arguably the most important in his life. There at the age of 27, his second published work, the *Réflexions sur l'état de l'Eglise en France pendant le xviiie siècle et sur sa situation actuelle*, was seized by the police. In the same year, Pope Pius VII was arrested in Rome by French troops and taken prisoner to France. And Lamennais made in the same year his first approach towards taking Holy Orders, although he did not become a priest until 1816 when he was 33 years old. Thus while on the road towards the priesthood he was rewarded for his scholarly pains in assessing the position of the French Catholic Church with brutal censorship, and he witnessed the second instance within a decade of the humiliation of a reigning Pope by France. Pius VII followed Pius VI into French captivity, thus demonstrating that the much celebrated Napoleonic Concordat could be as effective an instrument of religious oppression as the anti-Christian hostility of the French Revolution.[8]

The theme of the *Réflexions* is less important than the fact of its suppression by imperial censorship. The book discussed the evils of the Protestant Reformation and the Enlightenment in a rather conventional conservative Catholic way, seeing in them the fundamental causes of the French Revolution, and it portrayed the weaknesses of the Church and clergy in confronting the challenge of the *philosophes* with some understanding of the enervating effect of Bourbon absolutism on religious vitality. These themes would appear far more effectively in Lamennais' later work, but it was very important that he was forced by the experience of early censorship to reflect upon the supposed re-establishment of Catholicism by Napoleon, and he began the scholarly study and analysis which led him finally to place all his hope in the exaltation of papal power over the dynastic and territorial churches of Catholic Europe. In the wake of Napoleonic oppression and Pius VII's manly sufferings, Lamennais forged his commitment to Ultramontanism and the beginnings of what would become a deep aversion for the union of throne and altar.

It is most significant that it was Napoleon's *religious* policy in particular that made Lamennais a critic of the imperial regime, for unlike some of the purely political opponents of Napoleon, he would have little patience with the restored Bourbons when he concluded that they were continuing fundamentally the same Napoleonic policy towards the Church. Thus did Lamennais come to see that the legitimist alliance of throne and altar was identical to the Caesaropapism of Napoleon, to the religious policy of the revolutionary bourgeoisie in the early years of the Revolution, and to the Gallicanism of the Old Regime. In an era of considerable upheaval and radical change he was perhaps uniquely equipped to discover surprising and troubling continuities. He saw the Napoleonic restoration of the Church for what it essentially was: a parallel to Henry IV's apparent surrender to normative religious observance for the sake of a closer control of the power of the Church and clergy. Napoleon with Henry IV and his successors all had drawn the same conclusions: the Church could serve the State effectively and safely only if it were kept Gallican in spirit and in practice. It was this conclusion that Lamennais would spend half his life trying to undermine, in favor of a more prophetic role for the Church of France.

The Louis XVIII who ascended the throne in the wake of the collapse of Napoleon's empire was not the man who as the *émigré* comte de Provence had hoped in July 1795 to put an end to the Revolution. After more than twenty years of exile he had become something of a liberal. But if the Charter of 1814 reassured liberals and moderates that the restored Bourbons would not seek to endanger the major accomplishments of the Revolution by actually attempting to restore the Old Regime, those who had suffered in exile or hiding for their royalism hoped to push the monarchy into more reactionary policies. Since none had suffered more than faithful papal Catholics, clergy and laity alike, it was natural for an alliance to emerge between political legitimists and clerical conservatives. The excesses of the Revolution, however understandable, and the Napoleonic Concordat had worked together to undermine the confidence of those who had in the 1790s experimented with more up-to-date ecclesiologies and more progressive conceptions of the relationship of Church and State in a pluralistic intellectual environment. Restoration and reaction were the means widely believed able to prevent the recurrence of Revolution, and a throne–altar alliance was to be the indispensable underpinning of order. Lamennais began his priestly and literary career under the restored Bourbons as a brilliant and exciting expounder of traditionalist and reactionary ideas based on medieval nostalgia, something which he shared with such conservative publicists as Louis de Bonald and Joseph de Maistre and with young romantics like Chateaubriand and Victor Hugo. But Lamennais' faith in the Restoration was always rather tentative, and he quickly concluded that the Restoration had restored – more accurately, had continued – all too much in the realm of Church and State that was harmful; in a word, the Gallican tradition.

In 1830 Lamennais looked back on the fifteen years of Bourbon Restoration not only with distaste but with a recognition of its illusionary quality:

> After thirty years of convulsions, of civil and foreign wars, of glory without and sorrow within, of anarchy and despotism, suddenly the shadow of the old royalty appeared and all eyes were fixed on this and people thought the order was going to return and that future repose was assured henceforth, for the monarchy brought words of peace and reconciliation. People talked of an eternal alliance concluded between the past and the present: and from the enormous ruins of I know not how many past governments a new edifice arose, a hastily constructed temple, in which the parties, renouncing their old hatreds, were to unite and fuse. . . .
>
> When, after the tumults of the Fronde [in the seventeenth century], the last and weak effort of resistance to a government that would no longer recognize any limits, everything bent to the will of a single man, religion itself was enslaved and lost its dignity by losing its independence. The French clergy, despite the condemnations of Rome, received on its knees the servile doctrines that despotism insolently imposed upon it, corrupted in its own bosom the spirit of Catholicism, and, in the eyes of the people, rendered it the accomplice of the government that had pitched its tent on the last debris of Christian liberty. Finding servitude next to the altar, men grew frightened of God. . . .
>
> Catholics, instructed by experience, have recognized that the government was a bad support for religion; that religion has its strength elsewhere, that is, in itself, and that its life is liberty. Stifled under the heavy protection of governments, the instruments of their politics and the toy of their whims,

> it would have perished if God, in the secret counsels of His providence, which ceaselessly watches over the only society that will not end, had not prepared its liberation. . . .[9]

Here is Lamennais' most deeply held conviction: the hopes of Catholics for the Bourbon Restoration could not be realized because the Gallican theory and practice of the Old Regime had emasculated the Church and converted it into part of the bureaucratic administration; and the upheavals of Revolution were not accidental but the work of Providence watching over His Church and His People. Thus the conventional attack on the Enlightenment, as on the earlier Protestant Reformation, was only one side of the explanation for the chaos of Revolution. The decadence and weakness of Catholicism had also to be identified as the product of royal absolutism and domination. And a second convention of *émigré* and legitimist thought, that the Revolution had occurred as divine punishment for apostasy and was a means of expiation for sin, was transformed by Lamennais into a conviction that the revolutionary upheavals were "God present before our eyes in the world."[10] Thus like Alexis de Tocqueville, Lamennais would see in violent change the hand of Providence in history moving mankind towards a more egalitarian social order. Some of Lamennais' convictions were clearly common enough among many conservatives and reactionaries, but he radically transformed them. Some other of his ideas were seemingly conventionally liberal. Yet where his true originality lay was in his very early association of intransigent political and social ideas coming from the royalist emigration with democratic and socially utopian notions of Christianizing and transforming the social order. Before he had been a royalist, before he seemed to be a liberal, in his innermost being Lamennais had been an early Catholic integrist and intransigent ardently desiring to remake the world by Christianizing it.

The tragic irony of Lamennais' career has for many lain in his extreme advocacy of Ultramontanism and his eventual condemnation by the same papal authority that he had placed at the heart of Catholic regeneration. Liberals are always baffled, and rightly so, that he could ever have persuaded himself that papal authority might be the foundation of a modern Christian social order. They recall only too well not only Gregory XVI's condemnations of Lamennais' work but also the reactionary *Syllabus of Errors* and the papacy's congenital hostility towards modern life, a prophetic intransigence which has, with twists and turns, lasted even until the present time with Pope John Paul II. Liberals by definition are perhaps also unable to view with sympathy Lamennais' characteristically idealistic conception of the papal office. His view of the papacy was of a piece with his essentially romantic adulation of the Middle Ages as he assessed the problems of his own revolutionary era. He viewed the crisis of his own day in a way which, in certain specifics, might seem parallel to the analysis of liberals, but he viewed reality from a fundamentally different perspective. Where liberals exalted the autonomy of the individual and his reason in overcoming traditional oppression, Lamennais saw in the decline of the social power of the Roman Catholic Church the cause of the modern crisis and the key to European history.

Much as liberal historians and ideologists in the early nineteenth century might willingly or grudgingly praise the medieval Church for having defended liberty against the aggrandizement of secular rulers, they still believed that the victory of secular authority in the hands of princely rulers had been a necessary historical step in the emancipation of the individual. The Renaissance, the Protestant Reformation, the eighteenth-century Enlightenment, and the early years, if not the whole course, of the French Revolution were for them stages in the liberation of European men and women from the domination of traditional religious and political authority. Lamennais did not share any of this vision. Instead, he consistently held to a view of the course of history which identified the Roman Catholic Church as the only force ever to have defended liberty against arbitrary power. The Renaissance, the Reformation, the Enlightenment, and the French Revolution were all for him steps in the destruction of the spiritual power's ability to resist the rise of political tyranny, whether at first in the hands of princes or finally in the hands of the people. Disillusioned by the apparent restoration of authority under the Bourbons after Napoleon, Lamennais readily attacked the same secular authorities against which the Church had battled for centuries. As he addressed the seemingly sympathetic Pope Leo XII in the years before the revolution of 1830, Lamennais placed the blame for revolution squarely on princely power:

> It was the princes who first gave the example of rebellion against this salutary authority [of the Church] . . . They declared themselves to be the only interpreters, the only *judges* of divine law concerning the exercise of sovereignty. The Reformation seized upon this principle and extended it to all Christians, subjects as well as princes, and in that it was consistent. [Eighteenth-century] Philosophy, which is only a more developed form of Protestantism, in proclaiming in an even more general way the absolute independence or sovereignty of individual reason, has accomplished the overthrow of the basis of faith and the foundation of order.[11]

Thus, Lamennais' defense of papal authority was the defense of those heroic medieval pontiffs who had battled on behalf of the independence of the authority of the Church, and he very much prized the romantic view of medieval reality in which religion allegedly penetrated everywhere in society and could not be confined to a secondary role by the secular authorities. Ultramontanism for Lamennais was thus less a naive theory of theocracy than a means of insuring the reality of spiritual liberty and the freedom of the Church to play a major role in society.[12]

Lamennais was not the first, nor would he be the last, to entrust the Roman See with so elevated a role that even with its remarkable pretensions it was ill-equipped to play it successfully. It would be valid and easy enough to observe that his view of the medieval papacy, and worse, his desire to recreate it in the nineteenth century, were utopian and unrealistic. His thought was indeed always more prophetic than analytic. His condemnation of the Bourbon Restoration as "atheistic," where liberals and any empirical observers were considerably more impressed with, or frightened by, its extreme clericalism and commitment to anachronistic religious policies, was another sign of his predilection for utopian utterance. Because the Bourbon government tolerated and financially supported non-Catholic cults, Lamennais concluded that the State had become irreligious. The concessions and privileges granted to the Roman Catholic Church and its clergy were only designed, in his view, to tie the Church more closely to the supervisory State and its bureaucracy and to prevent it from freely taking initiatives towards the re-Christianization of society. What appeared to be governmental favor was really a slavish tutelage, and the essential policy of the State was religiously indifferent, hence atheistic. When viewing the secular authorities in his own day, or in the distant past, and comparing them with the policies of the Popes, Lamennais consistently refused to distinguish between conscious intentions and the historical consequences of certain policies. For him, what was all important was the inner meaning of an historical trend. This led him to see irreligion as the hallmark of Gallicanism and Ultramontanism as the cornerstone of a new social order.[13]

Lamennais managed to ignore the obvious – that the papacy was as much a temporal authority as the spiritual headship of the Roman Catholic Church and that it necessarily would find itself, along with other governments, in the position of making compromises with the political realities of the day.[14] What would more than any other factor finally cause Lamennais' total break with the papacy and the institutional Church was the papal attitude towards the Polish Revolt of 1831, for Gregory XVI's warning to the Polish insurrectionists was an affirmation of the Church's alliance with secular authorities against even a Roman Catholic people.[15] In his support of the established order, namely Tsarist Russian repression of Poland, Pope Gregory was essentially adhering to Metternich's policy of containing revolution. But Rome was, thereby, also abandoning a Roman Catholic people fighting for its liberty, as well as denying normative Catholic theology about the right to resist oppression. It was clearly in the throne–altar alliance that the papacy had placed all its hopes.[16] In his characteristically prophetic way Lamennais should perhaps also have condemned the Pope for "atheism," a charge at least as applicable here as when it had been hurled at the government of Charles X. In any case, for Lamennais papal support for oppressive regimes undermined the essential mission and very *raison d'être* of the papal office.[17]

In Lamennais' view the Popes were alienating the people by becoming firm allies of the secular rulers who had already achieved arbitrary power in the period between the Renaissance and the French Revolution. And the more that the people found itself forced by circumstances to adopt an anti-religious posture, the more the Church defensively felt it necessary to support the ruling authorities.[18] It was this cycle of disaster from which the Church and papacy refused to break:

> The Pope declares that in the war which exists everywhere between the peoples and the kings, he places himself on the

> side of the kings; he joins the cause of the Church to that of all European despotisms; he notifies the peoples that to be free, they must cease being Catholic. By means of this league of the two powers they flatter themselves that they can prevent the social transformation which time has rendered necessary; but they are grandly mistaken; it will be accomplished even more quickly, because in halting Catholic action the Pope delivers the world to the action of purely destructive forces. God has thus willed it, and the terrible persecutions which will be the consequences for the Church were also for her apparently the indispensable condition of a new life.[19]

At this point Lamennais understood that Popes and their curial officials were also men who were constantly tempted to place temporal considerations above spiritual goals. In his prophetic view, they "crucified [Christ] . . . in effect each day by *raison d'Etat* . . ."[20] For Lamennais the Popes were evidently not Ultramontane enough or Catholic enough to meet the challenges of a revolutionary age,[21] and he harshly concluded that Providence would make use of other men and other means to bring the Christian social order into being. In leaving the Church Lamennais abandoned not one part of his vision of a regenerated humanity; only the instrument of redemption might have to be different.[22] The papacy had tragically chosen to follow the example of Simon Peter literally by denying that it even knew the Christ.

Lamennais resolutely refused to deny the Christ, but his conviction that Providence would employ other means of creating a Christian social order led him to abandon all formal association with the Roman Catholic Church. He requested that upon his death he be buried in a common grave without religious ritual – at one and the same time to announce his solidarity with the poor and, no less importantly, to symbolize his conviction that the Church had fallen into desuetude. As early as 1833 he had expressed the conviction that "the more I have opened my eyes and the more I open them still further, it is impossible for me not to see in today's Rome an all too exact image of the Synagogue in the time of Jesus Christ."[23] Here he clearly contended that as the synagogue, according to normative Christian exegesis, had been found wanting at the appearance of the Christ, the Church in his day was also tragically misreading the demands of Providence.

It is interesting, as well as important, to note that none of Lamennais' associates and followers were courageous or impetuous enough to leave the Church with him. For a long time, all that remained of Lamennais' legacy within the Catholic Church was his Ultramontanism, and any surviving commitment to liberal ideas by his followers necessarily yielded to the dominant force within the French Church, to a combined Ultramontanism and legitimism.[24] Because his legacy was multi-faceted and ambiguous and his erstwhile disciples and friends tried to sustain it in various non-political ways, a Mennaisian might with equal plausibility have become a liberal, a democratic socialist, or a reactionary monarchist.[25] As Emile Poulat never tires of emphasizing, there is one and the same ancestry for counter-revolutionary Catholicism, Christian democracy, and even Christian revolutionary movements: they are all outgrowths of the same Catholic intransigence which always, first and foremost, desired to rebuild a Catholic social order.[26] Here was Lamennais' ideological home. His liberalism and Ultramontanism were actually less important than his prior commitment to intransigent Catholicism.[27] This was then his most basic commitment – to what may most appropriately be called *Social Catholicism* – and it is the key both to his historic importance and to his long isolation among French Catholics throughout the rest of the nineteenth century.[28]

Lamennais had demonstrated a concern with the social aspects of Catholicism quite early in his career. By 1822–3 he was already concerned about the situation of the urban working classes and seemed in a tentative way to understand that their condition constituted a new social problem. His preoccupation with the problems of Church and State and philosophical issues served for several decades to relegate these social concerns to the background. In a sense, liberalism and Ultramontanism, although he understood these doctrines in his own characteristic way, diverted him away from the social issues. For a time he ignored his own insights about the nature of modern "wage slavery." His determination to have the Church break with servitude to the monarchist legacy and turn resolutely towards the future caused him to ignore the relevance of a body of social doctrine which the Church already possessed. The turning away from traditionalism, which marked Lamennais' efforts during his association with the newspaper *L'Avenir* in the early years of the July Monarchy, made him temporarily oblivious of existing Catholic teachings about the Social Question.[29] He was not only preoccupied with liberalism at this time; his conception of liberalism was always different from that of the secular liberals, for he supported a fundamental authoritarianism they could certainly not share. He viewed liberty as a heady brew which could be safely imbibed only under the supervision of the Church: therefore, liberty for the Church to influence society was the first liberty needing establishment. His view was much like that of Bishop Chiaramonti before he was elected Pope Pius VII, who had on Christmas Day in 1798 welcomed the revolutionary armies of France to his episcopal city of Imola with a liberal Christmas homily on the Christian foundations of democracy. With him Lamennais emphasized that evangelical faith and discipline alone could guarantee the proper use of liberty. Only religion in general and Roman Catholicism in particular could persuade egotistical men to abandon their self-interest in favor of the general interest. In what must have been a deliberate challenge to the Voltairean sentiment of bourgeois liberals, Lamennais dared to praise the eighteenth-century Jesuit experiment in Paraguay as an example of the civilizing mission of Christianity. He thus refused to allow religion to be relegated, in typical liberal fashion, to a sphere of private concern. Religion was pre-eminently social and so it should remain.[30]

To extend the proper influence of religion to society as a whole was indeed the ambition of Lamennais, something bound to make conventional liberals very uneasy. Liberals typically wanted to limit the sphere of influence of religion and to control its expression closely: this was the essence of Voltairean religion and that which made ideological liberalism most hateful to the Church.[31] Lamennais wished instead to increase the ability of the clergy to work in society, for religion and its ministers alone, in his view, defended the poor and moderated the social effects of natural inequality. He came to understand clearly the narrowly bourgeois character of liberal ideology and advocated doctrines more democratic and social than liberal. In a conflict between liberty and equality Lamennais believed that equality came first, for liberty was possible only when it ceased being a selfish individualism and sought the general welfare under the guidance of equality and fraternity, which were the core of Christian faith. Nineteenth-century liberals naturally mistrusted such notions. And Lamennais' desire to increase the power and influence of the clergy, albeit in a constitutional arrangement where the State did not support any established cult, also made them uncomfortable; it went beyond Voltairean principles and even beyond the familiar sort of clericalism to which the French were accustomed. If religion became somewhat less a matter of individual salvation and more a question of the salvation of the social order, religion would henceforth be judged and legitimized most fully by its social efficacy. This would trouble clerics and laymen, believers and unbelievers alike.[32] But for Lamennais, liberty was always to be subordinated to a larger good:

> The welfare of society rests on two principles which rightly understood, comprise all its laws: "No liberty without religion" and "no religion without liberty." Now, our old Europe is divided into two parties of which one wants liberty without religion and the other religion without liberty, that is to say, both are striving to realize the impossible. The only remedy then is to attach the catholics to the cause of liberty, so as to win back the friends of liberty to catholicism.[33]

Not only secular liberals but also liberal Catholics were indifferent or hostile to the social concerns so well expressed by Lamennais once he broke away from purely political issues. Liberal Catholics and former friends and disciples like Montalembert and Falloux were complacently content with the bases of bourgeois society and welcomed the dictatorship of Louis Napoleon, making the defense of the established social order against the threat of social democracy or socialism *the* Catholic cause. If we compare their attitude to that of another follower of Lamennais, Dom Guéranger, who was totally identified with counter-revolutionary Ultramontanism and never in the least pretended to any liberal proclivities, we can see how poorly Lamennais was ultimately represented by the body of his friends and disciples. Dom Guéranger told the unbelieving bourgeoisie during the Second Republic that it ought to look more favorably upon the clergy which "represents order, even for those who do not believe . . . It represents at once moral order, political order, and national order."[34]

SOCIAL CATHOLICISM AND INTRANSIGENT CATHOLICISM

Social Catholicism as a response to changing economic and social conditions first appeared among those Catholics who were "intransigent" in their opposition to the course of modern life, among legitimists and conservatives for the most part. And even these, before 1848, were little concerned specifically with the Social Question. Catholics of all stripes were for many years, like non-Catholics, almost totally lacking in any understanding of the problems caused by changing economic and social conditions. The plight of workers and others in the lower classes and their alienation from religion tended to be analyzed in traditional spiritual fashion, because there was normative theological acceptance of the permanence and inevitability of suffering and inequality. Indeed, religion was often prized and defended precisely because, in the words of Cardinal d'Astros, it "'softens the power of those who command and ennobles the condition of those who obey,'"[35] a conception not as different from the classic Marxist position as it might seem. As Social Catholicism developed, it became obvious that it had many things in common with socialism, especially with what Marx called utopian socialism. It was the socialists' advocacy of class struggle which most importantly separated the social Catholics from the socialists.[36] Certainly Lamennais himself, as he well understood the common ground between himself and the socialists, always remained aware of what separated him from them: his opposition to class struggle and his acceptance of private property and the role of the family.[37] But before socialism became the great obsessive fear of Catholics and conservatives of all sorts, a common opposition to the rule of the newly victorious bourgeoisie had created much common ground between socialists and Social Catholics.

The concerns of Social Catholicism, while a response to the changing conditions of European life, involved less the displacement of more traditional Catholic concerns than a rediscovery of them, for the social element of Catholicism had traditionally been important, even if it had been somewhat submerged by the more individualistic emphasis given to Catholicism during the emancipation of the Catholic bourgeoisie in the Enlightenment. A leading scholar of French Catholicism puts it very well:

> The heart of Social Catholicism resides in the affirmation that there are social ramifications of dogma and that the Church is competent to speak about the problems of society. The specificity of Social Catholicism lies in the refusal of "liberal separatism."[38]

Or in the words of Henri Bazire, an early twentieth-century Social Catholic,

> [Social Catholics] are social not along with being Catholic, and they do not admit that one can see in the association of these two terms some sort of ingenious or accidental combination. They are social because they are Catholic, because in its fullness the idea of the social derives from the very essence of integral Catholicism and from the traditional interpretation of dogma by the Church. . . . It is not, as is claimed, a doctrinal excrescence: it is, instead, its natural flowering.[39]

Social Catholics looked back with approval to the centuries in which the Church had normally involved itself fully in the political, social, and economic life of Christians, to a time when the clergy had been an indispensable part of all activity and could not be readily marginalized by secular powers or preoccupations. In those days, it was totally inconceivable that religion could be a "private matter."[40]

Despite centuries of retreat and partial accommodation, the Catholic Church had nevertheless its own conception of the good society, one which claimed to reflect eternal truths and stood apart from any actual social system, but one certainly still influenced by all existing social systems. Emile Poulat reminds us that the Church has always had several different ways of seeking its objectives: it could support a return to a past social system with which it felt relatively comfortable but which actually only partially corresponded to its desires; it could seek through radical change to inaugurate the good society, but this would require its reliance on men whom it feared and over whom it had lost adequate influence; or it could choose to support existing social structures, thereby favoring the status quo. The Church could thus be reactionary, radical, or conservative, but its fixed objectives were actually at once more reactionary, more radical, and more conservative than any of the secular options theoretically available to it. Integral, intransigent Catholicism proposed to return society to the social influence of the Church, which therefore could not be content merely with the replacement of one political and social system by another; as if the return of absolute monarchy or aristocracy to replace the rule of the bourgeoisie would constitute a return to a true Catholic social order. The European monarchies were the ones first to begin to displace the Church and the bourgeoisie had inherited this role; the continuity between the Old Regime and the New was evident in the continuing privatization and marginalization of the Church and clergy. Intransigent Catholicism saw in liberalism the doctrine, and in the bourgeoisie the social class, which represented the culmination and final stage of a long war of secular authority against the influence of the Church. And in socialism, the Church saw the logical result of the social disorder which resulted from the rule of the emancipated and irreligious liberal bourgeoisie. The Church believed that it alone could save society from disaster.

As a result of its particular analysis of contemporary trends and events, the Church had not only to struggle against the bourgeoisie; it had also to persuade that élite that only the Church could save civilization and property. Thus while combatting the bourgeoisie on one level, the Church also sought on another level to convert it and to mobilize it in their mutual interest. The bourgeoisie was invited to abandon liberalism and anti-clericalism and to seek salvation, Social as well as individual, in and with the Roman Catholic Church. The Church could thus save even bourgeois civilization from itself – a serious temptation for the Church since, in the process of appealing to the bourgeoisie, it could easily become *merely* conservative and forget its true objectives. Modern Social Catholicism, the flowering of integral, intransigent Catholicism as it confronted the changing social order, could thus either concentrate on its ultimate goal of constructing the good society, in which case it would have to break with most existing political and social ideologies and groups; or it would work first to prevent the victory of radical social ideologies by allying itself with bourgeois and other élites with which it had only tactically a community of interest. How the Church has made these difficult choices is, of course, central to the history of how it has dealt with the modern world.[41]

Social Catholicism in France grew only among a small Catholic élite. It was never able, as in Italy, Germany, or Belgium, to become a mass movement because a truly *popular* Catholicism was lacking in France,[42] and the country was less urban and less industrialized than some of its neighbors. And whatever influence Social Catholicism was able to exert was narrowly restricted to those committed to the more reactionary versions of intransigent Catholicism. The condemnation of Lamennais and his subsequent abandonment of formal association with the Church served to leave in limbo his prophetic and utopian vision of how the Church could play a pre-eminent, or at least a more important, role in modern life. After his defection from institutional Roman Catholicism, his disciples and friends worked for the fusion of Ultramontanism and legitimism and pretended that he had really been a legitimist, although in fact he had during the Restoration quickly come to abominate the Bourbons. With each defeat at the hands of liberals, Orléanists, republicans, or anticlericals the Ultramontanists and legitimists came increasingly and ever more firmly to believe in a conspiratorial conception of history. Behind the attacks upon legitimate authority in Church and State they easily discovered Protestants, *philosophes*, Jansenists, Freemasons, and illuminati, all instruments of Satan; and from the 1830s on the Jews were always added to the list of Satan's servants. The Ultramontanists and legitimists violently opposed the parliamentary model in Church and State alike, exalting instead the vision of an all-powerful Pope dealing with an absolute king. In the hands of Louis Veuillot, the master of Catholic Ultramontanist and legitimist journalistic invective, intransigent Catholicism moved wholly in the opposite direction from Lamennais' intention. It was only the early Lamennais, the Lamennais of pure counter-revolution, which received any attention in these circles. Veuillot became more powerful and influential than many bishops, and he was one of only two laymen consulted officially by the Roman Curia as it prepared with the *Syllabus of Errors* the most coherent model of the intransigent Catholic ideology ever formulated.[43]

Even before the publication of the *Syllabus of Errors* (accompanied by the Bull *Quanta Cura*), it is possible to see in the 1854 papal definition of the Immaculate Conception of the Blessed Virgin Mary an amalgamation of the theological, devotional, and ideological concerns of Ultramontanist and legitimist circles. This dogma was defined by the Pope himself, intentionally without any recourse to a Church Council, thus anticipating the First Vatican Council's definition of Papal Infallibility. And the emphasis on the unique sinlessness of the Blessed Virgin reaffirmed the pre-eminently sinful condition of the rest of the human race which easily would go astray without the grace of God and the mediation of the Church and clergy. Thus the dogma could be seen as an attack on liberal views of human nature, liberal politics, and liberal disdain for the anachronistic temporal and spiritual power of the papacy.[44] One historian has suggested that the dogma of the Immaculate Conception also involved a prophetic tradition of eschatological significance in which an Age of Mary would precede the Second Coming itself, an hypothesis that the growth of devotion to Mary, including the belief in her appearance at Lourdes, La Salette, and other places in the nineteenth century, meant that Catholics responded to the challenge of modernity with eschatological hopes and expectations – in itself the mark of a counter-revolutionary mentality.[45]

It was significant that the enormously influential Veuillot made only hesitant movements in favor of working-class concerns during the Second Republic and then drew back with most Catholics in horror after the rise of socialism. He went so far as to attack all limitations on economic liberty, despite his hatred of liberalism as a whole and the fact that Social Catholics of whatever stripe were all agreed at least in opposing the depredations of economic liberalism. His newspaper, *L'Univers*, quickly abandoned any sympathy for Social Catholicism. Under Napoleon III, Social Catholicism became wholly dominated by its counter-revolutionary wing which looked entirely to the past, and its leading figures were without influence within the larger milieu of conservative Catholicism which tended to absorb the Social Catholics. Social Catholic leaders like Albert de Mun and La Tour du Pin were themselves incapable of understanding that the traditional aristocratic paternalism they sincerely believed to be the solution to the problems of the working class served only further to alienate workers who desired to manage their own affairs. The genuine concerns of the counter-revolutionary Social Catholics for the working class, and the equally genuine interest of Napoleon III and some of his entourage in the Social Question, were negatively received by the workers who were in any case moving towards socialism. The workers seemed to understand that "social" as used by the partisans of Social Catholicism meant the "defense of society" and hence the opposite of "socialist."[46] The reactionary wing of Social Catholicism suffered fundamentally from an inadequate sociological understanding of France, for it directed its appeal and good works entirely to the traditionalist élite on the one hand and to marginal workers and the destitute, not the industrial working class, on the other. In 1900 the Abbé Naudet, a leader in transforming reactionary Social Catholicism into progressive Christian democracy, observed that the faulty sociological understanding of the clergy made it ignore the really productive classes of society:

> The clergy of France has thought that it went to the people, to the workers, because with an admirable generosity it distributed alms widely and established hospitals, creches, and charitable institutions of all sorts. In this it deceives itself. For with all this it was not reaching the real people but those who had fallen below the people – the déclassé, the very poorest. It labeled as workers precisely those who could not work.[47]

If it was clear by the last third of the nineteenth century that the French working class as a whole had become alienated from religious practice and was effectively resisting the social and moral influence of the Catholic Church and clergy, historians are less than clear about when and how the Church "lost" the working class. By the last decade of the Second Empire most French Catholics were still largely indifferent to the Social Question and to the small movement of Social Catholicism. Misunderstanding the effects of industrialization and believing that poverty essentially had no solution, they took note of the Social Question only in their fear of socialism. Apart from this fear of the demands of the working class and for the sanctity of private property, they were mostly preoccupied with the fate of the Papal States at the hands of the Italian nationalists, with struggles over the control of education, and with the progress of Ultramontanism generally.[48] The two groups among Catholics with some knowledge and sympathy for the plight of the workers, namely the handful of Christian socialists in the period of the 1848 Revolution and the Social Catholics, were both without real influence in the Church. The Christian socialists tended to be very distrustful of the institutional Church, and because they were strongly anti-clerical they were regarded less as fellow Catholics than as enemies. The intransigent roots of Social Catholics guaranteed their being readily misunderstood and marginalized.[49] As a result, most Catholics could only conceive of two kinds of workers: docile Christian workers resigned to their miserable lives; and revolutionary workers seeking the overthrow of order, property, civilization, and the family. They could hardly conceive of militant Catholic workers striving for their own social and economic emancipation.[50]

Those historians who discuss how the Church "lost" the workers generally emphasize the enrollment of the Church, the clergy, and the lay Catholic élite in the anti-socialist movement beginning in 1848.[51] The Church only had traditional bromides to offer the workers desperately affected by economic change; it also tended to adopt the clichés of economic liberalism despite its theoretical hostility to the ideology of liberalism. As defiantly opposed to the course of modern life as Louis Veuillot was, he still did not hesitate to endorse economic liberalism by opposing State intervention in the economy.[52] The Church seems indeed to have tactically moderated its theoretical, but fundamental, hostility to bourgeois economic principles when the threat of socialism had frightened it sufficiently: it undertook an alliance with the bourgeoisie against socialism.[53] Here, the Church not only abandoned its own long-standing position; it also provided an ironic justification for the later alliance of the anti-clerical and Dreyfusard bourgeoisie with the socialist politicians in order to oppose the influence of the Church and finally to abrogate the Concordat entirely.

This alliance of the Church with the bourgeoisie unquestionably alienated the leaders of republicanism and socialism, men like Proudhon and Victor Hugo, and turned them from being Catholics or Catholic sympathizers into violent anti-clericals.[54] But it is not clear that the working class was similarly affected by the Church's advocacy of the status quo. The French working class only gradually became conscious of an identity distinct from that of the artisan class and of the differences between its interests and those of its employers. The social origins of the urban working class in the nineteenth century were diverse, like those of the *sans-culottes* during the French Revolution. In fact, workers were probably first alienated from the Church and clergy through their close association with their anti-clerical employers in the revolutionary bourgeoisie and their participation in *sans-culotte* culture long before the rise of industrialism.[55] Of course, working-class anti-clericalism and hostility or indifference to the Church were always in important ways different from the anti-clericalism and anti-Catholicism of the revolutionary bourgeoisie. Workers were particularly offended by the normative Catholic view that work and misfortune were punishments for sin and that inequality was natural and inevitable. They sensed what would later become painfully apparent to Catholics facing in more recent times the almost total de-Christianization of the French workers and other social strata – that the world of workers and the world of priests were totally alien to one another.[56] For Charles Péguy, writing just after the 1905 Separation of Church and State, the masses shunned the Church because "it is the official religion, the formal religion of the rich."[57] Eric Hobsbawm has observed in his important study of the religious origins of social protest movements that while the Church can often cling to reactionary policies without necessarily alienating the masses, its identification as "the Church of the rich" is fatally certain to render it incapable of appealing to them with any success.[58]

The Roman Catholic Church's hostility towards socialism was probably so disastrous for Catholicism because French socialism to a significant extent had grown out of a genuinely popular religious and moral sensibility, and it was at one and the same time the expression of working-men's religiosity and of a counter-culture in the midst of bourgeois society. Even during the Old Regime, the *compagnonnages* and other working-men's organizations had aroused suspicions on the part of the clergy who feared any recourse to religious terminology and ritual without clerical control or supervision. Workers and artisans had always had autonomous ways of expressing their religious needs, and they did not always interpret evangelical precepts in the socially approved ways of institutional religion. Often their religious instincts committed them to a collective search for improvement in their working and living conditions and to the cultivation of group solidarity. These tendencies were contrary to the clerical and bourgeois concentration on individual salvation. The workers were anti-individualistic and more this-worldly than otherworldly in their conception of religion. One can see this among the *sans-culottes* during the French Revolution, for in their social attitudes, including their apparent hostility to Christianity, there was also something derived from the traditional Catholic hostility to wealth, individualism, and selfishness. The Parisian *sans-culottes*, it might be worth recalling, were socially the same sort of people who in the early eighteenth century had been drawn in large numbers to the neo-Jansenistic movement of *convulsionnaires*; people defiant of respectable expressions of religiosity in favor of a more spontaneous and autonomous faith.[59] Socialism grew out of the religious, as well as the social and economic, needs of working men, and in time it came to be *the* religion of the masses, an alternative to the religion of the bourgeoisie and the priests. But by the time the Church was finally able to recognize the needs of a newly but slowly industrialized society, the workers had already been evangelized by a new church, namely the socialist movement.

Since for a long time the Church could bring itself to encounter socialism only by condemning it, the workers' devotion to socialism and hostility to institutional Catholicism correspondingly took on all the passion and intolerance of an *odium theologicum*.[60] French socialism in the nineteenth century resisted a fully Marxist orientation and preferred an approach which Marxists condescendingly labelled *utopian*. It is precisely this utopian character of French socialism and also of French republicanism which has enabled them to serve as alternative religions for Frenchmen and Frenchwomen who were ceasing to be Catholic. The Social Question was particularly susceptible to a religious critique, and the Church's long-standing failure to lead in this area served to deliver the working classes and much of the peasantry into the hands of radical republicanism and socialism.[61] Perhaps without actually realizing it, in battling against socialism the Church was struggling yet one more time against the religion of the masses, as during the Catholic Reformation it had sought to sanitize, rationalize, and supervise the expression of popular religiosity. By the nineteenth century, however, the Church and clergy could no longer employ the coercive power of a medieval Church or an absolute monarchy to enforce conformity. The Church's "loss" of the working class must therefore be seen less as a single event than as part of a very "longue durée."

It has been said that the Roman Catholic Church wishes at one and the same time to be a part of modern life and to bear witness to a higher standard which fundamentally challenges modern life. Therefore it can have a role which *attests* to the existing order or one which *contests* it. And sometimes it has been possible to play both roles.[62] A masterful examination of this dualism may be found in Ernst Troeltsch's classic study, *The Social Teaching of the Christian Churches,* where he demonstrated that the Christian attitude towards the existing order is normally both conservative and radical. It is generally submissive to an order which it nevertheless theoretically regards with either contempt or relative indifference. It may choose to submit to the world while it seeks to use the world for the achievement of its own goals, or it may more actively advocate radical change for the attainment of its highest objectives. Christianity, thus, can be revolutionary without intending revolution, and conservative without being able unconditionally to uphold the existing order.[63]

The French monarchy historically had stood up to a Roman Catholic Church which sought to pursue its own goals first, and it finally succeeded in taming the Church and clergy. Following this, the French Revolution so profoundly traumatized the Church that it came to look back to the period of its subservience to the monarchy as its halcyon days. When after the Revolution of 1830 Lamennais deplored the defensive alliance of throne and altar, he suggested that here the Church showed an essential lack of faith in God and in its own mission. Forgetting the promise of its Saviour that "the Gates of Hell would not prevail against it," the Church preferred to tie its fate to that of the equally endangered monarchy.[64] There was indeed here a certain loss of faith, or of nerve, among those Catholics who opted for a Catholicism of order. They feared to pursue the goals of Catholicism directly and preferred to rely on conservative principles and practices. They sought and forged alliances with unbelievers who shared with them little more than a Voltairean conviction about the utility of religion. With biting satire the ever perceptive Lamennais, this time the early Lamennais, had observed that each social class finds religion necessary for the social group below it, an attitude as destructive of true religion as it is tempting.[65] Perhaps no one has more opportunistically represented this viewpoint than the anti-clerical Adolphe Thiers who in 1849 expressed a willingness to allow primary education to be fully placed in the hands of the clergy:

> "It is necessary to bring to the school the social doctrine that must be imposed on the masses, such as religion. It would

> be notorious folly to believe that the great truths could be inculcated by reason. . . .
>
> "Oh, if things were as in the old days, if the school was run always by the *curé* or by his sacristan, I would be far from opposing schools for the children of the people.
>
> "I demand formally something beyond those detestable little lay teachers: . . . I wish to render all-powerful the influence of the clergy and make it much stronger than it is, for I count greatly on it to propagate that good philosophy that knows that man is here to suffer."[66]

The position of Thiers depended on the willingness of the Church and clergy to pursue moderation: support for the existing political and social order in exchange for a degree of privilege and official favor and benevolence. Gallicans and liberal Catholics generally made excellent allies for political moderates, while Catholics from the intransigent school were harder to trust not to pursue divisive policies. Under Louis Napoleon, during both the Second Republic and the Empire, the extreme Ultramontanism of much of the clergy and the Catholic press strained the alliance on behalf of order almost to the breaking point. The growth of clericalism, which was essentially the pursuit of the Church's own agenda first, endangered the alliance of the forces of order, and it compelled the government and its supporters to have recourse to a moderate dose of anti-clericalism to restrain the clergy from disastrous folly.[67] This moderate anti-clericalism, different from that of the working classes or the radical republicans, was a means of defense against excessive clerical pretensions. It was a weapon wielded in the manner of the kings and ministers of the Old Regime who wished to enjoy the usefulness of the Church without the risks of allowing it to endanger secular authority.[68] Intransigent Catholics were theoretically very bad allies for Voltairean moderates, since the former fundamentally contested the very foundations of liberalism. But the dread of social upheaval, in a word, the fear of socialism, persuaded the intransigent Catholics to throw in their lot with the tepid bourgeois Catholics and the unbelieving disciples of Thiers. In this fashion, the anti-capitalist, anti-liberal, and anti-bourgeois Catholic intransigents worked nevertheless in defense of their enemies.

The leadership role *manqué* of Lamennais is here highlighted all the more brilliantly, for he was virtually the only intransigent

Catholic to have proposed that, with faith in the divine promises made to it, the Roman Catholic Church undertake a truly revolutionary remaking of the social order. His failure to persuade anyone in the Church of the cogency of his prophetic vision left the Church with an unenviable choice: to play the role of Don Quixote in battling hopelessly against the windmills of modern life, or to serve the interests and defend the power of the established order. The first option might make the Church appear ridiculous, but the second, the role finally chosen, could only lead it into contempt. Until Christian democracy arose to pick up part of the legacy of Lamennais, whatever genuine concern there was within the Church for the plight of the masses was submerged in the general defense of bourgeois order. To rephrase somewhat the view of Emile Poulat: some Catholics wished to restore an old and presumably better order, while Lamennais wished to create a new social order. But what the Church finally settled for was the simple defense of the existing order.[69] Like the proverbial synagogue, the Church of France did not recognize the time of its Visitation. It is, therefore, possible and legitimate to consider Lamennais as the central figure, although unrecognized, of the post-revolutionary French Catholic Church – not because of his success, but because of the tragic failure of the Church to take him seriously, a failure he foresaw and whose implications he fully and fundamentally understood. Lamennais was nothing less than "the stone the builders rejected."

IV

French Catholics and the Third Republic. From Dreyfus to Pétain

By 1879 the Third French Republic seemed to be definitively established, despite the probable preference of a majority of Frenchmen for some kind of monarchical government. The republicans had triumphed not only over the royalists in general; they had also been victorious over the clergy and laity of Catholic France who were the mainstay of nineteenth-century royalism. The victory of the Republic was thus widely perceived as also the defeat of Catholic interests. This Third Republic went on resolutely to laicize the educational system, to restrict the work of religious congregations, and finally in 1905 to abrogate the Napoleonic Concordat with the papacy and thereby to end all public support of religion. Thus, by the beginning of the twentieth century France had become a lay Republic, more than 100 years after the first daring attempt during the French Revolution to sever the association of the Church with the State.

Catholics by and large needed no encouragement to view this course of events as disastrous. They had for a long time viewed a lay Republic as an instrument of de-Christianization, and it was normal for them to offer, at best, only a very limited allegiance to this irreligious State or, more typically, to seek its replacement. But no realistic opportunity for replacing it actually presented itself until French forces were defeated by Nazi Germany in 1940. The *Etat Français* established in the summer of 1940 was intentionally not designated a Republic, and the Chief of State, Marshal Philippe Pétain, was to be no mere republican functionary. Everything about the Vichy regime was designed to emphasize that it had replaced, not continued, the Third Republic. Most Catholics in 1940, the hierarchy, the lower clergy, and the laity alike, welcomed the advent of a regime which, however inauspicious its birth in military defeat, was embraced as the revenge for over sixty years of irreligion. Catholics in 1940 could readily persuade themselves that the defeat of France was only the defeat of the Republic and that they finally had an opportunity to restore Catholic authority and order to their country. If the establishment of the Third Republic had seemed a defeat for Catholic France, the complete disappearance of the hated Republic in 1940 seemed its long-awaited vindication.

THE *RALLIEMENT*

The hostility of Catholics towards the Third Republic – for the circumstances of its birth, for the course of its history, and for the fact of its ignominious defeat – was substantial but still far from the whole story. While there were Frenchmen, whether Catholic or not, who worked actively in monarchist parties and movements, notably in the very influential Action Française, most conservatives, Catholic or otherwise, by the time of the First World War were willing to consider the Republic as a possible instrument for defending their social and economic position. And they finally did come to find the Republic a means of defending the established order against radical and revolutionary change. The established bourgeois order (what Emmanuel Mounier, a radical Catholic intellectual, called "the established disorder") was indeed well defended by the Third Republic, and bourgeois Catholics, those Voltairean Catholics of order, found it possible to use the Republic effectively in their own interests. In this light, the Vichy regime should perhaps be viewed as an even more determined instrument of bourgeois social defense than the Third Republic. The story, then, of Catholics and the Third Republic is more complicated than a mere recitation of mutual hostility would suggest. It took conservative Catholics a long time to become reconciled with a Republic, but they took the plunge when they became convinced that the Republic was the best they could do in the defense of their vital interests.

The first half of the life of the Third Republic was marked by the continuing struggle of Catholics against it, while the second half was a time when significant reconciliation occurred between the Church and the bourgeoisie. It was paradoxically during the Vichy period that one saw both the zenith of cooperation between the Church and the ruling élites and the beginnings of significant dissent on the part of clergy and laity from this cooperation. The years in question here are chronologically defined by the Dreyfus Affair and the Vichy regime, and it is no accident that at both the beginning and end of this period the "Jewish Question" was intimately intertwined with the relation of Catholics to the political regime. Indeed, the attitude of Catholic France towards the Jews is an important aspect, perhaps a central one, in the development of both Catholic cooperation with and dissent from the bourgeois order of modern France. It was the Dreyfus Affair which revealed the lengths to which many Catholics would willingly go in their hostility to the established order, and it was the Vichy regime of Pétain and Laval which revealed to many Catholic clergy and laity how morally and spiritually compromising the defense of order could become. *From Dreyfus to Pétain* was indeed the period between the infancy and adulthood of the conscience of Catholic France.

The establishment of the Third Republic and the evident failure of royalism were as severe blows to French Catholics as the loss of its temporal power in 1870 had been to the papacy. As Pope Pius IX had withdrawn to the Vatican Palace, besieged and isolated from the currents of modern life, the defeat of royalism in France placed Catholics in a position of defensive isolation. Their first response was to cling with determination to their traditional allegiances and refuse all association with and participation in the Republic. Most Catholic élites indeed did remain hostile to the Republic for several decades, but even early in the life of the Third Republic it was becoming apparent that many ordinary Catholics were voting for republican candidates and thereby accepting the Republic. Regions of traditional Catholic strength were sending republicans to the legislature; thus the Breton *département* of Ille-et-Vilaine, with its population of overwhelmingly practising Catholics, in many communes returned republican candidates in similarly overwhelming numbers.[1] Since the bishops, by the terms of the Concordat, were chosen by the mutual agreement of the Vatican and the French government, a certain proportion of them were always at least moderate in sentiment towards the Republic. In the 1890s the government's *directeur des cultes* regarded approximately one-third of the bishops as satisfactory, one-third as unreliable, and another third as definitely hostile to the Republic. Conceivably, the proportion hostile to the Republic might have been even greater had the Roman authorities enjoyed complete freedom to make their own choice of bishops without the agreement of the French government.[2] In any case, by its own efforts the French Catholic leadership would have done little to seek accommodation with the Republic. It took the intervention of Pope Leo XIII – his famous encouragement of the *Ralliement* – to initiate the slow movement of Catholics away from intransigent royalism. And at that time papal encouragement, while necessary, proved insufficient; a true Ralliement finally required for success the unifying atmosphere of the First World War and an entirely changed domestic and international situation.

Leo XIII's encouragement for Catholics to accept the Republic has been somewhat misunderstood. Because this Pope is identified with the Church's belated attempt to come to terms with the vast economic and social changes wrought by capitalist industrial development, he has sometimes been miscast as some sort of liberal. It is true that his style of discourse avoided the intransigent and reactionary tones of both his predecessor, Pius IX, and his immediate successor, Pius X. Leo preferred a smoother, more soothing diplomatic approach where they specialized in flinty jeremiads. Nevertheless, he shared with them both and with dominant circles in the universal Church a desire to restore the historical social role of the Church which modern developments had undermined.[3]

There were, of course, some purely diplomatic motives in Leo's search for accommodation with the French Republic. The mutual hostility of the newly unified Kingdom of Italy and the Vatican was of serious concern to the Roman Curia, and the support which Germany and Austria-Hungary extended to the Italians placed the Vatican in a very weak diplomatic position. Leo saw better relations with republican France as a possible means of breaking out of this diplomatic isolation. He had already sought better relations with the German empire when Bismarck abandoned the anti-Catholic *Kulturkampf*. Leo had certainly not shied away from placing his own particular understanding of Catholic interests above the interests of the recently embattled German Center Party. He elevated his goal of a re-Christianized society carried out with the cooperation of the ruling élites above the mere interests of Catholics in individual countries. Thus he preferred to work with Bismarck rather than with the democratic and constitutionalist Center Party, and he abandoned Polish Catholic interest in Prussian Poland in the hope of placating Bismarck. Ludwig Windthorst, the great German Catholic leader, remarked that he had been "'shot in the back'" by papal diplomacy.[4] Still, diplomatic goals can only partly explain Leo's overtures. His greatest concern was always over the place of the Church in the modern world. More perceptive than the besieged Pius IX, Leo viewed modern civilization less as the enemy of the Church than as a seriously stricken body desperately needing the help of the Church to survive. He believed that the Church should exercise its "indirect power," that anachronistic postulate of Thomist political theory, by cooperating with established authorities. Both the civil authorities and the bourgeoisie would need to be persuaded that only the Church could save property, authority, and society; only the Church, mistakenly seen as an enemy of modern civilization, could in fact save it from the revolutionary consequences of its own disastrous ideology, liberalism.[5] With these goals ever paramount in his mind, Leo could with an easy conscience prefer to work with Protestant conservatives in Germany, to the scandal of the German Catholic Center Party. Despite the scandalized feelings of French Catholic royalists, he found it possible to urge acceptance of the increasingly lay Republic in the pursuit of goals which he believed the bourgeoisie, both Catholic and free-thinking, could in the end agree upon. Outraged or deceived German Catholics or French royalists might well be tempted to agree with a twentieth-century high official of the Roman Curia, Cardinal Tardini, when he remarked that "'Vatican diplomacy really began with Peter's denial of Christ,'"[6] but what looked to many like papal *raison d'état* was actually also the working out of a deeply held commitment to the intransigent Catholic goal of re-Christianizing society and restoring to the Church its traditional social role. The Ralliement, then, sought not the liberalization of Catholicism but the rallying of the bourgeoisie around the Church in the defense of the political, social, and moral order. However in the last decade of the nineteenth century neither Catholic nor free-thinking Frenchmen were yet ready for this great defensive endeavor. The Dreyfus Affair, whatever else it was, revealed how premature Pope Leo's grand strategy actually was.

THE DREYFUS AFFAIR AND THE ACTION FRANÇAISE

The Dreyfus Affair, *whatever else it was*! After almost a century of historical reminiscence, research, and analysis it is not entirely clear what the significance of the Dreyfus Affair was in the development of modern France. The dynamic course of historiographical controversy often results in undermining conventional wisdom and textbook-like assertions about the importance of certain allegedly key historical events. Historians of France have been capable of such disharmony on the meaning of the French Revolution, for example, as to cause laymen to throw up their hands in disgust at the antics of the professionals. The more important the event, the more the incentive for some to seek to strip it of its central importance. The Dreyfus Affair has been regarded since its beginning as classically important in the development and triumph of French republicanism. It also has been seen as marking the final defeat of the counter-revolution, the ideology of that portion of the French people that contested the French Revolution and all it had wrought. Historians today, however, are no longer as certain as they once were about the central importance of the controversy at the end of the last century over the guilt or innocence of Captain Alfred Dreyfus. It seems that its impact was always confined to the middle classes of Paris and a few provincial cities, with little resonance in the countryside of the peasantry or among the growing working class of the industrial centers. Nor is it any longer possible to claim that it definitively settled any political issues in France or altered its social structure.[7] But it can with considerably more certainty be claimed that for the story of the twentieth-century reconciliation of the Catholic Church and the lay Republic of France the Dreyfus Affair played an enormous role. At his trial in 1945 for collaboration with the German enemy, Charles Maurras, the leader of the Action Française movement which had been so influential among Catholics, replied to a guilty verdict against him with the cry: "It is the revenge of Dreyfus!" For him, at least, and for our understanding of the Catholic connection with the integral nationalism of the Action Française and its role in the reconciliation of the Church and the established order, the Dreyfus Affair cannot be underestimated. It was the Dreyfus Affair which gave birth to the movement led by Maurras, and the Catholic connection with the Action Française raised most fundamentally the entire question of the role of the Catholic Church in modern France.

There were not a few ironies in the association of the élites of Catholic France with the movement of Maurras, for he was not a Catholic, but an ex-Catholic; he appreciated those features of the Church which were Hellenistic and Roman – its order, its discipline, and its reliance on Greek intellectuality – but he feared and despised its original biblical, evangelical call to repentence and social justice. But perhaps the chief irony in the association of Catholics with Maurras lay in the fact that what launched Maurras' career with the Action Française in the first place was nothing less than the claim that, to use the very Gospel phrase itself, "it was expedient that one man should die for the people." Maurras was willing, indeed eager, to advocate in the defense of his political objectives what one Catholic scholar has called the equivalent of "ritual murder."[8] For Maurras, as for the priestly circles in the Jerusalem of Jesus, it was not unthinkable that an innocent man be punished for the greater objective of the general welfare.

Four years after Alfred Dreyfus had been condemned for espionage on behalf of Imperial Germany, suspicions that he had been unjustly accused and punished culminated in January 1898 in Emile Zola's "J'Accuse," an open letter to the President of the Republic. Within half a year Colonel Hubert Henry, an intelligence officer in the army who was responsible for forging documents to establish Dreyfus' guilt, committed suicide. The revelation of Henry's role as a forger gave life, as no other factor could, to the campaign of the Dreyfus family and others to seek a new trial for the unfortunate Alfred Dreyfus, and those who saw in any revision of the verdict against him grave danger for the welfare of the army and, by extension, of the French nation were thrown into consternation and confusion. It was at this point that Charles Maurras made his entry into public life with a public justification of Henry's forgery that would make him the chief ideological guide of nationalist thought and politics for the remainder of the life of the Third Republic. Maurras did not primarily concern himself with the details of the guilt or innocence of Dreyfus or with the details of Henry's death. He simply defended Henry as a martyr because he had forged evidence of Dreyfus' guilt in order to save the army and the nation from attack and ignominy, an essentially patriotic act in which the welfare of the nation was placed infinitely above the question of whether justice or injustice had been done to a single individual. Maurras thus elevated a *national lie* or *myth* to a position above truth or justice, and this would be a key concept of integral nationalism: that the individual's rights cannot be appealed to against the paramount rights of the State or nation.[9] The controversy about the guilt or innocence of Dreyfus offered Maurras an opportunity to give his ideas about the restoration of a strong France an immediate relevance. The campaign by Dreyfus' supporters, expressed as the defense of the ideology of the Revolution and the Republic, only convinced Maurras that the republicans were incapable of defending the interests of France. Indeed, whether Dreyfus were or were not personally guilty of the crime for which he had been tried and imprisoned was less important for Maurras than the fact that the Dreyfusards were from his perspective unquestionably themselves guilty of subverting the nation and, thereby, objectively guilty of treason. If the test of guilt or innocence were for Maurras the welfare of the community, then Colonel Henry the forger was clearly an innocent and exemplary patriot and Alfred Dreyfus a guilty traitor. The vindication of Henry was, then, the very foundation of the Action Française.[10]

It was not the trial, conviction, and sentencing of Dreyfus and his deportation to Devil's Island which constituted the heart of the Dreyfus Affair. The Affair, which took the form of a civil war fought in the press, on the streets of major cities, and in the courts of law, was more accurately about the attempt of the Dreyfus family and some of its supporters to win a new trial for the condemned traitor, and the violent opposition to revision on the part of many influential individuals and groups in French life. This attempt at revision was viewed by nationalists, conservatives, and most Catholics as a conspiracy against the army and the nation, a conspiracy financed and fuelled by the Jews and their allies and paid henchmen. Those working for Dreyfus' rehabilitation, in turn, became convinced that the anti-Dreyfusards aimed at nothing less than the overthrow of the lay Republic. Thus the judicial issue of whether Dreyfus had or had not received a fair trial was submerged in the renewal of the classic struggle between royalists and republicans, Catholics and anti-clericals, about what constitutional regime France should have. Twenty years after the apparent consolidation of the Republic, once again the basic lack of consensus among Frenchmen brought political contestation to a fevered pitch. And the fact that Dreyfus was a Jew, and that many of his firmest supporters were Jews, Protestants, or free-thinkers, induced the vast majority of Catholics who took an interest in the Affair to throw in their lot with the anti-revisionist movement; for they thought they saw in the forces aligned to defend Dreyfus the same combination of political and religious groups which had successfully worked for the laicization of public education and the curtailment of the influence of the Catholic Church on national life. Anti-Semitism, then, became for the first time in France a possible ideology for unifying the counter-revolutionary groups and tendencies in an attempt to restore a more traditional political and social order to France. It may well be, as claimed by a very respected and fair-minded Catholic historian, André Latreille, that the Dreyfusard and republican belief that the Church and the army intended to exploit the agitation over the Dreyfus Affair to overthrow the Republic had no more foundation factually than the not uncommon belief of Catholics and conservatives that there was a Judaeo-Masonic conspiracy to destroy the Church and rule France. Nevertheless, the level of verbal aggression on the part of many priests and Catholic journalists was so elevated that anticlericals could without yielding entirely to paranoia come to fear that the Church was seeking a disgraceful and dangerous alliance with the army to bring down the Republic. Nor was it hard for Emile Zola to believe that the Church was hoping to find in anti-Semitism what other approaches had consistently failed to provide, namely, the means of recruiting mass support for its political and religious objectives.[11] In dealing with the "Jewish Question" Catholics were indeed addicted to language so inflammatory and apocalyptic that the title of one of the books of arch anti-Semite Edouard Drumont might well serve to summarize all Catholic hopes, expectations, fears, and delusions: *The End of a World* (*La Fin d'un monde*).

ANTI-SEMITISM

Catholic historians and apologists once sought to deny Catholic support for the anti-Semitic movement in France at the end of the nineteenth century, but it has become clear to scholars, Catholics and non-Catholics alike, that a frank avowal of Catholic anti-Semitism is a necessary first step not only for ecumenical harmony but for genuine historical self-understanding. Catholic complicity in anti-Semitism before and during the Dreyfus Affair has at times been distorted – one thinks of the myth of Jesuit conspiracy to which Hannah Arendt, an otherwise perceptive historian of the Affair, fell victim[12] – but it is still very important to show how uniquely susceptible defensive Catholicism was to the multi-sided attractions of anti-Semitism.

Jacob Katz has persuasively argued in a number of places that modern anti-Semitism was basically a reaction to the incorrigible survival of Jewish identity. Traditional Christianity had a definite place for the Jews: it waited, for millennia if necessary, for their conversion, which was considered part of the divine mystery of redemption. This legitimation of a Jewish presence guaranteed Jewish survival within Christendom, albeit in a degraded and precarious condition. Modern, post-Christian society, however, had really no such place for the Jews. Emancipation was granted first in France and elsewhere thereafter in the hope and expectation that the Jews would respond to their liberation by vanishing as a recognizable group, but they did not, or could not, or would not disappear. Conservatives, troubled and challenged by rapid change, saw Jews as dangerous innovators, while socialists viewed them as capitalist exploiters, which was perhaps the same thing. Liberals viewed Jews as obsolete remnants of a barbaric tribalism destined in an enlightened age to disappear.[13] Few had any positive attitudes towards Jews *as Jews*.

As French Catholics after 1870 faced the alienation of the masses from the Church, the upheavals of economic change, and the rivalries between the great powers which placed French national interests in danger, they became susceptible to a *Weltanschauung* for troubled times which kept traditional beliefs and attitudes seemingly up-to-date with modern developments. Already inclined towards conspiratorial and apocalyptic belief, and led by a clergy whose mediocre educational foundation kept them ignorant of modern economic, social, and scientific thought, French Catholics could easily believe that secret groups of powerful and corrupt men controlled the destiny of nations.[14] Freemasons, financiers, Protestants, and Jews easily came to mind. The adoption of a modernized anti-Judaism, which is what anti-Semitism is, was a partial, if inadequate, coming to terms with the challenge of modernity. The struggle on behalf of the Church fell to men like Louis Veuillot and Edouard Drumont who brought together all the currents of mythic thinking, from the Left and the Right, into an apparently coherent explanation of present troubles. With the publication of *La France Juive* in 1886 Drumont had succeeded in concocting a heady brew out of the different currents of Jew-hatred; replacing religious anti-Judaism with a racial, national hostility to Jews as aliens, he was able to offer an explanation satisfactory for many different sorts of victims of modern times. All that was needed was the discovery of Judas in the person of Alfred Dreyfus. More than anyone else, Drumont was able to unite Catholic belief, feeling, and obsession by means of modern anti-Semitism. He preached with success among workers, clerics, and patriots: to the workers he observed that it was not capitalism but Jewish finance which oppressed them; to the poorly educated and economically strapped clerics he revealed that all the Church's woes came from the still unbelieving Jews who, however, were now equipped as never before with vast financial and economic power; and to the bewildered patriots fearful of France's rivalry with Britain and Germany he uncovered Jewish power in London and Berlin. Finally, Drumont warned the traditional believer who still awaited the conversion of Israel, that a few drops of baptismal water would not easily efface the taint of Semitic blood. For many he seemed, indeed, to unravel and explain the secrets of the contemporary world.[15]

Drumont's newspaper, *La Libre Parole,* and the organ of the Assumptionist Order, *La Croix,* accomplished the association of Catholicism with the new non-religious Jew-hatred so well that few Catholics thought it necessary or desirable to object. What Catholic dissenters there were from the new anti-Semitism came mostly from the thin ranks of liberal Catholics who had long opposed the more reactionary, intransigent, and irrational defenders of an embattled Church.[16] They were easily silenced by the mass of Catholic opinion which, whether reactionary or Social Catholic, was persuaded that the Jewish peril explained everything. The most bizarre, but in some ways the most revealing, defense of sanity came from the eccentric Léon Bloy, the later godfather and friend of Jacques and Raïssa Maritain, who raged against modern anti-Semitism because of its departure from the traditions of the Church.[17] Bloy exposed the radically new attitude towards the Jews which was being propagated within the deceptive appearance of Catholic theological continuity:

> One has seen more priests than one can count – many of them, without a doubt, sincere servants of God – become inflamed by the hope of some imminent violent reckoning in which the blood of Israel will be spilt on a scale to glut all the dogs in France. . . . The movement has been so sudden and the impulse behind it so compelling that, even today, none of them seem to have paused to ask themselves whether there is not the gravest danger for the soul of a priest in thus petitioning for the extermination of a people whom the Apostolic Roman Church has protected for nineteen centuries . . . and from whom have come the Patriarchs, the Prophets, the Evangelists, the Apostles, the early Disciples, all the early Martyrs, and, one hardly dares to add, the Virgin-Mother and Our Lord himself. . . .
>
> Antisemitism, something entirely modern, is the most horrible blow which Our Lord has received in his Passion, which lasts forever; it is the most bloody and the most unpardonable because he receives it on the face of his Mother and at the hands of Christians.
>
> Know that every morning I eat a Jew whose name is Jesus Christ, that I spend a part of my life at the feet of a Jewess whose heart is pierced and whose slave I have become; finally that I have given my entire trust to a pack of yids, one presenting the Lamb, another carrying the Keys of Heaven, and the third charged with the instruction of all nations . . . and know that one can be Christian only with such feelings.[18]

French Jews who were aware of Bloy's medieval defense of their right to exist did not understand his motives or appreciate his traditional attitudes towards them, which combined contempt with respect in the normative manner of Catholic theology, but his evident aloofness from the modern movement of anti-Semitism did reveal how ready many French Catholics were to throw off their faith and traditions for the temporal advantages of the new anti-Semitism.[19]

As the Dreyfus Affair developed and was finally brought to a conclusion with the rehabilitation of Alfred Dreyfus (although for some Frenchmen it has remained permanently without any definitive conclusion), it enabled those who believed that the Republic was in mortal danger from a plot of the army, the Church, and the extreme nationalists to unite on the one issue which could keep the republican forces of radicals and socialists together when economic and social issues badly divided them: the issue of clericalism. As the tide of public and parliamentary opinion turned in favor of the cause of Dreyfus, the parliamentary regime proceeded to purge the army leadership of anti-republican elements, to punish anti-republican plotters, and to take stern action against the Church. Whatever limited prospects for success Leo XIII's *Ralliement* may have once had, the Affair allowed French politicians to return to the old struggles of clericals against anti-clericals, at least for a time. If the Ralliement represented an attempt at the modernization of French political life – through its desire that the clerical issue be superseded by economic and social questions as the dividing line between Right and Left – the Affair allowed the Church to be singled out for punishment for its role in the agitation against Dreyfus and, hence, against the Republic. Although the hierarchy itself had carefully avoided taking sides in the Affair, the prominence of Catholic journalists and some priests in the anti-Semitic movement and the anti-revisionist campaign was a godsend to the anti-clericals. The Affair had the effect of persuading Frenchmen that the old political-religious alignments and prejudices were still meaningful. Some proponents of the *Ralliement* even found it possible to persuade themselves that the revisionist campaign was in the first place designed to destroy the *Ralliement*,[20] a tribute not only to their high suspicions of the base motives of the Dreyfusards but an indication of the damage done by the Affair to their fondest hopes of reconciliation between the Church and the bourgeoisie. In any case, it was the Church which would pay. The laws in 1901 against the religious congregations effected something akin to a dissolution of the monasteries. Diplomatic relations with the Vatican were soon severed, and in 1905 the Concordat was unilaterally abrogated by the French government, something which had been a stated goal of the radicals for several decades. All public support for religion was abolished, for Protestants and Jews as well as for Catholics. The Gallican Church thus came to an end.

THE SEPARATION OF CHURCH AND STATE

Although the Separation of Church and State in 1905 was the work of anti-clericals who had long sought this objective, and while it was debated in the spirit of taking revenge on a Church which had continually been associated with anti-republican movements, if not actual conspiracies, two important results of the Separation were as significant as they were perhaps unexpected. First of all, with the relegation of the Catholic Church to a private association of believers who ran their own affairs (or who had them decided entirely in Rome), the clerical issue was removed from the center of French politics to something like its periphery. Second, the Church became entirely dependent on its faithful laity for support, financial and otherwise, and it pursued a reconciliation with the conservative élites of France, Catholic and free-thinking, more resolutely than ever before. In a sense, then, the Separation furthered achievement of some of the objectives of the Ralliement: the Church's cooperation in support of a conservative political and social order, regardless of whether it was called republican or royalist.[21]

The politicians who voted for and supervised the Separation in the end pursued their objectives with a moderation and relative generosity which indicated that they did not intend to attack religion or deprive themselves of the socially conservative support of the clergy. They had simply – in the fashion of Voltairean anti-clericals under many of the regimes of the nineteenth century – taken measures to prevent the Church and clergy from attacking the established order. But by the terms of the Separation and by its manner of implementation they indicated that they had no further need to restrict the activities of the Church once it no longer had public financial support. The Separation, thus, was the *last* act of an official, governmental anti-clericalism which sought the disciplining, not the ruination of the Church. The agitation over Dreyfus had made it necessary to push anti-clericalism further than usual – to abrogate the Concordat which had always given the secular authorities a degree of leverage over the Church – but the republican politicians knew that it would have been foolhardy to have gone still further. Theodore Zeldin sums this up very well: "On the surface, the struggle of radicals against clericals was the dominant theme, and that struggle continued in party programmes. But beneath the surface, it was conciliation which triumphed."[22] With the Separation of Church and State a fact of life, and a fact clearly supported by French public opinion, the bourgeoisie felt itself free to contemplate what services the Church and clergy could offer it instead of fearing their disruptive influence on French Catholics. Except in the competition between lay education provided by the State and the Catholic education offered by the Church, the virulent issues between clericals and anti-clericals had been laid to rest.

In the several years before passage of the Law of Separation and in its aftermath, however, the very limited nature of this official anti-clericalism was not yet completely apparent. The French Church, clergy, and laity instinctively anticipated a campaign of persecution from the godless Republic, and the attitude of Rome and Pope Pius X encouraged them to prepare for a Gallic equivalent of the Bismarckian *Kulturkampf*. It would indeed be this atmosphere of expected persecution which permitted the Action Française and its non-Catholic, positivist, leader, Charles Maurras, to pose successfully as the most vigorous defender of Catholicism in France and to seek with considerable success to make the Church an adjunct of its own political program of integral nationalism. While the incompatibility of Catholicism with the social, philosophical, and ethical premises of the Action Française might have been apparent to any number of observers, it is very significant that the first Catholic to draw attention to these antitheses was a man of the Catholic Left, Marc Sangnier, the charismatic leader of the Sillon movement which sought the reconciliation of the Church with democracy and the Republic.[23] Sangnier, in other words, did not seek a Ralliement for socially conservative purposes; in the veritable tradition of Lamennais, he believed in a reconciliation of the Church with egalitarian, democratic belief and practices because Christianity was originally egalitarian and democratic. The Ralliement he contemplated and worked for was not one on behalf of the status quo, but one for substantial change.

Emerging from the thin but important ranks of Social Catholicism, Sangnier differed from many Social Catholics at the end of the nineteenth century in understanding the inability of Catholic paternalism to persuade the masses that they should submit themselves to the passive benevolence of priests and aristocratic and bourgeois Catholic laymen. Sangnier also understood that working-class youth could be won for Christian democracy only by being allowed to see it in action in the discussions about how to implement the social teachings of the Church stimulated by Leo XIII's encyclical of 1891, *Rerum Novarum*. His Sillon movement, which in later years would be viewed retrospectively as the forerunner of French Christian democracy, was a challenge both to a socialism which saw little good in Catholicism and to a Catholic establishment convinced that democracy was pernicious and inherently anti-Christian.[24] In the years of debate over the Law of Separation and in its immediate aftermath it was obviously all the more difficult to propagate these views among Catholics ready for a battle to the death against persecution from a godless regime of liberals, democrats, and socialists. Marc Sangnier and Charles Maurras recognized in each other a rival for the allegiance of Catholics, especially Catholic youth,[25] but they also recognized a more fundamental area of disagreement between themselves, their movements, and their followers. Maurras saw in Sangnier exactly that sort of Christian whose commitment to biblical and evangelical values and imperatives was revolutionary in potential. Sangnier was a Christian as well as a Catholic; he did not celebrate with Maurras the conservative restraints with which Hellenistic thought and Roman law had shackled Christianity. Sangnier, for Maurras, represented all the anarchistic, revolutionary currents which he believed were derived from Protestantism and ultimately from Jewish messianism and the biblical quest for social justice; he represented the Christianity of the *Magnificat* whose moral teaching Maurras feared and despised,[26] for it was a Christianity which could not, in his view, support order and hierarchy effectively. For his part, Sangnier deplored the association of Christianity and Catholicism with political authority, viewing, for example, the Romanization of faith through its adoption by the later Roman emperors as harmful – precisely the Romanization in which Maurras found the necessary restraints for the dangers of Semitic religion. One of Maurras' associates put the differences between the two men rather well when he found Sangnier optimistic about human nature and Maurras pessimistic.[27] Sangnier's political and social advocacy stemmed directly from his willingness to rely on the virtue found in men, while Maurras, the heir to a counter-revolutionary tradition going back to Joseph de Maistre (if not to St Augustine), found traditional hierarchies and a firm order necessary for the disciplining of anarchistic man. Christianity historically has found itself very much able to go in either direction, but it has usually chosen the path of order over the one of fundamental change.

Thus, Maurras and Sangnier understood each other very well indeed. But French Catholics generally, and certainly the hierarchy of the Church – in France and in Rome – were somewhat less perceptive. Many bishops were upset by the influence which the Sillon movement gained among their seminarians, but they had no such qualms about the greater influence of Maurras among an important segment of the clergy and laity alike. Bishops and officials in the Curia feared Sangnier's emphasis on the autonomy of the civic conscience from ecclesiastical control and his willingness to cooperate with men of different backgrounds, even with non-Catholics, in the pursuit of common goals.[28] That the Action Française also refused submission to ecclesiastical control and also cooperated with non-Catholics in the pursuit of its goals did not for many years concern the Church's leadership. Ultimately the Action Française would be condemned by the Church for the same dangerously autonomous proclivities found in the Sillon a generation earlier. But the conservative goals of the Action Française appealed so much more to conservatives in the Church's hierarchy than the democratic objectives of the Sillon ever could.

The condemnation of the Sillon movement by Pius X in 1910 was in no small way a tribute to the influence of Maurras among Catholics. Sillon's condemnation was consistent with Gregory XVI's censure of Lamennais in the 1830s: an attempt to create a more just social order on the basis of Christian values was condemned as anti-Christian by a papacy willing to absolutize the existing social order by giving it divine sanction and by delegitimizing Christian opposition to it. Unlike Lamennais, Sangnier readily submitted to Rome, but, whether submissive or not, he very much resembled Lamennais in representing a propheticism crushed by sacerdotalism.[29] The real difference between Catholics like Sangnier and those in the Action Française can be perhaps best expressed through a brief meditation on the words which the Gospel of Matthew attributes to Jesus: "On this rock I will build my Church and the Gates of Hell shall not prevail against it." Can Christians believe their Saviour that the power of evil will not triumph over the Church, or should they seek to buttress the Church by allying it with conservative forces and institutions?

Even if these forces and institutions are clearly inhospitable to the essential values of Christian faith? Is the Church supported by faith, or is faith supported by the Church? Action Française Catholics and integrist Catholics generally were pessimistic about the promise of Jesus; they felt they had to substitute order for the lack of faith. This is akin to the fear of the Grand Inquisitor in Dostoyevsky's *The Brothers Karamazov* that the return of Jesus would dangerously upset the delicate balance which the Church had created between prophecy and order. The Grand Inquisitor would have made a very good Maurrasian!

There were many affinities between the integrism of the Action Française and the Church's own integrism. As the heir to the *Syllabus of Errors* of 1864, Catholic integrism involved:

> a reciprocity between a political and a religious ideology which are in turn both cause and effect. The religion of Integrism is fundamentally authoritarian and pessimistic; it accentuates the dogmatic, hierarchical, and disciplinary aspects of Catholicism and especially the absoluteness of a truth to which the rights of man are not an alternative value; this religion seeks in a theology of Original Sin reasons for refusing the modern ideas of Democracy and Progress. From this religious to this political position the passage seems good but this religious position also seems tailor-made for this political position. The ideological circle is or seems exactly closed.[30]

As the Action Française in the period of the Law of Separation took upon itself a conspicuous role in defense of an embattled Catholic Church, the affinities between its integrism and the different but related integrism of the Church helped to conceal the dangers which Maurrasian thought held for Catholics. The defense of order indeed seemed able to excuse almost anything.

If Catholics of all political and social persuasions, felt it ritualistically necessary to denounce the Law of Separation, the greater portion of the episcopate nevertheless would probably have been willing to work within its provisions in order to achieve as favorable a result as possible for the Church.[31] But an intransigent Pius X preferred to inaugurate an integrist offensive within the Church, beginning in 1906 and lasting until his death in 1914. It was in this period that the adherents of the so-called Modernist movement within the Church were relentlessly pursued and then condemned. In France a few republican bishops were purged, firm integrists were named to vacant sees, recommendations by the French hierarchy on new appointments were ignored, and the Sillon became a favorite target of integrists and conservatives.[32] Bishops who met as a group to devise ways of coping with the end of the Concordat were kept on a very short rein by papal representatives, and very quickly the bishops' newly found freedom to convene, something not permitted without governmental permission during the century of the Napoleonic Concordat, was prohibited by a Rome no more desirous of an independent episcopate than the French government had been. Rome issued orders about non-compliance with the terms of the Law of Separation, and the bishops had docilely to accept these decisions. Priests who supported Christian democracy either in the legislature or in the Catholic Press were harassed and vilified.

One thorn in the flesh of the integrists was the Abbé Lemire, a priest and for thirty-five years a Christian democratic representative to Parliament from Flanders. As early as the 1880s Lemire had contemplated the eventual end of the Concordat with hope that it might be the first step in the Church's reaching out to the people, for the Concordat signified for him a bourgeois conception of Catholicism. He wanted the priest to be transformed into "a defender of consciences" and not to remain an "agent of the moral order salaried by the regime." He wished a bishop to become a true pastor, not "a functionary in a purple cassock as dreamt of by Napoleon I, this would-be head of the spiritual police sitting in his palace, like a prefect in his administrative office, between the dossiers of his parishes and those of the Minister of Cults." All this could be swept away, he anticipated, with the abolition of the servile Concordat which had made the Church, as Napoleon had indeed intended, into a department of State. With accents reminiscent again of Lamennais, the Abbé Lemire wanted priests to be citizens and to participate in all areas of life, no longer taking refuge in their sacristies, protected by their routines and their parishioners from contact with the real world. Thus, he himself found a parliamentary career perfectly appropriate for a priest, which earned him criticism from the hierarchy, as did his espousal of Christian democratic social and economic programs.[33] Men like Lemire, because they refused a policy of *Catholic defense*, which in the period of the Separation could only mean a defense of reactionary policies, incensed integrists and conservatives. They were very vulnerable to integrist persecution and to slander by the Action Française.[34] While there even were some integrists who had been opposed to the restrictions which the Concordat imposed upon the Gallican Church and were willing to foresee its end without fear,[35] for the most part Catholics felt obliged in the decade and a half before the First World War to see in the end of governmental support of the Church the clear sign of the evils of the godless Republic. What they probably might have more profitably seen in the Law of Separation and in the failure of their campaign – supported by the Sillon and the Action Française alike – to stop the government from taking an inventory of Church property was the sober fact that practising Catholics had now become a distinct minority in modern France.[36]

The critical insight of many of the early leaders of Christian democracy, particularly the "abbés démocrates" like Lemire, Gayraud, Naudet, Trochu, Garnier, and others, about the Church's need to break with the mere defense of a conservative social order unfortunately did not spare them from an addiction to the themes of economic anti-Semitism. Once French Christian democrats came to a more modern and scientific understanding of economic forces, in the period after the First World War and later, they eventually abandoned anti-Semitism. They would even come to claim that their real roots lay in the liberal Catholicism of the mid-nineteenth century, even though they actually resembled liberal Catholics only superficially by wishing to be up-to-date. More accurately, they owed far more to Catholic integrism, for with integrists and intransigents they desired most fervently to compel modern society to conform to their model of a Christian commonwealth, based on a union of the Church with the masses. Given their deficient education, their popular social recruitment, and their pessimism about the course of modern life, the Social Catholic and Christian democratic priests were easily persuaded by men like Drumont that the traditional enemies of Christendom, the Jews, were also responsible for the upheavals of modern society. Anti-Semitism appealed to them as an explanation and as a means of drawing the laboring classes away from irreligion and revolutionary socialism. The national congresses of Christian democracy held in 1896 and 1897 heard loud calls for anti-Semitic legislation along with popular measures to ease the economic oppression of the lower classes. The struggle against the Jews was viewed as part of a larger battle against financiers and capitalists. Social Catholics and Christian democrats generally did avoid the more blatantly racist aspects of anti-Semitism, but their progressive Catholic blend of radicalism and traditionalism freely utilized anti-Semitism to appeal to those forgotten or oppressed elements of modern French society impervious to more conservative appeals for order. Anti-Semitism seemed a logical outcome of anti-parliamentary and anti-capitalist thinking, and the forerunners of Christian democracy were very susceptible to this overall outlook.[37] It was one of the key themes of what one scholar has aptly called "Catholic Populism."[38] In many countries populist movements found it difficult, if not impossible, to avoid anti-Semitic appeals as they sought to mobilize social groups victimized by rapidly changing economic and social developments. Catholic social thought was susceptible to anti-Semitism also because it sought for simple solutions appropriate to static societies of scarcity and maintained a basically medieval and romantic conception of man and society. It was often more negative in emphasis than positive, lacking real understanding of modern economic forces. Catholic social movements shared what Eugen Weber has called the "traditional cultural baggage" of the masses, which always contained a large dose of hostility to Jews.[39] Thus in the dispute between traditionalists and progressives within the Church anti-Semitism for a long time was not a bone of contention.

A moderate application of the Law of Separation might have satisfied many French Catholics, which was precisely the intention of the moderate republicans for whom the old anti-clerical issues were increasingly less appealing. In any case, with the abrogation of the Concordat the fear of clericalism, except on the single issue of education, could no longer paper over the very fundamental disagreements between bourgeois and socialist republicans. Even in the face of mounting papal intransigence and provocation the moderate republicans refused to be bullied into taking a line with the Church which could be mistaken for persecution.[40] As papal fulminations during the pontificat of Pius X increased in number and intensity, the republicans showed what one could even call a truly "Christian" forbearance towards their ecclesiastical critics. It is not an exaggeration to contend, therefore, that the Vatican was essentially responsible for the rightward drift of French Catholics in the decade before the First World War and, therefore, for the enormous influence which the Action Française acquired over them. Rome discouraged and finally condemned any cooperation between Catholics and the godless Republic over the implementation of the Separation. Despite a 1914 condemnation of Maurras' anti-Christian philosophy by the Congregation of the Index, Pius X refused to make the condemnation public because, as he said, "'the Action Française . . . has done much good. It defends the principle of authority. It defends order.'" For his part, Maurras had already written that even as a non-believer he had no trouble defending and supporting the Catholic Church, "'the interests of Roman Catholicism and those of France being nearly always identical and nowhere contradictory.'"[41] This period between the Law of Separation and the mid-1920s was one during which the French bourgeoisie, Catholic and free-thinking, accepted much of the ideology of the Action Française and thereby came to see in the cooperation of the Church with it a key to the maintenance of order in a revolutionary age. It would be an era of a Voltairean Catholicism of order. And the Action Française, despite its reputation for disruptive and radical monarchism, would be the chief agent of this reconciliation.

THE IMPORTANCE OF CHARLES MAURRAS

The Action Française might appear an unlikely force for the reconciliation of the bourgeoisie and the Church. It was, indeed, vigorously hostile to the Republic, uncompromising in attacking its political and ideological opponents,[42] and unceasingly insistent about the certain guilt of the hapless Dreyfus – all factors likely, one might think, to make it unpopular with a conservative bourgeoisie dedicated to order. The Action Française's royalism, seemingly a futile anachronism, might also have been an insurmountable obstacle. But the attractions of Maurras and his movement need to be carefully appreciated in order to understand its important role in French Catholic history in the early twentieth century.

Despite what Charles Maurras and his disciples said and wrote about the restoration of the monarchy to a France weakened by republican ideology and parliamentary politics, it was clear to intelligent reviewers and critics from the beginning of that movement that its basic political doctrine was nationalism more than royalism. Royalism was a means of breaking with a Republic whose principles and practice had come to threaten order, but integral nationalism was a nationalism stripped of the dangerous principle of 1789. French nationalism had first come into being under the auspices of the Jacobins, but the ideology of the Revolution was being used to undermine the bourgeois order on behalf of socialism. Integral nationalism was a nationalism which could save the bourgeoisie from its own folly – and from its own revolutionary origins which now placed its position in jeopardy. The historic function of the Action Française was in fact not, as Maurras believed, to bring about a monarchic restoration; its actual role, clear at least in restrospect, was to give conservatives an attractive and militant ideology of social defense. The rhetoric of the Action Française could be radical, but its influence was conservative. As Maurras conceived of it, monarchy was to be the servant of integral nationalism and not the other way around: the cult of the fatherland took precedence over devotion to the person of the king. But Maurras's opposition to the Republic – which he persisted in referring to as *La Gueuse* ("the Tramp") – was understood by a bourgeoisie receptive to the appeal of the Action Française as essentially opposition to the *social* Republic, that is, to the use of republican ideology to justify the creation of a more popular and democratic social order. One could take or leave the monarchy but one still had available a justification for the defense of the social status quo.[43]

If the professed monarchism of the Action Française did not frighten the bourgeoisie into rejecting it as a radical movement, its integral nationalism could be misinterpreted as merely an enthusiastic form of traditional French patriotism. Although Maurras rejected the Revolution of 1789 and all its works, including that Jacobin nationalism which was signified by the *Fraternity* of the revolutionary trinity, he did not, despite an apparent traditionalism, view devotion to the monarchy or the French nation in traditional terms. His nationalism actually had deep roots in the positivistic social philosophy of Auguste Comte which believed that because individualism was destructive, the individual needed to be subject to a larger collectivity for his welfare and improvement. Maurras found in positivism an answer to his own loss of Christian faith and the anarchy of modern life and thought; it rescued him from a deep pessimism of cultural despair. But he appropriated Comte in his own special way, refusing to subordinate the individual to Comte's "Great Being," Humanity. It was, instead, in the nation that Maurras found the answer to destructive individualism:

> "Humanity does not exist – at least not yet. The largest group binding men together is still that which is given expression in the idea of nationality. If one is fully conscious of the truth of this, one becomes convinced that the Dreyfusards who seethe with indignation against Country in the name of Humanity are either fools or liars. He who defends his Country, his nationality and his State is engaged in the defence of all that is real and all that is concrete in the idea of Humanity."[44]

Maurras thus subordinated man to the nation; this was the essential core of integral nationalism. As one sympathetic but discerning Catholic critic observed,

> "the starting point is simple: the Country, this society to which an individual belongs through birth and education, must be understood by him as the essential condition of his development. . . . For a man concerned with his dignity and happiness, the highest reality that has call upon him is his Country."[45]

Here one is very close to Fascism, for the devotion of the individual to the collectivity is not limited by consideration of prior natural rights; the individual only has significance as part of the organic whole.[46] Yet as with Maurras's royalism, the bourgeoisie in search of an ideology of social defense could easily ignore such disquieting tendencies and focus upon the usefulness of integral nationalism in preventing change and disorder.

Charles Maurras and the other leaders of the Action Française viewed religion in the manner of Voltaire; it was a Catholicism of order which they appreciated for its support of authority, social hierarchy, and national tradition. One specialist in Catholic political thought has labelled Maurras a "belated Voltairian" because he wished to use religion for the "social discipline of the masses."[47] This is an important insight, for it explains how and why the Action Française could become the bridge of reconciliation between the French bourgeoisie and the Catholic Church. Though personally an unbeliever, Maurras believed that because the Catholic Church had for centuries contributed to the growth of the French nation, it would need to continue to play an important role in French life, although a *subordinate* one. He always used the word *religion* in its original Roman connotation of binding or social cohesion; his conception of the role of the Church was this-wordly and social, contributing to the binding of Frenchmen to one another in the national myth. As one critic observed, "The Church appears to him ... as at one and the same time the guarantor of civilization and the guardian of nationality."[48] Religion was not so much true as useful and necessary. This emphasis appealed to the free-thinking bourgeoisie, while for the Catholic bourgeoisie he could offer not only a vigorous defense of the Church as it faced the attacks of anti-clericals, but also a naturalistic justification for authority where merely theological or ecclesiastical arguments were embarrassing or no longer convincing. Appealing to Aquinas, Maurras supported the independence of the natural from the supernatural, thus propping up a waning faith in traditional theology with rational appeals. Certainly in revering Aquinas, Maurras really revered the thought of Aristotle, and the Aristotelian arguments he used, shorn of the normative Christian context insisted upon by Aquinas, left the individual in firm subordination to the community, something not entirely clear to Catholics who saw only his apparent "Thomism." Maurras, thus, provided ideological support for order where religion by itself seemed insufficient; he provided assurance for Catholics whose religious faith was waning, as his own had already been undermined, that their faith in themselves and their right to their social position did not have to rest solely on a supernatural justification. These could also be sustained by naturalism and realism.[49] Their principles, he implied, were not anachronistic after all, but *modern*.

Maurras was actually something of a disciple of eighteenth-century deism and a follower of Voltaire, much as he would have disputed the affiliation and dependency. Religion was useful, therefore it was true. Certainly integral Catholicism would not have been Voltaire's preferred form of social religion, but Maurras lived in far less optimistic times than had Voltaire. The attitude of Voltaire and Maurras towards Christianity certainly differed, but not their conception of how religion might justify itself and serve the community.[50] Maurras and the Action Française effected the final reconciliation of the bourgeoisie with the

Church on the principles of a Voltairean Catholicism of order. Many Catholics, to be sure, were persuaded to lend support to the Action Française mostly because of its role in defending the Church against the consequences of the Law of Separation.[51] But the way the Voltairean religion of the Maurrasians relieved the anxieties of lukewarm Catholics also should not be underestimated. The Action Française was able to nurture French Catholics at many different way stations on the road from belief to apostasy.

The First World War only enhanced the influence of the Action Française upon Catholics and conservatives, for its perfervid anti-Germanism largely replaced its attacks on the Republic, and it easily seemed to embody the most enthusiastic expression of wartime French patriotism. It was at this time that the Action Française was most effectively able to pose as the defender of conservative order without arousing fears about its ideological radicalism, and its conservatism indeed became its principal, characteristic appeal to Frenchmen. Despite its theoretical disdain for the electoral process and for the parliamentarianism of the Republic, the Action Française participated in the elections of 1919 by supporting congenial candidates around the country and, for the first time, by running three of its own candidates in Parisian electoral districts. Its electoral platform made no mention of the monarchy, preferring to appeal for the votes of patriots, chauvinists, conservatives, and Catholics with a more generally nationalistic appeal.[52] Its vitriolic journalistic voice, Léon Daudet, was actually elected to Parliament from Paris, and he lost no time in becoming the most extreme voice of chauvinistic nationalism in the legislature. The Action Française through its contribution to the war effort and the defense of order had finally become a leading component of post-war French conservatism. It was, therefore, necessarily also a leading force among French Catholics.

The 1920s have been perceived by a number of historians as the decade in which the French Church finally pursued a successful *Ralliement* to the Republic. Much is made of the support for or acquiescence in the Republic by the Catholic hierarchy, something allegedly evident by about 1930, and credit for this development is generally awarded to the policies of Benedict XV and Pius XI. And the chief sign offered of a change in French Catholic and Vatican attitudes is the 1926 condemnation by Rome of the Action Française. But many confusing issues are raised here. If the French hierarchy had really finally rallied to the Republic, why would it later be so enthusiastic in supporting the Vichy regime and in seeing in the aged Marshal Pétain the providential scourge of the godless Third Republic? Why was the Action Française publicly condemned by Rome in 1926 when condemnation was avoided in 1910? And why was the condemnation lifted in 1939, on the eve of the Second World War? If the Action Française had by the 1920s achieved a position of substantial importance among Catholics and conservatives, what exactly did its condemnation say about the drift of papal policies? What did the condemnation of the Action Française mean to French Catholics? And why was the movement of integral nationalism condemned after it had settled down as a force for conservatism and for reconciliation between Catholics and a conservative Republic, when it had not been censured in its earlier, more radical period of existence? In fact, it seems clear that the significance of the Roman condemnation of the Action Française, taken by many historians as extremely important, involved far less than meets the eye.

There *was* a Catholic *Ralliement* to the Republic in the 1920s, but it was not the *Ralliement* depicted in the very misleading book by Harry W. Paul entitled *The Second Ralliement: The Rapprochement between Church and State in France in the Twentieth Century*.[53] This book misleads when it concludes that Pius XI's return to the policy of Leo XIII, a policy marked by the appointment of conciliatory men to the French hierarchy and a willingness to work for friendly relations with the Third Republic, somehow involved a rupture with conservative politics, a rupture which was finally crowned by the condemnation of the Action Française, and a coming to terms with modern life and thought. Perhaps Paul and others have fallen into error through an initial misreading and misunderstanding of the motives and objectives of Leo XIII. Pius XI, for his part, understood what the abortive Ralliement of his august predecessor had been all about, and he in fact did pursue the same goals: reconciliation with a conservative Republic held out more hope for the restoration of the Church's influence than support for sterile ultra-reactionary movements. Pius XI was no more a liberal than Leo XIII had been, but he pursued long-standing objectives with new tactics and an appreciation of new political and social realities. The monograph of Oscar L. Arnal, *Ambivalent Alliance. The Catholic Church and the Action Française, 1899–1939*, here frequently cited, is a far more perceptive analysis of papal attitudes towards the politics of the 1920s and 1930s, and of the attitudes of Catholic France, because it understands more deeply the nature of the permanent objectives and concerns of the Catholic Church as it has confronted the radical upheavals of the twentieth century.

The encouragement given by both Benedict XV and Pius XI to the efforts of Aristide Briand and the League of Nations on behalf of international cooperation and Franco-German reconciliation had earned both these pontiffs the disapprobation of French nationalists, particularly of the members of the Action Française. Both Popes were defamed as pro-German. Indeed it was the extreme nationalism of the Action Française which created the earliest cracks in the façade of Catholic support for integral nationalism. But the apparent internationalism of the Vatican (indeed, how could a universal, *Catholic* Church be nationalistic?) urged European Catholics to overcome their nationalist rivalries in a common defense of order against the perceived threat of Bolshevism, from Soviet Russia and from domestic communists. French Catholics were urged to rely less on nationalist egoism than on cooperation with other Catholic and Christian states in defending Christian civilization from the godless threat from the east, a threat which the Church's unchanging outlook easily viewed as the final product of the dangerous liberalism against which the Church had never ceased battling. This internationalism, although it was distasteful to the Action Française, was not so much *liberal* as it was anti-communist.[54] Equally anti-communist in purpose was Pius XI's 1931 encyclical *Quadragesimo Anno* which, although it did advocate State intervention in the economy to regulate labor–management disputes when all else had failed and also certainly marked a reaffirmation of the Church's dislike of unregulated capitalism, still found Marxism a greater danger than capitalism. It also struck at working-class independence by denying the right of workers to engage in strike action.[55] Pius XI continued to wish, in the tradition of Social Catholicism, to undertake the re-Christianization of the working classes and to persuade capitalists and the bourgeoisie that only the Church could save them from socialism or communism. In this he was also totally at one with Leo XIII. Thus the appeals to workers, capitalists, and internationalists were ambiguous signs of an acceptance of the modern world; papal policy still was largely motivated by the intransigent Catholic goal of re-Christianizing society, and in this effort anti-communism was in the 1920s becoming a principal element. For French Catholics, this meant approval of efforts towards reconciliation and cooperation with a conservative Republic. Even those Catholics in the Christian democratic wing of the French Church were highly nationalistic and anti-communist,[56] and papal initiatives easily met with their support. There could, thus, be considerable confusion about the thrust of papal policy; it could be mistaken as actually more accepting of modern life than it really was.

It is probably erroneous to ascribe the Church's eventual condemnation of the Action Française to the growth of liberal or progressive convictions in Rome. Probably Pius XI simply believed that he and the Church had a better answer to the calamities of modern life than the doctrine of integral nationalism:

> To this Integral Nationalism the new pope opposed Integral Catholicism, the only solution to all the problems of society. For the Action Française modern errors stemmed from 1789 and it put in opposition [to these errors] the virtues of the Old Regime. The pontifical genealogy reached farther back and placed the Golden Age in the Middle Ages which the Renaissance shattered with its attack on the social role of the Church. In the eyes of Pius XI it was inconsistent to battle against contemporary modernity in the name of an earlier modernity. The Catholics of Action Française could not accept the Republic on principle; the Pope was indifferent to this: monarchy, if one desired it, a Republic if one wished – but a Christian order of society![57]

The last real outburst of anti-clericalism in France, more farcical than significant, occurred in 1924 with the victory of the Left in legislative elections. The newly formed ministry of Edouard Herriot intended to subject the rewon provinces of Alsace and Lorraine to the Law of Separation, from whose consequences they had been spared by their incorporation in 1871 into Bismarck's Germany, and also to break off the newly re-established diplomatic relations with the Vatican. French Catholics of all political stripes reacted to this renewal of a hoary anti-clericalism with an equally outmoded general defense of Catholic interests. The result was not insignificant, however, for it led to the creation of the Fédération Nationale Catholique (the FNC) which, under the leadership of General de Castelnau, was able to exert firm conservative control over most Catholic organizations. The FNC was to be very influential in the elections of 1928 when almost half of the deputies sent to Parliament supported a number of measures designed to appease Catholic interests. In 1929 Pius XI extended to the FNC his highest approval as the guide to Catholic Action, which was the umbrella organization under which Rome and the hierarchy intended to exert a close control over all Catholic groups and movements.[58] The FNC had benefited from the last blast of traditional anti-clericalism in much the same way that the Action Française had waxed mightily among Catholics in the aftermath of the Separation. Their memberships overlapped in a number of regions and in many activities. FNC rallies were sometimes protected by members of the Camelots du Roi, an Action Française organization, and General de Castelnau actually did not even hesitate to appear in court on behalf of some Camelots who had physically attacked Marc Sangnier; thus the FNC even condoned the brutal physical violence, and not merely the verbal violence, of which some members of the Action Française were capable – and even against a leading Catholic like Sangnier, an exemplar, at once, of Catholic charity and obedience. And the man who would be notorious under Vichy for the enforcement of its anti-Semitic legislation, Xavier Vallat, was at the same time a lawyer for the Action Française and a leading FNC orator. The political and social program of this new organization of Catholic defense actually differed from the Action Française only in its somewhat more subdued expression of anti-Semitism and royalism.[59]

From the Vatican's point of view the FNC had an important advantage over the Action Française. The FNC was part of Catholic Action and therefore subject to the supervision of the French hierarchy. The Action Française had never officially been a Catholic organization, and however sympathetic an ally of the Church it was in battles against anti-clericalism, it did not submit to ecclesiastical discipline. Indeed, the Action Française always jealously guarded its freedom to criticize high churchmen and to pose as more integrally Catholic than some Popes. All this would be painfully clear to Pius XI after the condemnation of the Action Française when Maurras and his associates defied the Church and reverted to an almost instinctive Gallicanism which preferred a French to a Roman Catholicism. In condemning the Action Française, the Vatican condemned not only the little understood pagan cultural doctrines of Maurras, something unknown to most Catholics, but also the strategy of utilizing the Church in defense of political and social positions without any prior belief in the dogmas of the Church or a readiness to submit to its authority. The Fédération Nationale Catholique was far more amenable to Church discipline and obedience and thus could much better serve the interests of the Vatican.

Since the political and social program of the FNC hardly differed from that of the Action Française, the condemnation of the latter hardly could constitute any endorsement of more liberal or progressive Catholic initiatives. The Roman attack on the Action Française was more the reassertion of the Church's own authority over the Catholic laity than a repudiation of political or social conservatism. Liberal Catholics wanted desperately to see in the repudiation of the Action Française an important sign of change in the orientation of the Church, and they sought to make the most of papal initiatives towards the working classes and towards international cooperation, but in every case they exaggerated the possibly liberal implications of Pius XI's strategy and failed to see that in attacking Maurras the pontiff was attacking not conservatism but a Gallican-like independence on the part of Action Française Catholics. Nor were they the only ones misled, for many historians of this period have also overestimated the impact of the break with the Action Française, forgetting in the process the extremely conservative policy of the FNC.[60] It is true that both Benedict XV and Pius XI were less sympathetic to the ultra-reactionaries in the Curia than Pius X had been,[61] but liberal Catholics always drew more favorable consequences from the discredit of certain kinds of clerical reactionaries than the facts warranted. Their folly would be amply demonstrated in the 1930s when the evident rise of Fascism as a threat to civilization elicited from Rome only a more frenzied concern with communism.

The slowness and evident unwillingness of many French Catholics to obey Rome in the matter of the censure of the Action Française only seemed to justify the increasingly outraged Pius XI in his conviction that he had nipped a dangerous neo-Gallicanism in the bud, and he insisted on obedience with renewed asperity. He was above all defending the Church's authority. He did succeed in breaking the hold of the Action Française over French

Catholics, and the circulation of the Action Française's daily newspaper and other publications did significantly decline. Yet the claim that French Catholics were thereby freed from thraldom to conservative politics is difficult to accept because the FNC in many ways simply continued to uphold the Action Française doctrines under the protection of Catholic Action.[62] One might indeed question whether the condemnation of the Action Française actually made any real difference, since in the 1930s the more liberal and progressive Catholics continued to have great difficulty in being heard over the chauvinism of the FNC.[63] In any case, the disciplinary penalties levied against French Catholics who refused to heed the Vatican condemnation of the Action Française and the placing of its newspaper on the Index were more often than not applied with moderation. The many bishops who acted indulgently towards Catholics who were Action Française members were not censured or punished, and only two highly placed French clerics living in Rome were publicly humiliated for their disobedience to the Pope; indeed, they were intentionally made an example of. It is true that Catholics who publicly and with great obstinacy refused to acknowledge the right of the Church to demand that they detach themselves from the Action Française found themselves in the position once held by Jansenists in the seventeenth and eighteenth centuries: their public challenge to the Church was met by refusal of the sacraments, in many cases causing distress and serious division within families. But compliant priests were often found to moderate the theoretically harsh penalties imposed by the Church; there was no Louis XIV here to enforce the decrees of Roman tribunals. Many Catholics obeyed the Vatican with considerable mental reservation, waiting for a change, and by the mid-1930s the tide indeed began to turn.

In 1934 the Cardinal-Archbishop of Paris permitted religious funerals for Catholics from the Action Française and for Camelots du Roi who had been killed in the 6 February riots against the Parliament, riots with which many Catholics sympathized for a variety of reasons, even on the progressive Catholic Left. Paris's Cardinal Verdier evidently felt that in the changed political context no scandal would result from his remarkable leniency, whereas earlier Action Française members had normally been denied religious burial.[64] Indeed Verdier's conciliatory attitude towards the Action Française was part of a process of reconciliation between the integral nationalists and the Church, a process which would culminate in the lifting of the ban on the Action Française by Pius XII in 1939, just two months after his election as Pope. With an irony which his own mistaken analysis of papal policy necessarily concealed from him, Harry Paul commented on the rehabilitation of the Action Française by observing: "Once the Vatican had reached a modus vivendi with Mussolini and Fascism in Italy in 1927, and with Hitler and Nazism in Germany in 1933, it became ridiculous to maintain such an intransigent attitude towards Maurras and Action Française."[65] How true! – if the Vatican were correct in seeing the communist, and not the Fascist, threat as the greater danger. Indeed, it is quite possible to see papal attacks on Mussolini (*Non Abbiamo Bisogno*, 1931) and Hitler (*Mit Brennender Sorge*, 1937) as more moderate and qualified than the papal condemnation of communism (*Divini Redemptoris*, 1937).[66] With the rehabilitation of the Action Française, Voltairean Catholics of order were more than ready for the regime of Marshal Pétain.

THE CATHOLIC LEFT

The very real sympathy of Pius XI for the plight of the working classes, as expressed in encyclicals based on the Church's Social Teaching, easily got lost in the period between the two world wars. Papal attacks on unbridled economic liberalism fell on deaf ears as the Catholic bourgeoisie rallied to the conservative Republic. The Catholic laity of France was led by men whose private financial support in the local parishes was vital for a Church deprived twice in little more than a century of its property and all public financial subsidies. These bourgeois Catholics naturally preferred French nationalism to papal internationalism (however deeply anti-communist the latter was), the traditional defense of religious rights to the more modern program of Catholic Action, and a privatized religion to Social Catholicism. They were impervious to the social concerns of the modern Popes and saw in papal pronouncements only what they wished, justification for their continued conservatism and anti-communism. The originally reactionary roots of the Church's Social Teaching made it easy for the bourgeoisie to ignore what it also contained that sanctioned a truly radical transformation of the social order. They could always point with alarm to "red Christians," men who took too seriously the Church's opposition to capitalism and economic liberalism.[67] And the Christian democrats, those who tried to utilize the Church's traditional Social Teaching in a new, less reactionary direction, had only modest success in the 1930s; they found themselves constantly in serious controversy with the Catholic bourgeoisie. The need to proclaim opposition to Marxism on every suitable occasion seriously prevented the Church from influencing those de-Christianized or un-Christianized masses it sincerely wished to reach.[68] The overtures made to Catholic workers during the Popular Front by Maurice Thorez on behalf of the French Communist Party were rebuffed by all but a fringe group of leftist Catholics, leading Emmanuel Mounier to note the irony of the Catholic rejection of Thorez's "extended hand." In his view, Fascism always began with an "extended hand" to spiritual forces and inevitably found receptivity among Catholics in the forging of a conservative alliance.[69] As a prophet Mounier was much misunderstood in his own time, but he was very important for the eventual re-orientation of French Catholicism after the Second World War. One historian has called his journal, *Esprit*, "the most persuasive voice of the French Catholic Left," while another views him as "a prophet of Christianity as the most radical of counter-cultures."[70] Some discussion of Mounier is very important in understanding the dilemmas of French Catholics before the Second World War and their new departures in the post-war era.

Mounier – along with Jacques Maritain, but in a more radical way than Maritain – influenced seminarians, clergy, and Catholic intellectuals in the pre-war and post-war years by urging them to understand the need for a break between Christianity and "Christian civilization," between the authentic Gospel and the temporary forms which Christian faith took in different societies. Even Catholics on the Left were much too tied to outdated conceptions, institutions, and problems.[71] Or as Georges Hoog, an important Catholic on the Left, complained in 1938, French Catholics were always in the unenviable position of "ralliés," always a generation late in catching up with reality.[72] Characteristically, Mounier would reserve much of his scorn for the Christian democrats whose reformism made them as much a part of what he termed "the established disorder" as the conservatives. Even the hated Action Française, he felt, at least had courage, something of which no one could accuse the timid Christian democrats.[73] Where the fledgling Christian democrats had once been bold in desiring to accept the Republic, such acceptance had by the interwar years become part of the bourgeois conservative consolidation, and Mounier refused the choice of rejecting the Republic, and thereby supporting reaction, or accepting it, since that meant accepting a very imperfect bourgeois order, "the established disorder." He wanted to go beyond these distasteful alternatives. From the traditional stance of intransigent Catholicism, Mounier opposed the liberal notion of religion as a private affair; he wanted religion to realize fully its fundamentally radical potential in remaking the social order.[74] Above all, Mounier deplored the role of the bourgeoisie in Catholicism, especially its modern support for religion. Its former hostility to religion was both more honest and less harmful. Writing in 1933, in the very month Hitler came to power in Germany, Mounier continued to attack reformism and to preach revolutionary change, a position which in the words of Jean-Marie Domenach, a later editor of Mounier's *Esprit*, can be deemed, "'a little remote from reality'" and certainly "'utopian.'"[75] But it was precisely the prophetic quality of Mounier's thought which impressed many observers and allowed him to be seen as something of a latter-day Lamennais, whose reputation and significance also does not rest on mere political wisdom or prudence.

Mounier's definition of *the bourgeois* was less a matter of his socio-economic position than of his psychological or spiritual condition. For him, the bourgeois individual was a believer only in the utility of religion, but not in God. Thus he was the Voltairean *par excellence*.[76] Mounier surveyed with bitter irony the role of the bourgeoisie in French Catholicism:

> Sometimes under its own name, [but] here in France anonymously, there exists in many countries a Catholic party, and this party is found almost regularly to coincide . . . with the forces of reaction. . . . The bourgeoisie was born in opposition to the Christian spirit. . . . It grew firm with the [rise of the] individual, then at the time of the revolutionary ideology it gave itself noble credentials: the Declaration of Rights, the code of conformity for the perfect egoist. . . . It found its natural metaphysics in Voltaireanism: a God, creator of worlds, indifferent and a technician like one of themselves, and who for the comfort of the bourgeois established

> this inimitable confidence in indefinite progress, the guarantee of all risk, the continual enrichment of the chief shareholders, ... as is proper in a well-run enterprise. The apparent union, through the throne, between the bourgeoisie and the Church, under the Restoration, was really only apparent.... Louis-Philippe replaced Voltaire, the umbrella triumphed over the pen, [but] to be a good natured fellow didn't mean one was any less daring.... Everything changes: the bourgeois now goes to Mass, he even has his very own proper Mass, when the sun is already high in the sky between a yawn and a good midday meal. Conversion? Not at all. The bourgeois was afraid: afraid of the Republic first of all and of its democratic elements; then, today he has created for himself a Republican comfort, fear of Communism.
>
> One knows the rest. In each of our provinces ... the equation is established between Catholic newspaper and conservative newspaper, Catholic candidate and conservative candidate. The bourgeois is clever. Having assumed in his own program all the Catholic causes, but [in a form] sterilized, naturalized, and rigidly fixed, as soon as some character makes a move to be Catholic without being bourgeois, he cries for union on the "pure ground of religion...."
>
> ... The bourgeois, who is master of the game, does not change camp except to guarantee the mediocre permanence of his aims: yesterday [he was] with the people against religion, because religion would have destroyed his commerce; today [he is] with religion against the people because the worker threatens to destroy his factory.[77]

Mounier's position was so squarely based on the tradition of Catholic intransigence that it was only after the Vichy period that he emerged clearly on the political Left. In the 1930s he had sought, consistent with Catholic Social Thought, a "third way" between capitalism and socialism. This anti-capitalist and anti-Marxist stance led many to flirtation with various forms of Fascism, for Fascism also claimed to seek an alternative to capitalism and socialism. Mounier did flirt with Vichy's National Revolution briefly, but he ultimately was able to take advantage of the campaign mounted against him by the Action Française and also of his brief imprisonment by the Vichy regime to emerge finally and fully on the Left of the political spectrum, where he remained until his death in 1950.[78] But whether on the Right or the Left, Mounier always consistently opposed the bourgeois Catholicism of order, which is what made his thought exciting to many French Catholics in the period after the Second World War.

CATHOLICS, VICHY, AND THE OCCUPATION

The Vichy regime was welcomed by Catholics, as it was by most Frenchmen seeking to understand and cope with the disaster of military defeat. But the Catholic leadership also saw in the new regime a final vindication of all the struggles of Catholics during the lifetime of the Third Republic. They were quick to locate the blame for the defeat of 1940 in the spiritual and moral defects of a godless Republic and society, an indictment which was firmly part of conservative tradition but was also based ultimately on the entire Judaeo-Christian prophetic tradition of exposing the moral causes of personal and national disaster. In an important collection of essays entitled *After Auschwitz*, Richard L. Rubenstein observed how this prophetic tradition about divine vengeance for unbelief and immorality can lead to monstrous theories of culpability.[79] Certainly, the use of this tradition in 1940 offered a terrible legitimacy to the Vichy regime as it proceeded to punish those groups it held responsible for the errors of French national life. Churchmen were quick to praise Pétain's use of moralizing themes without considering how little his own personal history really conformed to Catholic models of private or public life. The Vichy politicians shamelessly played on the themes that the Catholic leadership was bound to receive with enthusiasm, and the hierarchy collaborated with the Pétain regime to a degree far beyond the Church's normal support of constituted political authorities.[80] Pétain, himself, never paid a visit to a provincial city without a public welcoming ceremony at the local cathedral, and clerics persisted in publicly lauding him as France's "providential man." The non-Catholic press was indeed just as effusive about the marshal as the Catholic press and clergy, and for some time only the collaborationist press of occupied Paris was in a position to ridicule this excessive adulation. And the pro-clerical policies of the Vichy regime in questions of public aid for Catholic education, while they were consistent with the appeasing trends of the last two decades of the Third Republic, did have the unfortunately clear effect of associating the Church publicly with the victory of a vindictive Right over a prostrate Republic.[81]

Georges Montaron, a leading Catholic progressive, has described the role of the Catholic leadership during Vichy with biting asperity:

> For the mass of Christians Pétain was also the symbol of a certain recognition and a renaissance of Christianity. For the bishops and the majority of Catholics it was the revenge for 1905: the Church was finally going to recover the position of privilege which the Republic had denied to it. The Catholics with the hierarchy in the lead had only accepted the Republic out of necessity, and they applauded when Work, Family, and Fatherland replaced Liberty, Equality, and Fraternity . . . Passing from acceptance to support, the Catholic hierarchy became one of the pillars of Vichyism.[82]

As always, this hostile interpretation of official Catholic relations with Vichy may be contested, and it is again in René Rémond's work that a contrary view can be found, a view more favorable to the Church. Rémond has been skeptical of the alleged integrism of the hierarchy and has cautioned:

> It is a simplification to reduce the behavior of the bishops to an expression of traditional clericalism or to explain their sympathy for the government of Marshal Pétain with reference to their satisfaction at revenge against the lay and anti-clerical Republic. How could this episcopate have been able so quickly and so completely to deny itself, having in part been marked by a refusal of extremist politics and having in its youth defined itself in opposition to the Action Française? In expressing loyalty to the established government it did not believe itself out of step with its earlier acceptance of the Republic: did it not remain faithful to a policy of relevance? It had not changed, the regime – France had changed by miraculously returning to the Church. They had suffered too much from the isolation which resulted from the Catholic emigration from politics and the hostility of the politicians; for nothing in the world would they again be relegated to the position of *émigrés* or a minority. They also intended to continue to work closely with

> those in power. Without realizing that the political personnel had radically changed, the meaning of such cooperation had also radically changed.[83]

Rémond's indulgent, Panglossian, assessment is based on a more general view that the condemnation of the Action Française really liberated French Catholicism from conservatism, a view which should be all but demolished by the persistence of conservative positions in the dominant FNC and by the Catholic proclivity for the Vichy counter-revolution. Another look at the "Jewish Question" should demonstrate that the Catholic leadership persisted in its traditional positions until the eleventh hour, and that it was ordinary priests and laymen rather than prelates who, before it was too late, redeemed the reputation of Catholic France.

It is clear from recent research[84] that the Vichy regime needed no German pressure or persuasion to enact discriminatory legislation against the Jews of France. Frenchmen committed to the myth of the Resistance, whose core was the denial of any overwhelming French support for Vichy and the minimization of the extent of collaboration with the German occupiers, have preferred to believe that the Germans were mostly responsible for the anti-Semitic legislation and acts of Vichy. Someone as well aware of the native French tradition of anti-Semitism as Jacques Maritain wrote in 1942 from his American refuge that Vichy anti-Semitism was the result of German pressure.[85] It is possible that the excuse of German pressure was not entirely a matter of self-deception, for the assigning of German blame might have been a way of discrediting the Vichy regime in general and its anti-Semitic program in particular; it was perhaps a means of exposing Vichy's supposed autonomy as farcical.[86] In any case, before the massive deportations of Jews to Nazi death camps began in 1942, protests to the Vichy government over the anti-Jewish measures were confined to Protestant officials and some Catholic priests and laymen but certainly did not come from the Catholic hierarchy.[87] The initial anti-Jewish legislation was not an object of official Catholic protest at all. Immediately after the 1940 defeat, in a number of areas the diocesan publications called "Semaines Religieuses" urged such measures as the revision of the naturalization of foreigners, the dissolution of secret societies, the reform of education, and the repression of communism, a program quite consistent with the Action Française and the FNC. And as late as Easter 1941, the Bishop of Grenoble, Mgr Caillot, was including Jews and Freemasons in his list of enemies of Catholic France. Bishop Caillot would later offer some assistance to the persecuted Jews of his diocese, but his rhetoric reflected the experiences of his youth when belief in the negative influence of Jews upon France was standard fare among Catholics. Many of those like Caillot who would later offer aid to Jews had been at least theoretically in favor of legislation to curb their allegedly harmful influence.[88] Those most responsible for the drafting and the enforcement of the anti-Semitic legislation, Xavier Vallat and Raphaël Alibert, were fully imbued with the anti-Semitic ideology of the Action Française. Indeed, the legislation "was inspired by and generally sponsored by friends and allies of the Action Française."[89]

The first protest over treatment of the Jews by the assembled cardinals and archbishops of France came in 1942 after the 16–17 July round-up of foreign Jews in Paris. It was delivered in private to Pétain by Cardinal Suhard, the Archbishop of Paris, but it was widely distributed to parishes all over the country, was published clandestinely, and was even known abroad. The round-up of non-French Jews in the Unoccupied Zone made an even greater impression, and important rescue operations began in Lyon, a city which quickly became the Catholic capital of Unoccupied France. The role of the Archbishop of Lyon, Cardinal Gerlier, is hard to evaluate, for while he maintained a conspicuous loyalty to the Vichy authorities, he did allow considerable clandestine help to the Jews on the part of his clergy. Some bishops and other clergy protested against the separation of children from parents who were subject to deportation, without understanding that the removal of the children was a necessary cruelty to save their lives. Despite considerable confusion, it seems clear that the Vichy authorities, particularly those in the Commissariat aux Questions Juives under Xavier Vallat who enforced the anti-Jewish measures in the Unoccupied Zone, and the collaborationist press in Paris, were upset by the protests and feared the widespread influence they might have. Somewhat fewer than half of the bishops of the Unoccupied Zone made public protests from the pulpit over the deportation of Jews. None of the bishops in the much more tightly controlled Occupied Zone did so, not even Cardinal Liénart of Lille who had before the war denounced anti-Semitism and had been sympathetic to a more progressive

Catholic attitude on a wide range of subjects. It is true that his diocese of Lille was under German military occupation from Brussels, which left him little freedom of action. In any case, although these protests were short-lived and were not renewed when deportations resumed in February 1943, they did mark the beginning of Catholics distancing themselves from the Vichy regime.[90]

The deportation of the Jews, mostly non-French Jews among whom some French Jews were included, did finally arouse great opposition at all levels of the French clergy. Along with the question of what attitude to take towards the obligatory labor service in Germany and the rise of armed resistance to the Germans, the deportations "placed too many moral, even religious, principles in the balance for the Catholic organizations to pretend to ignore them."[91] While anti-Semites and collaborators complained bitterly that the clergy was apparently inadequately anti-Semitic,[92] the clergy's general support for Vichy did not make it tolerant of real, murderous, racial anti-Semitism. The clergy was found, as Hannah Arendt once remarked, not really anti-Semitic after all,[93] or at least it was compelled by its own principles to test its traditional ideological positions against the empirical facts of deportation and extermination. Theoretically able to stomach the anti-Jewish legislation of the Vichy regime, it was finally humanly unable to stand by and see its hereditary belief in Jewish malfeasance exploited to justify deadly persecution. This victory of empirical fact over ideology, prepared by the slow modernization of Catholicism, was finally the victory of life over myth.[94] Maurras and his coterie might claim that the Jews in unoccupied Vichy France behaved even more objectionably than before the war, but ordinary priests, members of male and female religious orders, Catholic laymen and laywomen, and even an occasional prelate saw only the men, women, and children of Israel pursued like wild beasts by the German and French police. And in the end they did their Christian duty. Everything in their history and tradition had prepared them for the discriminatory legislation of Vichy; nothing had prepared them for the Final Solution. It was in the crucible of the Second World War – and not before – that the conscience of Catholic France reached adulthood.

The persecution and deportation of Jews from Occupied and Unoccupied France was of course not the only question that troubled the conscience of French Catholics during the Second World War. The Vichy government's acceptance of German demands that Frenchmen be sent for terms of obligatory labor in Germany raised many difficult moral dilemmas. Bishops weighed their belief in the legitimacy of the Vichy regime against a disinclination to have Frenchmen sent to support the German war effort; they had also to consider that those who refused the labor service and disappeared into the *maquis* thereby left the weakest members of the working class, who had no means of evasion, entirely exposed to forced labor in Germany. Some bishops encouraged priests to accept labor service in Germany in order to have them minister clandestinely to the spiritual needs of their fellow laborers, thereby initiating the worker-priest experiment which would have importance in post-war France. The advice of the clergy in this matter of obligatory labor service was often contradictory and not always very helpful to perplexed Catholic laymen. Protestant authorities were more unambiguous in their advice here, as they had been for the most part on the question of Jewish deportations; generally, French Protestants had awakened to the Nazi peril much earlier than French Catholics, and they had usually been immune to reactionary ideology.[95]

On the question of whether normal obedience to constituted authority applied any longer to the Vichy regime after it had effectively lost any real autonomy following the German occupation of all continental French territory late in 1942, the Catholic clergy officially clung to outmoded positions which deepened terrible moral conflicts among many of its flock. The irony was not lost on thoughtful Catholics that in the last days of the Vichy regime bishops flocked with eagerness to attend the funeral of assassinated Vichy minister Philippe Henriot, a member of the FNC and for many years a leading Catholic personality who had been struck down by the Resistance for his pro-collaborationist activities; while Catholics in the Resistance often lay mortally wounded without any priests to give them the last sacrament, since priests who aided Resisters usually did so without the sanction of their ecclesiastical superiors. In 1942, during his brief imprisonment by the Vichy authorities who had mistaken his intellectual opposition for actual political opposition, Mounier was denied Holy Communion by the prison chaplain who believed, with the support of his ecclesiastical superiors, that obedience to the authority of the government was a necessary prerequisite for reception of the sacraments.[96] Mounier at first feared that the blatant clericalism of the Vichy regime and the fawning adulation of the Church for the discredited National Revolution would cause a great resurgence of anti-clericalism. As many Catholics increasingly distanced themselves from Vichy, however, he noted: "'Happily for religious peace the Laval–Darnand regime substituted teams of killers for teams of *bien-pensants*, and numerous Catholics entered the Resistance.'"[97] For the most part, it was the question of obligatory labor service in Nazi Germany which finally persuaded significant numbers of Catholics to oppose Vichy actively, especially members of the important Jeunesse Ouvrière Chrétienne. It was also important that Catholic opposition to Vichy and to the Germans was undertaken without episcopal sanction and was led in large part by laymen, a factor which would help to de-clericalize French Catholicism in the post-war period.[98]

It was not during the *Ralliement* proposed by Leo XIII, nor during the so-called Second *Ralliement* after the First World War, that the French Catholic Church entered the modern world. Its initial reception of Vichy's counter-revolution, and the persistence of its ecclesiastic and lay leadership in continuing to support the government of the ageing Marshal Pétain, undermine any such Panglossian interpretation of modern French Catholic history. It was only the moral, ethical, and spiritual delinquency which the Vichy regime and the German Occupation required of Catholics that finally removed the blinders from the eyes of enough of them to enable them to see the modern world as it really was. As long as French Catholics were unable to face reality empirically, they were captives of myth and bound to surrender to dangerous programs for the restoration of an impossible Golden Age of Christendom. Arno J. Mayer aptly reminds us that

> reactionary political actors propose to lead a retreat back into a world both lost and regretted. At the same time that they epigrammatically idealize this past, in order to stimulate political action in the present, they denounce all their antagonists as devious conspirators sworn to the corruption of contemporary man and society. This conspiratorial view enables reactionary leaders and their followers to ignore the economic and social causes for the erosion of their own expendable stations in life.[99]

It has taken Catholic France so long to recover from the traumas of the Bourbon monarchy and the French Revolution that one might exclaim with the author of a late nineteenth-century novel about the French clergy: "Oh Holy Catholic Church! It must be that something divine resides in you, for your priests have not been able to succeed in destroying you."[100] This perennial cry of a certain Catholic anti-clericalism testifies to an exceedingly useful truth about the Roman Catholic Church.

V

The Church in contemporary France

No group of Frenchmen, from 1944 to the present, has found it easy to digest the "lessons" of the Second World War and the Occupation. The myth of the Resistance[1] has for a long time permitted the French to pretend that the period 1940 to 1944 was one in which most of them, though defeated, pursued the struggle against the German enemy by other means until the arrival of the Allies and the forces of General de Gaulle, much like the Austrians have been able to persuade themselves that they were simply the first victims of Hitler's aggression. In both cases, the existence of a civil war between citizens was essentially denied in the interest of national unity. The long-standing differences between Frenchmen, illuminated by the defeat and Occupation, were as intense within Catholic France as within the nation as a whole, and Catholics could be found in virtually every group from 1940 to 1944, from participation in the ranks of collaborators with the Germans and supporters of Vichy to membership in the active Resistance and the overseas Free French. The Church as a supporter of Marshal Pétain had no privileged position of moral rectitude from which to sermonize about the experience of the Occupation. Only individual clerics, certainly excluding most members of the compromised hierarchy, and individual laymen could credibly confront such questions. And it was not long before issues of moral seriousness indeed arose to disturb the placid forgetfulness of Frenchmen in all spiritual and ideological camps. It was directly on the issue of decolonization, particularly in Algeria, one which would bring down the Fourth Republic after only a decade of life, that the "lessons" of the Occupation would be first and most pointedly applied. A number of prominent Catholics spoke out strongly enough to demonstrate that the experience of the Occupation had not simply passed them by. The Catholic community could not simply return to the "normalcy" represented by the pre-war period; some portion of it at least had learned something. And while Catholics, clergy and laity alike, faced the Algerian problem with less than single-minded moral clarity, as a whole Catholics came off very well during the decolonization of the French empire. One may reasonably hold that the most consistent opposition to the Algerian war came not from secular intellectuals, radicals, or communists, but from the ranks of French Catholics.[2] And it was these men and women who would work to sever the old connection of the Catholic Church with an outmoded political and social order and to bring it into dialogue with modern France, something finally sanctioned by the work of the Second Vatican Council, whose receptivity to French theological thought was generous and profound. The years of defeat, foreign occupation, and shameful collaboration might for most of the French be best forgotten, but for a determined group of Catholic militants as well as for militants in a number of other social and ideological camps, the "lesson" of those years was that they must not be forgotten but must serve as the foundation of a new France.

CATHOLICS AND COLONIALISM

Frenchmen of all ideological persuasions had been for at least a century agreed that France had a civilizing mission overseas. Both traditional Catholicism and Jacobin nationalism were intensely missionary, and whatever hostility anti-clericals might express towards the religious orders and their work in France itself, they never ceased to see in Catholic missionaries abroad the vanguard of France's imperial mission. Rightists and leftists shared, if nothing else, a belief in the benefits that French institutions and practices would bestow on less developed peoples. Assimilation by native peoples to French culture and civilization meant a hard-won membership in civilized humanity itself. Such widely held, normative attitudes towards the French possessions abroad made it extremely difficult for Frenchmen to contemplate the loss of their empire. Indeed, the empire had been the staging area for the liberation of the mother country itself, the place where a defeated nation could regroup morally and militarily in preparation for a victorious return to Europe. Here Frenchmen could easily be blinded by their deepest beliefs and passions into misreading the direction of historical development and even the basic requirements of democratic life. Thus the demands for self-government and independence by Indochinese, North African, and sub-Saharan African dependants, coming as they did right on the heels of the liberation of France itself, encountered firm determination by large numbers of Frenchmen that the empire must be maintained at all cost. A 1946 public opinion poll showed that French Catholics were more pro-colonialist than non-practising Catholics or non-Catholics.[3] French communists shared with Catholics a commitment to France's civilizing mission, and the Communist Party found it as difficult as the Catholic hierarchy to forge a strong, united, unequivocal position on the movements for independence, especially in Algeria. Both the Church and the Communist Party were torn by contradictory goals, the dead hand of tradition, and the need to satisfy strongly-held, but conflicting demands from their adherents.[4] Those Catholics who came publicly forward to urge the dismantling of the empire, particularly those who opposed the drastic measures taken to defeat the Algerian nationalists, had the forces of patriotism and religion entirely against them. It was only their keen memory of the moral dilemmas of life under German Occupation and Vichy collaboration which gave them the courage to persist.

Probably the most eminent Catholic personality to take a strong position against the violation of human rights in North Africa was François Mauriac, a member of the Académie Française since 1933 and the 1952 Nobel laureate in literature. Basing his position squarely on the experience of his countrymen and co-religionists during the Vichy period and the German Occupation, he insisted that the French military's use of torture and other violations of human rights to defeat the nationalist movement in Algeria was nothing more than the same *racisme* which the Nazis and their collaborators had practiced. He contended that all victims of racism, whoever they were, were the brothers of the same human Christ worshipped by his fellow Christians. More than the existence of torture itself, what especially outraged Mauriac was the readiness of Frenchmen, including Catholics, to regard it as necessary and to cover it up. He easily associated this with the sins of omission which his countrymen had committed towards the persecuted Jews in their midst during the war years.

And just as during the war, now moral considerations again placed Christians in a dilemma: should they obey orders which might lead them to commit atrocities, or should they resist the demands of their own government? Young men drafted and sent to Algeria looked in vain for clear answers from their spiritual guides in much the same way as those who were drafted into forced labor in Germany had contemplated the choice between obedience and resistance without clear guidance from Catholic authorities. As in the period of the Occupation, ordinary priests and laymen often took courageous positions and acted against manifest evil while members of the Catholic hierarchy sought refuge in tortured syllogisms and evasion.[5]

The Fourth and Fifth Republics were still free societies, and men like Mauriac could speak out freely. Nevertheless there were consequences. Mauriac was bitterly attacked by rightists, and in terms reminiscent of the attacks on the defenders of Alfred Dreyfus a half-century earlier. Mauriac was accused of insulting the army, like the Dreyfusards of 1900, but certainly unlike the Catholics of that era, he replied that the best way to defend the army and France was to defend justice.[6] And he went on to defend priests and others who objected to the repression in Algeria on moral grounds with the insights gained from the painful experience of the Occupation.[7] As the French military increasingly resorted to a policy of retaliation much like the brutal reaction of the Nazis to the deeds of the Resistance, many on the Catholic Left defended the human rights of the Algerian Muslims; these included such organizations as the Action Catholique Ouvrière, the Association Catholique de la Jeunesse Française, and the Mission de France which directed the worker-priest experiment; such periodicals as *L'Esprit* and *Témoignage Chrétien*, the former founded by Mounier and the latter a public opponent of anti-Semitism in Lyon during the war; and such Catholic personalities as Louis Massignon, Jean-Marie Domenach, and Jacques Madaule, along with François Mauriac. Mauriac clearly did not speak for all Catholics. There was Catholic support also for the colonialist position. Many Catholics indulged in tortured disputes about the teaching of the Church on Just War and its application to the Algerian situation. Some like Georges Bidault, once a prominent Catholic member of the Resistance and a leading member of many post-war government ministries, tried to pretend that the Algerian war was a struggle between Christianity and Islam, cynically hoping thereby to get religious sanction for a reactionary political program. He was not alone in seeking to justify the maintenance of a French Algeria with slogans about a crusade to defend the west. Catholic collaborators had once defended Nazi Germany's war in Russia on these grounds, and while the Vatican did not officially endorse such crusading notions during the Second World War, Pius XII did indeed bless the Cold War against "atheistic communism." Rightist Catholics felt quite at home in bogus crusades against communism. One priest labelled opponents of the Algerian repression as followers of the "Voltairean philosophy," while even the venerable Cardinal Saliège of Toulouse, one of the few prelates to have spoken out publicly against Vichy and Nazi anti-Semitism, supported the maintenance of a French Algeria.[8] The force of Catholic integrism and integral nationalism was evidently still far from spent, but on the issue of decolonization the Vatican had moved more quickly than the French hierarchy away from European ethnocentrism. Conscious of its "catholic" mission Rome worked to weaken the traditional nationalism of the French clergy and expressed sympathy for self-government in the colonies of European powers.[9]

Mauriac himself had not always been fully against colonialism, and in 1960 he was critical of some Catholic opponents of the Algerian war who continued to recommend resistance to government orders on the part of soldiers and officials, for he had placed all his hope in the policies of President de Gaulle. But even when he disagreed with some radical Catholics on specific measures he still found Catholic heroism a positive step in the desired eventual reconciliation of the Church with the working class and the colonial peoples. He was much more bitter about what he considered the excessive caution of the French hierarchy in 1961 when the terrorism of the Fascistic Secret Army was at its height:

> We are surrounded by Christians, by practising and faithful Catholics of the sort who would not kill a fly, but who are at one with the men of blood. And they give them their support, their prudent and deaf approval. . . . But who speaks to us today? We are, after all, not sheep without pastors. When the archbishops and bishops of France assemble, there is a crowd. But what word do we receive from them? . . . There is not one of them to my knowledge who with a clear and intelligible voice pronounces the word which we

> await. A single voice would be enough to break the silence. Alas! We miserable sheep never hear that cry which I loved so much in my childhood, when the old shepherd gave out that bizarre and guttural cry, and the whole treading flock pressed around him. That cry which would rally all of us, it would need to fall from one in authority, from the mouth of a single one of our spiritual leaders, or it would be expressed by a small number of bishops ready to risk everything. When the cardinals and archbishops of France, after having assembled, then adjourn, we read with respect the communique that they publish and which always condemns violence "wherever it comes from." The purpose of a communiqué is to bind no one by name. An assembly even as august as that one, as it is in fact no one, its resolutions blow neither hot nor cold. I doubt if they allow the members of this venerable body to have a clear conscience and if there is a single one of them who believes that the wishes expressed by their full assembly have ever stayed the hand of a single murderer.[10]

Whatever the disappointments of Catholics with the degree of support they received from the hierarchy in their opposition to the Algerian war, it was significant that Catholics joined non-Catholics in the pursuit of their aims. Because the Church, the clergy, and the laity were deeply divided over issues of decolonization, as indeed they were over all political issues, Catholics began more and more to work together with non-Catholics. This contributed to the abandonment of the Catholic "ghetto" and the full integration of Catholics into national life, the de-confessionalization of Catholic activity. It also was consistent with the ever larger role of Catholic laymen in political and social life. The French Church would never be the same, with active laymen who did not wait for directions from clerical supervisors and who freely joined with men and women lacking Catholic ties in the pursuit of common objectives.[11] Catholic involvement in the controversies over the Algerian war was one of several movements which changed the face of the Catholic Church in France. If the Church was no longer to be feared, it was hoped that it also would no longer present an image of futility and desuetude, the popular image of the Church which a noted Catholic leftist in 1960 offered for final interment:

> It is an old structure half in ruins, lost out in the countryside. In the interior of a sort of barn a visitor would notice that half of the windows are broken, the seats almost demolished, the altar in a pitiful state. When the wind blows during winter, attending Mass is not recommended for persons with weak lungs. The parish priest is an unsteady old man who functions each Sunday in four different parishes and travels around on a sort of motorbike from a bygone age which seems likely at any moment to expire for good in one last backfire. The responses in the liturgy are exchanged in a nave three-quarters empty. Six old ladies, three awful young women gone to seed sitting around an organ, and two gentlemen and four boyscouts with a sanctimonious air make up the public of this strange assembly. That is the Church![12]

This was the Church that time forgot, as the freeway or *autoroute* of modernity bypassed an old village which had once stood at the crossroads of economic and cultural life. Avoiding such a fate would be the challenge of the Catholic Church in a modernizing France.

THE WORKER-PRIESTS

If the "lesson" of racism refused to go away, and indeed was by the Algerian war raised to prominence in the lives of many Catholics, the problem of the role of the priest and the Church's relationship to the working class also took on added importance because of the Occupation. The worker-priest experiment had been begun during the Occupation, and in the immediate post-war period it also became a prominent issue for Catholics, because it raised two fundamental questions which could never again be ignored: what was the possibility of collaboration between Catholics and communists? and what was the nature of the priestly role in a society where traditional clerical identity was becoming extinct? The worker-priest movement and the controversy it generated were not merely examples of change, but a fundamental *critique* of the French Church, a challenge to its long-held insistence on the distinction between the laity and the clergy, the temporal and the spiritual.[13] Over 700,000 French workers were sent into forced labor in Germany during the Occupation, and with them were secretly sent priests who were ostensibly conscripted workers. Among the workers were included some 10,000 Catholic militants, of whom about a third were seminarians. The decision of the French hierarchy in April 1943 to send worker-priests secretly into Germany stemmed from the German government's unwillingness to allow priests to participate in the program of forced labor. The French hierarchy's concern was to provide for the spiritual needs of those workers whose obedience to the Vichy government's decision it had essentially urged. The dispatch of worker-priests was to have far-reaching consequences.

The presence of French priests and seminarians at the front during the First World War had done much to lessen the anticlericalism of Frenchmen, ending as it did a certain separation between laity and clergy. But the Vatican authorities had looked with much less benevolence upon fraternization between laity and clergy. Rome reaffirmed the incompatibility of sacerdotal and secular activities and treated priests returning from the war like men in need of ritual purification. This pattern was repeated in 1940: full participation of the clergy in the war effort was followed by a return to clerical "normalcy." The clergy demobilized in 1940 was demoralized by more than the military defeat. A Church periodical in Marseille put these words in its mouth:

> The Church, it is the assembly of the faithful, that is to say the *people*. We are the religious servants of this people. . . . *How are we going to penetrate this people?* . . . There is still something that now separates us from the people. In the armies we shared the life of men; we were in the midst of them; they gave us their confidence and their friendship. . . . Today we have returned to our parishes, to our neighborhoods; we have put our cassocks back on and have resumed our religious functions. . . . And once again, there is an emptiness around us. *Why* is it so? What still separates us from men, from the people?[14]

This bewilderment was overcome notably among those priests who participated in the worker-priest experiment. The experiences of worker-priests, and also of other priests who were deported or prisoners of war, reduced them all to mere workers, to "men among men." For the first time these priests experienced at first hand what working-class insecurity involved. A French

Jesuit in wartime Germany described his experience on behalf of his fellow priests in this way:

> We unanimously have blessed God for having made us live the life of a proletarian in Dachau. The hard life, in inhuman conditions, which we have led has made us ourselves experience all the spiritual problems which similar conditions pose to millions of men. To work without a wage commensurate with the effort involved, to work more than strength permits and less than ability demands, to work without the least interest in the work, for hated masters, under brutal surveillance. That makes singularly easy, if you wish, an heroic Christian life but singularly difficult a normal Christian life. How much would the priest gain to be able to realize concretely through personal experience the conditions of life of those he seeks to evangelize!

The Bishop of Montauban, himself briefly imprisoned by the Germans, testified in a similar vein; he learned through his experiences the meaning of work, poor lodging, inadequate clothing, and the lack of human dignity, the life which the urban proletariat endured even in normal times. It is difficult to overestimate the influence of such experiences on priests and militant laymen who returned to France with a changed vision of the role of the Church and clergy.[15]

The French clergy had been aware for at least some fifty years that France had become largely de-Christianized, and the initiation of the clandestine worker-priest movement among the French workers in Germany occurred at the same time as the publication of an influential book by two priests, Henri Godin and Yvan Daniel, entitled *La France Pays de Mission?*, a book which uncovered the false optimism of all previous Catholic attempts at outreach to the workers of France. The Church's mission to the workers had not understood that the working class lived in its own world, with its own values and its own particular trials. To seek to convert workers to Catholicism and to have them participate in "normal" parish life meant unavoidably also to require them in some sense to abandon their comrades and join the bourgeoisie. Godin and Daniel, for all their insight, probably still were unable entirely to leave behind their own bourgeois condescension towards the "pagan" workers. The workers, missionaries would need finally to understand, were not pagans hungry for the good news of the Gospel, which simply needed to be presented to them more effectively, more cleverly. The workers, rather, were already convinced by their own culture, experience, and history that Christianity and the Church were obsolete. The worker-priests, whether first in the midst of forced laborers in Germany or thereafter at home in French factories, docks, union halls, and cabarets, were seeking out men they were ill-prepared to encounter on the basis of their narrow seminary education and theoretical theological horizons. These priests were not prepared perhaps for the economic and social insecurity and cultural deprivation of the workers, but poverty they at least were supposed to know something about. What truly amazed them among the working class, however, what they had not been in the least prepared for was the possibility of moral and spiritual grandeur in a working-class environment. The worker-priests discovered a vitality which contrasted favorably with the routine, anemic life of most Catholic parishes. They saw, even more shockingly, that the Marxism denounced by the Church from the beginning was able to inspire an enthusiasm and joy in many workers which many Christians back in Catholic parishes had never experienced. In a word, they discovered a world for which their traditional clerical routines had not prepared them, and perhaps even the possibility that the workers might know more about *real* Christianity and could apply it more effectively than the priests could preach the Gospel to them.[16] The priests had come to the workers to enlighten them and save them, and it was the workers who brought clarity to their own shadowy lives.

It was painful for the priests of the Mission de France to face the fact that the Catholic clergy was still being trained for a medieval, rural civilization which no longer existed. The Church had fallen behind cultural, economic, and social change to such a degree that its ability to speak at all to the modern age was in serious question. It had also not understood how material conditions fundamentally affected the way people felt and thought, having seen in "materialism" something to battle against rather than a fundamental human insight from which it might learn. Many worker-priests were able at once eloquently and poignantly to express the "conversion" which their contact with the working class brought about. Let one description suffice:

> "I have understood that all these men [the workers] . . . would find themselves cramped for room at our sermons and in our churches, before our moral exhortations about individual salvation. . . . I have also understood that the 'Catholic' faith was not from the start a personal tie between the soul and God, but a belonging to Jesus Christ, Saviour of the world, and a participation in his work of creation and love. . . . For me, it is the companions of the workshop and workers' hostel who have made me turn towards Him whom I unconsciously called the All-Powerful. And the 'communards' who surround me have given me back hope in my priesthood and the vision of a cosmopolitan Jerusalem of Pentecost, of an earth renewed by a salvation finally found again. . . . The word revealed by God shut itself up in the Apocalypse in an immense marching song towards unity through the victory of Christ. Karl Marx was needed to take up this song again and to teach it to the modern masses. Faith in a saved Humanity, regenerating Hope in a New World, universal and constructive Charity – here are the three theological virtues which the world of workers has revealed to my priesthood."[17]

Despite widespread support for the worker-priest experiment influential circles among French Catholics and suspicious observers in the Vatican were fearful that the priests who became workers might succeed all too well, that they might come to sympathize with Marxist movements. In 1947 when a group of representatives from the Mission de France had met with Pius XII to explain their experiment the Pontiff had given them no more than seven minutes of his time. They returned home from Rome much like Lamennais a century earlier, so enthusiastic about their mission that they misread the level of support they had in Rome. The Pope and his entourage, in any case, were at the time more concerned with the threat of communism in the forthcoming Italian elections. With communism and the Cold War the first priority in the Vatican, the danger that worker-priests would become associated with communism finally would lead to a suspension of Rome's approval for the experiment. Until Rome in 1953 forced the Mission de France to alter its approach to the working class, the Vatican had been bombarded with French complaints about the activities of the worker-priests.

Worker-priests and Catholic lay militants during 1945–50 found themselves inseparably bound together with members of the Communist Party which played so central a role in the lives of French workers. As the worker-priests and Catholic militants sought a clearer understanding of their relationship to the communists, they came to see that there was no possible avoidance of some degree of participation in communist-sponsored activities and organizations; some acceptance of communist ideology was also unavoidable. In the hands of conservatives, the Holy Office in the last years of Pius XII's pontificate proceeded without restraint to discipline French theologians, and the condemnation of the worker-priest experiment was one of several casualties of the Roman commitment to the Cold War.[18] Whatever its impact on the working class to which it directed its mission, the worker-priest movement had evidently the greater effect within the Church. It precipitated a spiritual crisis and changed the Church in important ways.[19] The Parisian Action Catholique Ouvrière asked on behalf of all workers and many Catholics: "What is there so diabolical about our working-class life that within it priests cannot remain priests?"[20]

The leading role taken by the Vatican in the justification of the Cold War against communism was a response of the Roman Catholic Church to the Sovietization of eastern Europe and the electoral successes of communist parties in western Europe. It also was consistent with its long-term suspicion of socialism and communism as the bastard offspring of the philosophy of liberalism. Catholics had thereupon easily fallen into collaboration with reactionary, conservative, and Fascist movements in the struggle against socialism and communism, and the condemnations of Marxism under Pius XI had been sharper than the criticisms of Fascism in Italy and even of National Socialism in Germany.[21] In France, in the aftermath of the Second World War, a mass Catholic political party, the Mouvement Républicain Populaire (MRP) arose for the first time, and like its counterparts in West Germany and Italy it enthusiastically supported United States interests in Europe, the defense of the west against a feared Soviet aggression, and an ultimately united Europe. The very early demise of the MRP, once Gaullism had begun its ascendancy, demonstrated that there was actually no long-term mass support for Christian democracy in France and that the MRP simply had temporarily occupied the right-wing of the political spectrum, while the classic Right was still discredited and embarrassed by its associations with Vichy and the National Revolution. The MRP received the votes of conservatives who had nowhere else to go politically, while the Church was more than happy to urge Catholics to support it, seeing in Christian democracy the means of effacing all trace of its own close ties to the Vichy regime. Whatever strength the Resistance myth had among the leadership of the MRP – an influence that normally was expected to push the party in a progressive rather than a conservative direction, based as it necessarily was on a high degree of cooperation with socialists and communists – the MRP electorate was solidly conservative, centered principally in the conservative Catholic east (Alsace-Lorraine) and west (Brittany). The MRP strongly supported not only United States interests in Europe but also the maintenance of French colonial possessions. Its stand particularly on the Algerian war brought it into acute conflict with left-wing Catholics, while right-wing Catholics in any case continually deserted it for Gaullism. The MRP thus lost both parts of its clientele, demonstrating that Catholics in France, unlike those in Italy, West Germany, Holland, or Belgium, did not have the unity needed for a Catholic political party to flourish.[22]

There were only small groups of Catholic "progressistes" in France who actively sought cooperation with the Communist Party, and these were vigorously denounced by the hierarchy. The 1949 Vatican condemnation of cooperation with communists was effective in Italy and Spain, but it had limited meanings in France where most Catholics continued to avoid the communists; only a few militants on the Catholic Left were affected by Vatican strictures. Still a somewhat larger number of French Catholics did have hopes or illusions about reconcilation between the Church and Marxism, at least on the practical level. Worker-priests participated along with communists in anti-American demonstrations, thus placing themselves in direct opposition to many of the political objectives of the Vatican. One noted "progressiste" offered an uncomfortable choice for Catholics raised in the tradition of Social Catholicism:

> In political life it is impossible to be simultaneously for capitalism and against it. To denounce the abuses of capitalism, as the Church does, leaves room for two distinct policies: either to endeavor to correct the abuses without

> challenging the validity of capitalism itself and thus really to defend capitalism; or else to put an end to the abuses by removing their cause. . . .[23]

Generally, the last decade of the pontificate of Pius XII was a repressive one for French priests and laymen who sought innovative approaches to the challenge of modern life. The condemnation of Catholics who supported communist causes was followed by the encyclical *Humani Generis* in 1950 which struck at the theological innovation championed by French Dominicans and Jesuits. This repression, however, related as it was in part to the Cold War, was only temporary, and it made the flowering of progressive Catholicism after the encouragement of the Second Vatican Council and the later development of a Vatican *Ostpolitik* all the more startling. In fact, Pius XII had silenced the French Church only to have its experiments in theology and social action ratified by the receptivity given them by the Council and the honor extended to the censured theologians of France. The Council indeed seemed to be approving thirty years of labor by the embattled militants of the French Church.[24]

EMMANUEL MOUNIER

The most important voice on the Catholic Left in the period after 1945 was Emmanuel Mounier. In all his early contradictions and apparent political variability he can be said to have prefigured most adherents of the Catholic Left in the years after the Second World War. Mounier drew a generation of young Catholics away from reaction, royalism, nationalism, bourgeois complacency, and even Christian democracy. His undefinable philosophy of *personalism* sought to offer a Catholic and Christian alternative to these bankrupt ideologies, and hope to those seeking to be both Christian and modern at the same time. It also sought to be an alternative, or perhaps it would be more accurate to say a *necessary corrective,* to Marxism. Where to Mounier Marxism seemed clearly superior to personalism in its understanding of social and economic development, personalism was more humanistic and had more to offer the individual concerned about transcendence. Mounier actually was close to favoring a friendly, mutually fruitful, cooperative competition, perhaps a "peaceful coexistence," between Marxism and personalism.[25]

Mounier's *Esprit* was the first periodical to be published in

France after the Liberation. It rose from its pre-war circulation of 3,000 to 4,000 to a post-war high between 15,000 and 19,000 by 1964. Although *Esprit* was not officially Catholic and therefore not under Church control, it nevertheless was in fact one of the leading Catholic reviews, certainly equal in circulation to the influential and official publications of the Dominicans and Jesuits.[26] For the last six years of Mounier's life and for a long time thereafter *Esprit* reflected Mounier's concern with the problem of communism. He believed that the principal task of the post-war era was to follow the path of the Resistance in seeking to reintegrate the communists into French life, since the Communist Party had played a pre-eminently patriotic role during the Occupation and enjoyed the confidence of the oppressed strata of French society. He no longer identified his journal and personalist philosophy, as before the war, with the search for a political program that was "neither Right nor Left." He claimed instead that his true inspiration came from the humanistic and Christian socialism of 1848. Periodically frustrated and disappointed by the brutalities of Soviet power in eastern Europe and the difficulties of dealing forthrightly with the Communist Party at home, Mounier nevertheless refused to return to his pre-war anti-communism. He feared Fascism and Gaullism in France more than any movement on the Left and held that anti-communism whatever its source or motive always worked against the underdog and in favor of the Establishment, culminating in the isolation of the masses and the consequent victory of Fascism. Even the general outrage over the trial and imprisonment of Joseph Cardinal Mindszenty in communist Hungary left Mounier still sympathetic to the Hungarian government's position; he found the cardinal a thorough reactionary and no martyr to religious freedom. Subsequent Vatican embarrassment over the cardinal's strident anti-communism, during his fifteen-year residency in the American Embassy in Budapest and his final removal to Vienna, when its own *Ostpolitik* had finally caught up with reality may indicate that Mounier was after all fairly clear-headed about the dynamics of the Catholic crusade within the Cold War.[27]

Mounier's views of communism also placed him clearly in the anti-American camp, and while this may have been a leftist position after the Second World War, it actually had been common with intellectuals on both the Left and Right before the war and under Vichy. Mounier decried the American appropriation of the cause of "Christian civilization," which the Vatican managed easily enough to swallow, and he suggested that if the Church really wanted to strike at godless materialism it should begin with the United States.[28] The pro-American policy of the MRP was of course anathema to Mounier, as was its essentially bourgeois program, however reformist. Officially the MRP claimed to seek "to end the disastrous split between Right and Left." Such a goal was for Mounier the touchstone of reaction since it would only end by defending the existing order; to join men under the banner of religious unity could only play into the hands of the Right, and indeed the MRP did split the Left and strengthen the Right with its insistence on raising the divisive issue of public support for Catholic education.[29] A true disciple of Social Catholicism, Mounier recoiled from the tepid faith of bourgeois Catholicism and was attracted to those with revolutionary fire, including a brief flirtation with Vichy "revolutionaries" after the 1940 defeat and with the communists after 1945. Since he never actually had, like the "progressistes," advocated active collaboration with the Communist Party Mounier did not fall under official Vatican sanction with the 1949 prohibition on collaboration with communists, but it was clear at his untimely death in 1950 that he and his cause were fundamentally estranged from official Catholic policies.[30]

Many of the heirs of Social Catholicism had identified themselves with the political Left even earlier than Mounier, notably during the Popular Front of the 1930s. In the thirty years before the work of the Second Vatican Council Catholic militants had come to accept the world as part of God's creation and the scene of His presence. This meant an abandonment of the traditional Catholic preoccupation with conversion of a pagan, sinful world in favor of a Christian "presence" in the world or a Christian "witness" to it. It also meant a liberation from confessionalism and clerical tutelage in favor of cooperation with men and women of good will from any number of spiritual and ideological camps. The goal of their social action was no longer a Quixotic restoration of a "Christian social order;" the more realistic goal of humanizing the existing world was sought.[31] Traditional Catholics frequently denounced worker-priests and lay militants and complained that the interest of Catholics in political and social change distorted the faith. A typical expression of this complaint can be found in the address of the Archbishop of Bourges to the Plenary Assembly of Bishops in 1957:

> Wherever one turns one finds the political *first*, the economic *first*, the social *first*. [The Gospel] is reduced to the founding of justice and brotherhood among men. There is nothing here drawing souls to become converted to one humanism above another. Marxism is more alluring.[32]

But three short years later the French episcopate officially recognized that there was in fact no hope of re-Christianizing society as such, and the believer was advised to leave the Catholic "ghetto" for full participation in the life of his community; only by its actions and the "fruits" thereof might the Church recover its lost credibility.[33] Catholic militants thus were working for "the kingdom of God on earth," something the Church had since St Augustine treated with suspicion and had postponed to the end of time.[34]

CATHOLICS AND MARXISM

The Vatican's 1949 condemnation of collaboration with communists was hardly able to outlive Pius XII himself. Catholic–Marxist dialogue, something Mounier could urge only with great caution and some dissimulation, became a reality during the pontificate of John XXIII. His 1963 encyclical *Pacem in Terris* facilitated such a dialogue by its position that the claim of truth in dogmatic matters should not be used to violate the respect due to persons; thus while doctrinally antagonistic, Catholics and Marxists as persons of good will could engage in respectful dialogue with one another.[35] Dialogue was also greatly facilitated by the abandonment of triumphalism and of support for a Roman Catholic religious monopoly by the Fathers of the Second Vatican Council in favor of clear approval, for the first time in Catholic history, of religious freedom. By 1972 the French episcopate was even willing to concede that the venerable Marxist doctrine of "class struggle" need not obstruct dialogue and in any case deserved more than traditional Catholic anathemas. According to the bishops assembled at Lourdes in that year:

> The Gospel law of love does not invite men to resign themselves to injustice. . . . It is a false theology of love that is invoked by those who would want to camouflage situations

> of conflict, to preach attitudes of collaboration confusedly, minimizing the reality of collective antagonisms of all sorts. Evangelic love demands lucidity in analysis and the courage of confrontations which allow progress really towards greater truth.
>
> . . . Christians from various walks of life – workers, rural people, intellectuals – express what they experience with the phrase "class struggle." This expression represents for them a concrete situation which they have neither invented nor chosen. Many of them do not merely intend thereby to describe a fact of life; for them the expression is the fundamental key to understanding and explaining concrete reality. It also characterizes a type of efficacious and operative collective action.[36]

And this striking tolerance for the concept of "class struggle" was not really weakened by a degree of moralizing by the bishops concerning a Christian attitude towards conflict:

> It is evident that this analysis in terms of class struggle has allowed many militants more precisely to besiege the structural mechanisms of injustice and inequality. . . . Faith exerts a critical role in the antagonisms which pit men against one another. The Christian, whatever the analysis to which he ascribes, has to live these conflicts and struggles with respect for men and groups, including those who are adversaries. His faith certainly does not divert him from resolute combat in putting an end to injustices, inequalities, and oppression so long as he acknowledges the right of his adversary and the portion of truth which is in him however terrible the confrontation.[37]

By 1977 it was clear that what the French bishops feared most about Marxism was its totalitarian tendencies rather than its emphasis on class struggle as the moving force of history. In other words, the bishops mistrusted in the Communist Party what had been until recently the characteristic feature of their own Catholicism, the opposition to pluralism.[38] One could hardly imagine a more graphic sign of how far the Church had come.

SINCE THE SECOND VATICAN COUNCIL

How far has the Church of France really come? It is sometimes frustrating or exasperating for laymen, particularly non-Catholic laymen, to investigate change in an institution which constitutionally and viscerally always prefers to claim continuity rather than to admit change, which sees *restoration* where others see *revolution*. Yet the change in the French Church in the years since the Second World War has been enormous. It has excited those who never expected to see the Church truly enter the modern age, while many Frenchmen, including non-believers, who believed with Voltaire and Maurras in a Catholicism of order have been immeasurably chagrined. As one non-believer wrote in *Le Monde*, "'The balance of societies demands that institutions remain faithful to their calling. A church has for its calling the dispensing of certainties, not the spreading of doubts. . . .'"[39]

In the years after the close of the Second Vatican Council in 1965, the Church of France has:

- altered its hierarchical style of leadership.
- seen a striking decline of religious practice.
- suffered a crisis in vocations.
- lost whatever intellectual influence it had with great effort acquired.
- abandoned a fortress or "ghetto" mentality.
- transformed its clergy by abandoning the cassock, making it outwardly indistinguishable from other Frenchmen.
- seen the decline of the parish as the center of Catholic activity.
- allowed the individual conscience to replace the teaching Church as the highest moral authority on many important questions.
- applied the papal condemnation of Communism as "intrinsically evil" equally to capitalism.
- and been receptive to Marxism as a tool of social analysis.[40]

The Church in this period has, above all, lost its *unity*, or at least the appearance of unity and relative unanimity within a hierarchical structure, a façade which not only concealed diversity and disagreement but which also usually threw the institutional weight of the Church on the side of the Establishment. This had been the foundation of "Catholic" politics, whose perversions so aroused the prophetic ire of Mounier. Jean-Marie Domenach recalled from his days with the Resistance in the Vercors that a young *résistant* might be found in Church taking Holy Communion alongside a uniformed *milicien*.[41] Unity might thus come at too high a price. In any case, by 1972 the French Church officially came to recognize *pluralism* in political and social concerns, a clear admission that it no longer could dogmatically command assent from Catholics on these questions. There was no longer a "Christian" or "Catholic" politics, only a Christian or Catholic *practice* of politics, and Catholics like others had to work out their responses to public issues that lacked clear Catholic answers.

Because the Church had traditionally been conservative, the espousal of pluralism actually constituted an opening to the Left.[42] Thus when the Church intervened publicly in the early 1970s with declarations against sacred cows like nuclear weapons, the rightist government resented it, and individual Catholics with military associations readily embraced anti-clericalism, telling the Church to mind its own business; if it could not defend order as it had in the past, it should at least stick to "spiritual" matters.[43] Thus the Church is no longer able or willing to claim a *total* answer to the problems of modern life; it has opted instead to be a point of reference for the defense of certain human values, and it maintains its customary intransigence only in defense of violated human rights as it seeks to mobilize moral indignation and to comfort the afflicted.[44] Jean-Marie Domenach, the heir of Mounier, can better than anyone characterize the new position of the Church:

> One must first of all recognize what has been gained. The Church of France is no longer today that reactionary force which it was from the start of the 19th century. She no longer places herself automatically on the side of the established order. A growing number of Catholics have understood that the chief sin of their Church for 150 years has been . . . a political sin. . . . The bishop is no longer automatically at the side of the prefect. . . .
>
> They range themselves in increasing numbers against concrete injustices: they are often in the forefront of

> struggles for immigrant workers, for refugees, for the oppressed of all sorts. They no longer fear in doing this to leave their own milieu to act together with others. It seems that Non-denominationalism [*laïcité*] no longer makes for difficulties. And one no longer isolates them with the rotten sophisms of neutrality because they have recognized, as Mounier invited them to do, that violence does not only reside in struggle but also and first of all in that "normal" oppression which covers itself with the tranquillity of order.[45]

Analyses of social trends in today's modern industrial societies have come to depend heavily on public opinion polls, and in the use of this tool modern France has not lagged behind in the slightest. Most books and articles on French social developments in the last two decades, including those on the role of religious institutions and their teachings, rely strongly on the results of public opinion polling. It is estimated that between 1944 and 1976 the French public was asked 1,687 questions in 288 polls about religion in the broadest sense.[46] While there are differences of opinion about the causes and implications of various trends in the life of Catholic France, the results of the polling efforts do demonstrate clearly the striking changes which Catholicism has undergone in France during the last several decades. Where a degree of caution is necessary, however, is less in interpreting current data than in predicting future developments, for scholars of secularization and other observers of religious trends unfortunately have often enough been tempted by temporary developments into incautious and erroneous predictions about long-term future behavior.[47] Nevertheless, the findings of public opinion polls on the state of French Catholicism have, on the whole, provided very informative and reliable information about what has happened to the Church, the clergy, and the laity since the Second World War and, particularly, since the Second Vatican Council.

Although over 80 per cent of the French above 18 years of age consider themselves Catholics or have, at least, been baptized in the Catholic Church, the number of those *practicing* their faith has always been much lower. In the early 1960s, parish surveys indicated that about 25 per cent of adults attended Sunday mass regularly, a figure somewhat lower than those found in public opinion polls which sometimes inflate attendance at mass. By the end of the 1970s, however, attendance at Sunday mass had fallen to somewhere between 10 and 15 per cent of adults.[48] Although such categories as "cadres supérieurs," "cadres moyens," and "agriculteurs" can over a decade or two mix together people of very different educational, social, and occupational backgrounds, particularly in the years after 1960 when France was rapidly becoming modernized, and thereby can distort the meaning of the raw data, it would appear certain that between 1966 and 1977 the change in religious practice was markedly downward in all social categories except that of "agriculteurs."

Groups	*Level of mass attendance* *Year*	*Per cent*
Cadres supérieurs	1966	29
(management)	1977	19
Cadres moyens	1966	19
(middle management)	1977	14
Employés	1966	11
(employees)	1977	9
Ouvriers	1966	13
(workers)	1977	6
Agriculteurs	1966	27
(farmers)	1977	29

While workers have for a long time been less inclined to practice the Catholic faith than the rest of the population, where they most strikingly differ from the general population of France is less in their pattern of attendance at mass than in their greater imperviousness to the influence of the Church on their personal lives; they are able to appreciate the greater interest currently of the Church in progressive causes dear to them without in the least allowing themselves to become involved with the institutional Church on a personal basis.[49] But what is probably even more important than the relative isolation of the working class from the Church is the increasing inability of the Church to reach the young. While the percentage of male and female heads of household above the age of 40 who attended mass regularly dropped moderately from 1966 to 1978, the percentage of those under 40 years of age dropped dramatically, from 18 to 4 per cent among males and 17 to 7 per cent among women. In the same survey it appears that in 1978 about 25 per cent of males under 40 years of age were willing to list themselves as "without religion," not caring to claim a conventional Catholicism by virtue of baptism as an infant; this was an increase from 14 per cent in 1966. Only between 13 and 14 per cent of men over 40 years of age claimed in 1978 to be "without religion," a figure hardly different from that of 1966. The figures for women under 40 years of age also show a great increase between these years in those claiming no religion, while figures for older women "without religion" remained quite stable.[50]

More spectacular than the drop in the number of practicing Catholics is undoubtedly the crisis in the recruitment of priests for the French Church. Between 1956 and 1968 the number of ordinations of secular priests dropped dramatically; in 1956, 825 men were ordained, while in 1968 the figure had dropped to 461. By 1977 the number of men ordained dropped to 99 and in 1987 was at 106. Correspondingly, between 1940 and 1965 the number of resignations from the secular priesthood averaged 40 per year. By 1972 the average was 225 per year. Thus the number of secular priests in France declined from 42,500 in 1948 to 28,000 in 1985. By 1972 the number of priests voluntarily leaving their functions equalled the number newly ordained, thus transforming the normal death rate among priests into a permanent loss. The priests are thus increasingly and overwhelmingly of advanced age, without any adequate replacement by younger men. This massive decline in the number of priests, 34 per cent between 1948 and 1985 and 22 per cent between 1975 and 1985, is more than matched by a decline of 35 per cent among monks from 1975 to 1982 and 54 per cent among female religious in the same period.[51]

In the last twenty-five years secular priests have been recruited increasingly from the managerial classes and the upper levels of the working class and dramatically less massively from the peasantry, shopkeepers, and artisans, as had been the case for a long time. As this clergy speaks of the *people* and takes up its concerns and causes, it actually is becoming increasingly less representative of it socially. More and more priests are recipients of degrees in higher education, but because of the encouragement of theological studies by the Second Vatican Council tensions have increased between different generations of priests who have different sorts of training as well as social origins.[52] Generally, the clergy, by its training, education, background, and attitudes, is divided among itself and increasingly unsympathetic to the major concerns of its parishioners. Despite the growth of the "middle classes" since the Second World War, the Church and clergy and lay militants have preferred to work with workers and peasants. This may have something to do with the clergy's feelings of discomfort with the "liberalism" of the middle classes. Thus the social groups which make up the bulk of its parishioners are ironically the ones with which the clergy feel least comfortable.[53]

Politics also significantly divides the clergy from its parishioners. Political analysts have found that while the Church has moved massively to the Left since the Second World War, that is to say, away from traditional conservative positions and attitudes, and while the clergy sympathizes increasingly with the Socialist Party, the bulk of practicing Catholics has remained massively on the Right. Through the middle of the 1970s, the greater the level of integration of individuals into institutional Catholic life, the greater the likelihood of their voting for the Right. Correspondingly, the greater the detachment of individuals from religion, the greater their vote for the Left.[54] Practicing Catholics who support the parties of the Right obviously do so to register their non-radical political preferences, either reformist or conservative, and they are very much aware of the fact that the clergy generally, and the priests particularly with whom they are personally acquainted, do not share their political views. According to a 1976 poll of adult practicing Catholics, a plurality of these Catholics believe that priests were on the Left: 29 per cent of practicing Catholics considered priests to be on the Left, 21 per cent of them placed priests in the Center, and 14 per cent considered them to be on the Right. Those polled believed that bishops were somewhat more moderate than their priests; only 12 per cent of those polled believed bishops to be on the Left compared with 29 per cent who placed them in the Center and 19 per cent on the Right. If one realizes that 34 per cent of priests themselves are believed to have voted for the Left in 1973, with a much higher percentage on the Left among the younger clergy; if one understands that when leftists were polled about the politics of priests, 28 per cent of communists and 25 per cent of other leftists said that they believed priests to be on the Right, with only

11 per cent of communists and 18 per cent of other leftists believing them to be on the Left, what is one to conclude? At least, that the priests who are considered leftists or progressives by their own parishioners are considered to be on the Right by the people they most earnestly want to evangelize and to help![55]

The laymen with whom French priests get on the best are generally the left-wing militants of Catholic organizations concerned with workers and peasants. In May 1977, the national convention of the Action Catholique Ouvrière (ACO) elected two members of the Communist Party to its national committee. It also declared itself against episcopal warnings over Marxism. A survey of the political affiliations of 12,000 of its 25,000 members in the previous year revealed that 75 per cent were socialists, some 13.5 per cent members of the PSU (Parti Socialiste Unifié), and 9.5 per cent communists; in 1968 less than 2 per cent had been communists.[56] A poll of priests in April 1976, in *Le Point* asked them which function of the priest was the most important: 37 per cent answered that the most important was *work with militant adults*. 37 per cent, not necessarily the identical people, agreed that the obligation of weekly mass should be weakened while another 17 per cent agreed it could be made optional. It therefore should come as no surprise that the Catholics with whom the priests have the most in common come to mass the least frequently. This has led Michel de Certeau to note a radical phenomenon: "more and more numerous Christians are all the more less faithful in practising [the faith] as they are more believing. It is their faith itself which distances them from sacramental or liturgical practice."[57] Thus the people with whom the priests agree the most are also those least likely to attend mass and participate in parish functions. This same poll of priests also revealed that 25 per cent of them refused to affirm the Resurrection of Christ and the Real Presence in the Eucharist. A greater proportion, about one-third, were against the expression of traditional popular Catholicism, namely statues, medals, candles, etc., and about one-fourth generally were more concerned to deal professionally with social rather than personal sins.[58]

If a large number of priests are interested in social questions, their parishioners generally are less enthusiastic about clerical positions on public affairs. The clergy, priests and bishops together, are generally equally divided between sacramental and socio-communitarian activities when they define the principal role of the clergy, while the laity is overwhelmingly in favor of priests sticking to ceremony, catechism, and charitable activities.[59] A 1971 poll about the clergy's role in public affairs had asked a cross-section of the French whether priests and bishops should take public positions on a number of issues. In general, the public was most supportive of clerical intervention on moral issues such as pornography and the war in Vietnam, evenly split on issues of general social and economic policy and reproductive issues, and least supportive of intervention on partisan political issues like strikes and electoral campaigns.[60] The differences between clergy and laity over political questions and the proper role of the clergy are important because they demonstrate the changed prestige of the clergy in its relationship with its parishioners, but any concern about the clergy's involvement in politics may be overdrawn. Polls seem to indicate that the clergy has a very modest influence on the opinions or actions of laymen. When asked in February 1973, whether the positions of the Church since Vatican II and the declarations of the French hierarchy on "Faith and Politics" has an influence on their political views, 73 per cent of those polled replied that they had no influence on them at all, while only 7 per cent admitted some important degree of influence. In the same poll, 61 per cent said that faith had little or no importance in their professional or political life, while only 34 per cent admitted some importance of their faith in these areas. A poll two years later asking the same question about the influence of faith on political allegiances received similar impressions of the unimportance of religion: 62 per cent said faith played no role in political allegiance, while only 20 per cent claimed it played some role, whether important (8 per cent) or secondary (12 per cent); thus those claiming some importance for their faith in this realm declined by one-third between 1973 and 1975.[61]

The transformation of the French Church and clergy from reliable defenders of order into what John Ardagh has called "a loose network of semi-autonomous groups . . . splintered into highly varied tendencies"[62] has upset conservatives greatly, and conservative politicians and observers see in the radical or Marxist proclivities of many clergy a "neo-clericalism" which they seek to combat with the old weapons of anti-clericalism. As anti-clericalism long served the radicals, republicans, and socialists in defending secular values and progressive social causes and in papering over their own internal divisions, it now is found mostly on the Right.[63] Another form of opposition to the leftward drift of the Church was the growth of a traditionalist movement, some elements of which were clearly Maurrasian in emphasis, while others like the "Silencieux de l'Eglise," founded in 1969, were more moderate. The public revolt against the Vatican by Mgr Marcel Lefebvre in the summer of 1976 and his movement's continuing ability to get the attention of the media demonstrate the seriousness of the crisis within the French Church. While integrism is not especially strong in France, it has benefited from its association with the defense of a certain popular Catholicism which is strong. Lefebvre's political views come directly from the Action Française, but many supporters of Lefebvre are attracted less to rightist positions in Church or State than to his challenge to a Church they feel no longer understands them.[64]

There has always been within Catholicism the coexistence of a popular with a clerical religion, usually in relative harmony. Popular religion is a faith practiced with what more educated people call *superstition*, and it concerns itself with the daily needs of individuals and families and with communal festivals. Those French Catholics who are labelled "seasonal Catholics" because their contact with the Church is confined to baptisms, First Communions, marriages, funerals, and major holidays are essentially attached to popular Catholicism. A more clerical form of Catholicism has often sought to control or abolish certain manifestations of popular religion, most notably during the Catholic Reformation when an urban and upper-class leadership with partial success imposed many of its values on popular Catholicism; what reformers called "abuses" were in large part quite simply the traditional practices of a popular cult of Catholic faith.[65] The liturgical changes brought about by the Second Vatican Council were similarly a reform by an educated élite imposed upon a popular mass of Catholics, and this widened the gap between "seasonal Catholics" and an avant-garde laity and clergy.[66] The use of French in the liturgy of the Church favored a certain theologically educated élite, including laymen, over the rural and popular masses for whom Latin ritualism and theatricality were the highest expression of popular Catholicism, even though the Latin liturgy itself represented the preferred formal worship of still an earlier élite.

The use of French in the mass and a number of other changes

provided an opportunity, sometimes an excuse, for expressing long-repressed attitudes towards the traditions of conservative French Catholicism.[67] In the 1960s an innovation was made in the baptism of infants of non-believers or "seasonal Catholics." Polls indicated that three-quarters of Frenchmen resented the clergy's attempt to tie the baptism of their children to greater parental participation in the Church. Priests were more evenly divided on the question of baptism, but the decision of the hierarchy did demonstrate a certain disdain for popular Catholic expectations. A new form of clericalism was seen arising, as baptisms were delayed, candles and statues were suppressed, processions were discouraged, and the blessing of houses and religious medals were treated as superstitious.[68] The denial of baptism to the children of Catholics who rarely attended mass could be seen as a new form of Jansenism, the denial of sacraments to non-heroic Catholics. The bishops finally relented and urged moderation in the requirements for baptism, and the clergy as a whole remains split in its attitude towards popular Catholicism. The greater the dedication to working with Catholic militants on social questions, the less patience priests normally have had for the needs and feelings of "seasonal Catholics." As the clergy has come to treat Catholics more like adults and has therefore demanded more of them, some have responded with a more personal and fervent practice of their faith, while many others have been alienated from the Church and have abandoned attendance at mass.[69]

Polls indicate that the French population as a whole has changed in its attitudes towards the Second Vatican Council. In 1973, 53 per cent of Frenchmen were still positive about the changes in the Church; communists and socialists were among those most positive. In 1976, 48 per cent of practicing Catholics polled thought the Church had gone too far, although 40 per cent of them still favored continuing reform. 56 per cent of practicing Catholics called themselves "traditional" while 33 per cent wanted to be called "modern." Another 1976 poll, stimulated undoubtedly by the rebellion of Lefebvre, found that 29 per cent of Frenchmen and 31 per cent of Catholics believed that Vatican II had done more harm to the Church than good, while 24 per cent of Frenchmen and 27 per cent of Catholics thought that the Council had done more good than harm. Despite this, however, some 56 per cent of Frenchmen polled still said that they viewed the work of the Council favorably, compared with 10 per cent who were hostile.[70] Apart from their opinions on the Council, however, a poll for *Panorama aujourd'hui* in the same year found that 41 per cent of the French public agreed with the contention that the Church is an outmoded institution, while only 25 per cent thought that it had adapted successfully to modern times.[71] Where once the institutional Church was the model of hierarchic power, it has come instead to be viewed as out of touch with both democracy and managerial expertise in all areas of modern life, political, familial, educational, and economic. Likewise, the clergy's own expertise is questioned where priests do not receive special training in professional skills, like those of psychological counselling for example. Theological knowledge is clearly not much in demand. It is thus no longer sufficient to dress up clerical anti-modernism in up-to-date clothing; modernity is now perceived to be not merely an option for the Church but an undeniable fact of life.[72]

The Roman Catholic Church in a France less and less Catholic is thus in considerable disarray. Many have abandoned Sunday mass and other formal contact with the Church. Some have lost their faith, while others are uncomfortable with the pace of change in the Church – too rapid for some, too slow for others. Many have been told by priests at war with their own Church that mass is no longer obligatory; over half of the clergy opposes the Sunday obligation of attending mass. When asked whether former members of the working-class Jeunesse Ouvrière Catholique who had ceased practicing the faith were still Catholics, one priest in the Moselle replied benevolently that "'no one is excluded from the Kingdom of God'" – an answer marking a significant departure indeed from Catholic history and tradition.[73]

A type of class struggle exists within the Catholic population of contemporary France: young priests are on the Left while the mass of practicing Catholics is on the Right. The bishops seek to reassure both the Left and the Right and to govern the Church from dead center; they have interpreted the growth of support for Mgr Lefebvre in the last decade as a sign that in the recent past they may have perhaps allowed the Left within the Church to exert too much direction and influence.[74] The masses to whom the priests wish to go are divided between workers who are the most institutionally irreligious of all the French and the rural population which is the most Catholic, but both groups are largely interested only in traditional rites of passage, in popular Catholicism, if at all, and they have no interest in the concerns of the activist priests. Thus the masses escape the influence of a clergy which has the modernization of the faith permanently on its agenda but little sympathy for what either the masses, the conservative bourgeoisie, or the newer managerial middle classes seek from religion.[75] Those who seek the Kingdom of Heaven as an earthly attainment increasingly prefer to work in de-confessionalized groups (like the non-Catholic CFDT, the Confédération Française des Travailleurs, whose members left the Catholic CFTC, the Confédération Française des Travailleurs Chrétiens) where they cooperate with non-Catholics on common objectives and have assumed leadership roles. Voltairean Catholics increasingly find the Church and clergy less supportive of their fundamental social concerns and are ill at ease in the Church.

The Catholic Church today thus has no longer any real unity, nor any authoritarian means of enforcing unity or even of pretending to it. The events of May 1968, had revealed the impotence of the Church. While there was little emphasis directly on religion during the abortive student cultural revolution, there certainly was considerable messianic revolutionary rhetoric. But as the political crisis developed, the hierarchy, while vaguely sympathetic to the grievances of students and workers, understood that French Catholics – both clergy and laity – stood on both sides of the struggle, and the beleaguered bishops sought through moralistic and ideological terminology to paper over the serious differences between them. They evidently feared that any real analysis of the fundamental social issues involved would alienate too many people from the Church. As a result the Church was able to avoid confronting the real issues of the social upheaval of May 1968, but at the price of increasing and embarrassing irrelevance.[76] It is difficult to see how unity could be imposed from above upon French Catholics, how either papal or episcopal authority could accomplish this. John Paul II's visit to France in 1986 was met with only tepid enthusiasm. For Catholics who have learned during the Occupation to work out the consequences of their moral and ethical commitments without the help of bishops and often without the help of any clergy at all, a unity which would place *miliciens* and *résistants* side by side at the altar rail would remain unacceptable. Once the Church had opened itself up to the world, all the conflicts of the world entered into the Church.[77] It is hard to see how the doors and windows could ever be shut fast again.

Afterword

According to a leading modern sociologist of religion, the "classical task of religion" is "that of constructing a common world within which all of social life receives ultimate meaning binding on everybody."[1] This is a definition close to the conception of religion which prevailed in classical antiquity, in the ancient world of individual *poleis* and great empires. The men of the Enlightenment, for their part, and most notably Jean-Jacques Rousseau, doubted that Christianity could really perform this binding function because of its other-worldly emphasis; they did not have any fixed view about the this-worldly revolutionary impact of Christianity, since by their time Christianity had long since been thoroughly tamed. Charles Maurras, first and foremost a classicist and a disciple of Aristotle, feared that authentic Christianity was more apt to loosen than to bind the ties between men because it did, at least originally, have some definite and revolutionary this-worldly goals, and he was persuaded that the Roman Catholic Church had particularly found an effective way, nevertheless, of mobilizing Christianity in the service of order. Those, on the other hand, who valued Christianity for its revolutionary message of equality and justice were persuaded that Christianity had paid too heavy a price for benevolence and support from political authority, that it had in the process of upholding order become largely denatured. Some of them would locate the time of the harnessing of Christianity to political purposes in the Renaissance, while those with a broader conception of the sweep of history went farther back, back to the adoption of Christianity by the Emperor Constantine. The papacy always wished the independence of the Church from the control of temporal rulers, but because the Popes were until the late nineteenth century temporal rulers themselves, they never could or would convincingly sound the call for Christian revolution, being necessarily committed to the upholding of the existing political and social order.

Whatever remained of the revolutionary potential of Christianity found a home in Christian social movements and especially in secular socialism. In the Catholic Church the Social Catholics were the authentic heirs of those theologians and churchmen who had wished the Church to play an active role in the realization of the Kingdom of Heaven. But the Bourbon monarchs of France and their ministers succeeded remarkably well in making the French Church into the instrument of their control, while the papacy consistently failed to play a prophetic role in the lives of European Catholics. As a result, the Roman Catholic Church became a force for conservatism and order, and in fear of the modern world it confined its millenary strivings in the strait-jacket of reactionary and monarchist politics, which rendered it increasingly quixotic and irrelevant. Those who most strongly supported the Catholic Church in France did the cause of religion the most harm. In the words of Herbert Luethy, a respected and perceptive observer of French life,

> the loyalty to the Church of the French right has perhaps done more harm to French Catholicism than republican hostility; for it has been directed to the Church, not as a religious but as a political institution, not as a religious community but as the only surviving symbol of the old order, a *corps d'état* of the monarchy. . . .[2]

The Roman Catholic Church, in Europe as a whole and in France, was always found in the position of fighting the battles of an earlier generation, as when it directed its talents and energies in the eighteenth century against Jansenism while the men of the Enlightenment, more unopposed than not, struck mortal blows at its very foundation. It little understood that the monarchs whom it so fulsomely had lauded as the face of Divinity itself had already completely compromised the mission and autonomy of the Church. As a result, it could neither welcome the changes brought about by the revolutions of the eighteenth and nineteenth centuries nor oppose them in any authentic and effective way. It could only cling all the more desperately to traditional practices and institutions whose doom was inevitable. Religion under the impact of modern social and economic change and intellectual emancipation was bound to become "privatized," a matter of individual or group "choice" or "preference" and something necessarily irrelevant to public life.[3] In France it was probably only in the generation following the Vichy interlude and the Second World War that the privatization of French Catholicism was really understood in all its seriousness. Cardinal Feltin, Archbishop of Paris from 1949 to 1966, noted that

> "the world indeed still wants a Church, but on the condition that its cult be so little public and so inoffensive that business can continue as usual and that men can thereby benefit without being hampered in their dealings or projects – that its doctrinal authority not concern itself with the real problems of life but remain in the sphere of mysterious speculation."[4]

It would appear that such a realization of the plight of French Catholicism in the middle of the twentieth century came unfortunately far too late. Those who still look for the Church of France to play a public role often seek only an associate or ally in a particular cause, whether of the Left or the Right, but are unwilling to submit to its moral authority or guidance. The number of its clergy and the prestige of its hierarchy diminish without pause. One cannot know whether a refusal in the seventeenth century to serve the royal will; a willingness in the eighteenth or nineteenth centuries to baptize the democratic age; or a real repudiation in the twentieth century of the Fascism for which the Church bears some responsibility, in the place of its shameful indulgence for all rightist movements, might have made any difference in its present predicament. The voice of the Roman Catholic Church is everywhere in the industrialized world little heard or heeded, and in France, the Eldest Daughter of the Church. The majority of the population which desires its presence at the important milestone of life little understands its doctrine, its history, or its mission. It has no enemies without, because it has lost the power to inspire or frighten; all its enemies are within – in the different factions of Catholics who deny one another the very name of Catholic.[5] No intellectuals, no philosophers, no important literary figures adorn its ranks. There is no Bossuet, no Lamennais, no Maritain, no Blondel, no Teilhard de Chardin, no Mounier, no Bernanos, no Mauriac. At no time perhaps in its long history has the Catholic Church of France been so impoverished and so inconsequential in the sight of the French nation. It seems reduced to a mere historical artifact. The crisis of the French Church seems to this observer to be without any possible resolution, but religion is so capable of taking up unexpected roles and adorning itself with unexpected finery that any prediction of its demise would be hazardous. In any case, historians do well not to predict the future on the foundation of their necessarily subjective encounter with selected episodes of the past. We know a little of what the French Church has been. What it will be remains to be revealed.

My own extended encounter with the French Church has clarified a good deal for me about France, the French, the Roman Catholic Church, the course of history, and the dilemmas of modern life. If this book has done any part of this for my readers I should feel that my efforts have not been entirely in vain.

If the heroic personalities of this book include such men as Lamennais and Mounier, and if one of the chief villains is Charles Maurras, I make no apologies. And if I have been more understanding of socialists than of Catholic integrists or integral nationalists, I can only plead my intuition that in the musty recesses of integrism one encounters less the supposed odor of sanctity than the infernal miasma of Fascism.

Notes

FOREWORD

1 Theodore Zeldin, *France 1848–1945*, Oxford, Clarendon Press, 1973–7, II, 1039.

I TOWARDS A ROYAL RELIGION: THE ESTABLISHMENT OF CONFORMITY. FROM THE CATHOLIC LEAGUE THROUGH THE REIGN OF LOUIS XIV

1 La Bruyère, *Oeuvres complètes*, Paris, Gallimard, 1951, 239–40. Mme de Sévigné in 1674 also described the lack of reverence on the part of the courtiers. According to her account, when the king was not present in the royal chapel they behaved as if God also were absent. E. Pilastre, *La Religion au temps du duc de Saint-Simon, d'après ses écrits*, Paris, Félix Alcan, 1909, 28. *Mémoires de Saint Simon*, Paris, Gallimard, 1983–5, V, 614–15.
2 G. Goyau, *Histoire religieuse de la France*, Paris, Librairie Plon, 1922, 396.
3 Joseph Lecler, "Le Roi de France 'Fils ainé de l'Eglise'," *Etudes*, vol. CCXIV (1933), 22–3.
4 Pierre Pithou was the author of the "Harangue de d'Aubray" in the *Satyre Ménipée* (ed. Ch. Marcilly), Paris, Garnier Frères, 1882, 267.
5 Ralph E. Giesey, *The Juristic Basis of Dynastic Right to the French Throne*, Transactions of the American Philosophical Society, n.s., vol. LI, part 2, 4–6, 17–22, 39. Lionel Rothkrug, "Religious Practices and Collective Perceptions: Hidden Homologies in the Renaissance and Reformation," *Historical Reflections/Réflexions historiques*, vol. VII, no. 1 (spring 1980), 12–13. J. W. Allen, *A History of Political Thought in the Sixteenth Century*, London, Methuen, 1928, 283–4.
6 Sanche de Gramont, *Epitaph for Kings*, New York, G. P. Putnam's Sons, 1967, 32.
7 Claude de Seysell, *The Monarchy of France* (ed. Donald R. Kelley), New Haven, Connecticut, Yale University Press, 1981, 51–2.
8 Peter Brown, *Augustine of Hippo*, New York, Dorset Press, 1986, 239.

9 Jean Delumeau, *Un Chemin d'histoire. Chrétienté et christianisation*, Paris, Fayard, 1981, 233–4.

10 Myriam Yardeni, *La Conscience nationale en France pendant les guerres de religion (1559–1598)*, Louvain and Paris, Nauwelaerts, 1971, 100, 106, 118.

11 Joseph Lecler, *Histoire de la tolérance au siècle de la réforme*, Paris, Aubier, 1955, II, 98.

12 Frederic J. Baumgartner, *Radical Reactionaries: the Political Thought of the French Catholic League*, Geneva, Librairie Droz, 1975, 103–4, 119–20, 222.

13 Roland Mousnier, *The Assassination of Henry IV. The Tyrannicide Problem and the Consolidation of the French Absolute Monarchy in the Early Seventeenth Century*, New York, Scribner's, 1973, 89–103. Baumgartner, op. cit., 240.

14 L. W. B. Brockliss, *French Higher Education in the Seventeenth and Eighteenth Centuries. A Cultural History*, Oxford, Clarendon Press, 1987, 299.

15 Mousnier, op. cit., 104–18, 224.

16 W. J. Stankiewicz, *Politics and Religion in Seventeenth-Century France*, Berkeley, California, University of California Press, 1960, 16.

17 William F. Church, *Constitutional Thought in Sixteenth-Century France. A Study in the Evolution of Ideas*, Cambridge, Harvard University Press, 1941, 260ff. J. H. M. Salmon, *Society in Crisis. France in the Sixteenth Century*, London, Ernest Benn, 1975, 235, 273.

18 James Broderick, SJ, *Robert Bellarmine, Saint and Scholar*, Westminster, Maryland, The Newman Press, 1961, 295. John Courtney Murray, SJ, "St. Robert Bellarmine on the Indirect Power," *Theological Studies*, vol. IX, no. 4 (December 1948), 528–32.

19 Pierre Blet, *Les Assemblées du clergé et Louis XIV, de 1670 à 1693*, Rome, Universita Gregoriana Editrice, 1972, 348, 360–2, 586.

20 Roland Mousnier, *Les Institutions de France sous la monarchie absolue, 1598–1789*, Paris, Presses Universitaires de France, 1974–80, I, 245–51. Aimé-Georges Martimort, *Le Gallicanisme de Bossuet*, Paris, Editions du Cerf, 1953, 66–7, 72–3, 134–41. Pierre Blet, *Le Clergé de France et la monarchie*, Rome, Librairie Editrice de l'Université Grégorienne, 1959, I, 59–62, 81–2; II, 428. L. W. B. Brockliss, op. cit., 272–4. For a discussion of the changing nature of Gallicanism, see Norman Ravitch, *Sword and Mitre. Government and Episcopate in France and England in the Age of Aristocracy*, The Hague, Mouton, 1966, 16–20.

21 Charles Augustin Sainte-Beuve, *Port-Royal*, Paris, Gallimard, 1952–5, III, 660.

22 ibid., I, 98–9. Lucien Goldmann, *Le Dieu caché. Etudes sur la vision tragique dans les pensées de Pascal et dans le théâtre de Racine*, Paris, Gallimard, 1955, 156.

23 Victor Martin, *Le Gallicanisme et la réforme catholique*, Geneva, Slatkine Reprints, 1975, 213–14, 226–71. François Lebrun (ed.), *Histoire des catholiques en France du XVème siècle à nos jours*, Paris, Privat, 1980, 96–8.

24 Nigel Abercrombie, *The Origins of Jansenism*, Oxford, Clarendon

Press, 1936, 174, 188. Ronald Knox, *Enthusiasm. A Chapter in the History of Religion*, New York, Galaxy, 1961, 184.

25 William F. Church, *Richelieu and Reason of State*, Princeton, New Jersey, Princeton University Press, 1972, *passim*.

26 ibid., 54, 86–97, 311–16, 384–9. Louis Cognet, in H. Jedin and J. Dolan (eds), *History of the Church*, New York, Crossroads, 1981, VI, 3–33. Jean Orcibal, *Jean Duvergier de Hauranne, Abbé de Saint-Cyran et son temps (1581–1638)*, Paris, J. Vrin, 1947, 30–1, 517–61. René Taveneaux, *Jansénisme et politique*, Paris, Armand Colin, 1965, 13–14.

27 Abercrombie, op. cit., 188.

28 Goldmann, op. cit., 127. Goldmann is not even consistent in his contention that Richelieu feared the withdrawal of the élite from public service, for he admits that neither the cardinal nor Saint-Cyran probably foresaw the appeal of a program of renunciation for the *noblesse de robe*, believing rather that its only likely appeal would be for the higher clergy who might thereupon return to purely spiritual affairs in the spirit of the Council of Trent. ibid., 130.

29 Knox, op. cit., 185.

30 A. Latreille, E. Delaruelle, J.-R. Palanque, and R. Rémond, *Histoire du catholicisme en France*, Paris, Editions Spés, 1957–62, II, 344–5. Taveneaux, op. cit., 15, 57, 71. Cognet, op. cit., 46. Alexander Sedgwick, *Jansenism in Seventeenth-Century France. Voices from the Wilderness*, Charlottesville, Virginia, University Press of Virginia, 1977, 67. Richard M. Golden, *The Godly Rebellion. Parisian Curés and the Religious Fronde, 1652–1662*, Chapel Hill, North Carolina, University of North Carolina Press, 1981, 129, 132ff. P. Jansen, *Arnauld d'Andilly, Défenseur de Port-Royal (1654–1659). Sa correspondance inédite avec la Cour conservée dans les Archives du Ministère des Affaires Etrangères*, Paris, J. Vrin, 1973, 19–24. Jean Delumeau, *Le Catholicisme entre Luther et Voltaire*, Paris, Presses Universitaires de France, 1971, 177–8.

31 Taveneaux, op. cit., 33. Abercrombie, op. cit., 283–4. Cognet, op. cit., 46.

32 Lionel Rothkrug, *Opposition to Louis XIV. The Political and Social Origins of the French Enlightenment*, Princeton, New Jersey, Princeton University Press, 1965, 286–98, 458–63. Louis Cognet, *Crépuscule des mystiques*, Tournai, Desclée, 1958, *passim*. Michael de la Bedoyere, *The Archbishop and the Lady. The Story of Fénelon and Madame Guyon*, London, Collins, 1956, 102–23. See also J.-R. Armogathe, *Le Quiétisme*, Paris, Presses Universitaires de France, 1973.

33 W. J. Stankiewicz, op. cit., 58, 110

34 ibid., 111, 115–16. Latreille *et al.*, op. cit., II, 298.

35 Emile Léonard, *Histoire générale du protestantisme*, Paris, Presses Universitaires de France, 1961, II, 333.

36 Stankiewicz, op. cit., 140–1. It is of course ironic that the Huguenots also shared something of the fate of the English Presbyterians who not only failed to establish their preferred form of church government but were also reduced in the late seventeenth century to marginality by a "dry" persecution, becoming merely another English Protestant sect.

37 Elisabeth Labrousse, *"Une Foi, une loi, un roi?" Essai sur la Révocation de l'Edit de Nantes*, Geneva, Labor et Fides, 1985, 40–1.
38 *Dictionnaire historique et critique de Pierre Bayle*, new edn, Paris, 1820, article "Amyraut," 507–19. I am very much indebted to Professor Larry Bryant for having brought to my attention this matter of the kneeling of Huguenot ministers.
39 Labrousse, op. cit., 41–3, 116. Stankiewicz, op. cit., 146ff.
40 *Mémoires de Louis XIV pour l'instruction du dauphin* (ed. Charles Dreyss), Paris, Didier, 1860, II, 454–7.
41 Michael G. Finlayson, *Historians, Puritanism, and the Religious Factor in English Politics before and after the Interregnum*, Toronto, University of Toronto Press, 1983, *passim*.
42 Jean Orcibal, *Louis XIV et les protestants*, Paris, J. Vrin, 1951, 57, 67.
43 Orcibal, *Louis XIV et les protestants*, 91, 102–3, 110. See also Orcibal's essay "Louis XIV and the Edict of Nantes," in R. Hatton (ed.), *Louis XIV and Absolutism*, London, Macmillan, 1976, 154–76.
44 Orcibal, *Louis XIV et les protestants*, 156–8.
45 Burdette C. Poland, *French Protestantism and the French Revolution. A Study in Church and State, Thought and Religion, 1685–1815*, Princeton, New Jersey, Princeton University Press, 1957, 26.

II "A FRENCHMAN WITHOUT BEING A CATHOLIC": CATHOLICISM AND CITIZENSHIP IN THE EIGHTEENTH CENTURY

1 Burdette C. Poland, *French Protestantism and the French Revolution. A Study in Church and State, Thought and Religion, 1685–1815*, Princeton, New Jersey, Princeton University Press, 1957, 83.
2 Bernard Plongeron, *Conscience religieuse en révolution. Regards sur l'historiographie de la Révolution française*, Paris, A. & J. Picard, 1969, 202–4.
3 Timothy Tackett, *Religion, Revolution, and Regional Culture in Eighteenth-Century France. The Ecclesiastical Oath of 1791*, Princeton, New Jersey, Princeton University Press, 1986, 73–4.
4 J. C. D. Clark, *English Society, 1688–1832. Ideology, Social Structure and Political Practice during the Ancien Regime*, Cambridge, Cambridge University Press, 1985, 9.
5 ibid., 207.
6 Henry Kamen, *The Rise of Toleration*, New York, World University Library, 1967, 145–60, 216.
7 *Oeuvres de Turgot* (ed. Gustave Schelle), Paris, Librairie Félix Alcan, 1913–23, I, 406.
8 It is sobering to note that the one modern historian of the French Church who in two excellent books has successfully reasserted the importance of ecclesiastical and religious issues for an understanding of eighteenth-century France, Dale Van Kley, may have himself successfully avoided the dangers of modern secularism only to fall perhaps into a Protestant bias when he writes of the "bureaucratization of the sacraments" during his discussion of the controversy concerning the refusal of sacraments; and also when he suggests that

both sides in this controversy could have avoided furthering the secularization of society if they had only favored the separation of Church and State. Dale Van Kley, *The Damiens Affair and the Unraveling of the Ancien Regime, 1750–1770*, Princeton, New Jersey, Princeton University Press, 1984, 108, 163–5. See also his stimulating book, *The Jansenists and the Expulsion of the Jesuits from France 1757–1765*, New Haven, Connecticut, Yale University Press, 1975.

9 Bernard Plongeron, *Théologie et politique au siècle des lumières (1770–1820)*, Geneva, Droz, 1973, 91–2, 184–9.

10 John Bossy's book, *Christianity in the West 1400–1700* (Oxford, Oxford University Press, 1985) is a healthy reminder of things modern European or western man has forgotten about his religious heritage.

11 Poland, op cit., 61–3.

12 David D. Bien, *The Calas Affair. Persecution, Toleration, and Heresy in Eighteenth-Century Toulouse*, Princeton, New Jersey, Princeton University Press, 1960, 58–67, 114–15, 157.

13 Michel Richard, *La Vie quotidienne des protestants sous l'ancien régime*, Paris, Hachette, 1966, 299.

14 Poland, op. cit., 65–8. Richard, op. cit., 287–8.

15 Poland, op. cit., 75.

16 Poland, op. cit., 81–5. R. Mandrou *et al.* (eds), *Histoire des protestants de France*, Paris, Privat, 1977, 232–3. Richard, op. cit., 305–6.

17 Dale Van Kley, "Church, State, and the Ideological Origins of the French Revolution: the Debate over the General Assembly of the Gallican Clergy in 1765," *The Journal of Modern History*, vol. LI, no. 4 (December 1979), 642–5. Plongeron, *Théologie . . .*, 91–2.

18 Quoted by Van Kley in *The Damiens Affair . . .*, 163.

19 ibid., 162–3.

20 ibid., 116–18. Norman Ravitch, *Sword and Mitre. Government and Episcopate in France and England in the Age of Aristocracy*, The Hague, Mouton, 1966, 24–50.

21 Robert R. Palmer, *Catholics and Unbelievers in Eighteenth-Century France*, Princeton, New Jersey, Princeton University Press, 1939, 10. For a thorough discussion of religion and citizenship see Jeffrey Merrick, "Conscience and Citizenship in Eighteenth-Century France," *Eighteenth-Century Studies*, vol. XXI, no. 1 (fall 1987), 48–70, and also his book entitled *The Desacralization of the French Monarchy in the Eighteenth Century*, Baton Rouge, Louisiana, Louisiana State University Press, 1990.

22 Peter Gay, *The Enlightenment. An Interpretation*, London, Weidenfeld and Nicolson, 1966, I, 338.

23 René Pomeau, *La Religion de Voltaire*, Paris, Librairie Nizet, new edn, 1969, 24–78. Ira O. Wade, *The Intellectual Development of Voltaire*, Princeton, New Jersey, Princeton University Press, 1969, 8–22, 120–1.

24 Pomeau, op. cit., 110–11.

25 Voltaire, *Le Siècle de Louis XIV*, in *Oeuvres historiques*, Paris, Gallimard, 1957, 1066–82.

26 Pomeau, op. cit., 400ff. Philip T. Hoffman, *Church and Community in*

the Diocese of Lyon 1500–1789, New Haven, Connecticut, Yale University Press, 1984, 93–6.

27 Daniel Blackstone, "A la Recherche du lien social. Incrédulité et religion d'après le discours janséniste à la fin du dix-huitième siècle," in J. R. Derré *et al.* (eds), *Civilisation chrétienne. Approche historique d'une idéologie, XVIIIe–XXe siècle*, Paris, Editions Beauchesne, 1975, 63–87.

28 Peter Gay, op. cit., II, 522–8.

29 ibid., II, 546. Despite the many differences between Voltaire and Rousseau, they shared a belief in natural religion. Despite his upbringing in Geneva, Rousseau's Protestant legacy must have been more moralistic than theological. In his *Confessions* he remarked about the terrors of damnation which he for the first time had found in the works of the Jansenists and Oratorians. It is hard to believe that someone educated in a Calvinist city and one who for two years as a boy lived with a Protestant pastor had to learn of austere Augustinianism from Catholic writers – unless the dissolution of orthodox Calvinism which d'Alembert celebrated in 1756 had already occurred at least a generation earlier. See *Rousseau, Religious Writings* (ed. Ronald Grimsley), Oxford Clarendon Press, 1970, 9–10; and Jean Guéhenno, *Jean-Jacques Rousseau*, London, Routledge and Kegan Paul, 1967, I, 10–12. I am not sure I should agree with R. R. Palmer that in religious questions Rousseau's spirit was often more Protestant than rationalist. See Palmer, op. cit., 98.

30 Palmer, op. cit., 226.

31 Bernard Groethuysen, *The Bourgeois. Catholicism vs. Capitalism in Eighteenth-Century France*, London, Barrie & Rockliff, 1968, 131–73.

32 Friedrich Engels, *Socialism, Utopian and Scientific*, New York, International Publishers, 1935, 17–22.

33 Ernst Troeltsch, *The Social Teachings of the Christian Churches*, London, George Allen and Unwin, 1931, I, 254–6, 285–302.

34 Amintore Fanfani, *Catholicism, Protestantism and Capitalism*, New York, Sheed and Ward, 1955, 206–9.

35 Hoffman, op. cit., 93–6. See also Jean Delumeau, *Le Catholicisme entre Luther et Voltaire*, Paris, Presses Universitaries de France, 1971, *passim*.

36 Jean Quéniart, *Les Hommes, L'Eglise et Dieu dans la France du XVIIIe siècle*, Paris, Hachette, 1978, 158.

37 Groethuysen, op. cit., 21–5.

38 Maxime Leroy, *Histoire des idées sociales en France*, Paris, Gallimard, 1946–54, I, 84.

39 Groethuysen, op. cit., 32. The growth of intellectuals as a specialized part of the élite involved their resentment of the clergy as the directing *caste* of society. See Emile Faguet, *L'Anticléricalisme*, Paris, Société Française d'Imprimerie et de Librairie, 1906, 93.

40 Hoffman, op. cit., 170.

41 Quéniart, op. cit., 166.

42 ibid., 100–4, 138.

43 ibid., 73–6. François Lebrun (ed.), *Histoire des catholiques en France du XVème siècle à nos jours*, Paris, Privat, 1980, 229.

44 Quéniart, op. cit., 279–309. William H. Williams, "Voltaire and the Utility of the Lower Clergy," *Studies on Voltaire and the Eighteenth Century*, vol. LVIII (1967), 1874ff.

45 Groethuysen, op. cit., 45–6. Lucien Goldmann, *The Philosophy of the Enlightenment. The Christian Burgess and the Enlightenment*, London, Routledge and Kegan Paul, 1973, 55.

46 Robert Mauzi, *L'Idée du bonheur dans la littérature et la pensée française au XVIIIe siècle*, Paris, Armand Colin, 1967, 281–4.

47 Gay, op. cit., I, 351–7.

48 Palmer, op. cit., 129, 221. Mauzi, op. cit., 180–215. Norman Ravitch, "Catholicism in Crisis: the Impact of the French Revolution on the Thought of the Abbé Adrien Lamourette," *Cahiers internationaux d'histoire économique et sociale*, vol. IX (1978), 359–62.

49 René Taveneaux, *Jansénisme et politique*, Paris, Armand Colin, 1965, 49–50, Palmer, op. cit., 74–5. Van Kley, *The Jansenists and the Expulsion of the Jesuits . . .*, 226–8.

50 Daniel Mornet, *Les Origines intellectuelles de la Révolution française*, Paris, Armand Colin, 6th edn, 1967, 471–2.

51 Van Kley, *The Jansenists and the Expulsion of the Jesuits . . .*, 224.

52 Pierre Sage, *Le 'Bon Prêtre' dans la littérature française*, Geneva, Droz, 1951, 148, 274–5, 443.

53 Bernard Plongeron, "Recherches sur 'l'Aufklärung' catholique en Europe occidentale (1770–1830)," *Revue d'histoire moderne et contemporaine*, vol. XVI (October–December 1969), 578ff. Owen Chadwick, *The Popes and European Revolution*, Oxford, Clarendon Press, 1981, 391–444. Derek Beales, *Joseph II*, vol. I: *In the Shadow of Maria Theresa 1741–1780*, Cambridge, Cambridge University Press, 1987, ch. 14.

54 Douglas Dakin, *Turgot and the Ancien Regime in France*, London, Methuen, 1939, 13–15, 216–21. *Oeuvres de Turgot*, IV, 557–68.

55 M. G. Hutt, "The Curés and the Third Estate: the Ideas of Reform in the Pamphlets of the French Lower Clergy in the Period 1787–1789," *The Journal of Ecclesiastical History*, vol. VIII, no. 1 (April 1957), 89–92.

56 Bernard Plongeron, "Permanence d'une idéologie de 'civilisation chrétienne' dans le clergé constitutionnel," *Studies in Eighteenth-Century Culture*, vol. VII (1978), 271ff.

57 Régine Pernoud, *Histoire de la bourgeoisie en France*, vol. II: *Les Temps Modernes*, Paris, Editions du Seuil, 1962, 358–62.

58 Tackett, op. cit., 40–3.

59 Pernoud, op. cit., 271.

60 "Grand Colère du Père Duchesne sur le refus du Roi de sanctionner le décret concernant la Constitution civile du clergé," quoted in Alec Mellor, *Histoire de l'anticléricalisme français*, Tours, Mame, 1966, 89.

61 Gary Kates, *The Cercle Social, the Girondins, and the French Revolution*, Princeton, New Jersey, Princeton University Press, 1985, 103.

62 Plongeron, *Conscience religieuse en révolution . . .*, 196–208. The great patriarch of the Constitutional Church the Abbé Henri Grégoire, supported the separation of Church and State in 1794–5 only in a desperate attempt to prevent the official establishment of a non-Christian revolutionary cult. See Norman Ravitch, "Liberalism, Catholicism, and the Abbé Grégoire," *Church History*, vol. XXXVI (December 1967), 425, 438.

63 Norman Ravitch, "The Abbé Fauchet: Romantic Religion During the French Revolution," *Journal of the American Academy of Religion*, vol. XLII, no. 2 (June 1974), 261–2. Ravitch, "Catholicism in Crisis . . .," 379–80, 382–3. Kates, op. cit., 111–13. This explains a great paradox in the historical interpretation of the French Revolution by Aléxis de Tocqueville, where he claimed that it was not Catholic faith but the social position of the Church in the Old Regime which the revolutionaries most vigorously attacked; he nevertheless considered the ideology of the Revolution as akin to a religion. See Tocqueville's *L'Ancien Régime et la Révolution* (ed. J.-P. Mayer), Paris, Gallimard, 1952–3, I, 83–90. The religion of nationalism, thus, was both the product and the rival of Catholicism. As for socialism, John McManners reminds us that "the renegade clergy of France deserve a greater place in the history of socialism than the very modest niche so far allowed them", McManners, *The French Revolution and the Church*, New York, Harper & Row, 1969, 91. Patriotic Catholicism during the Revolution sought relevance by transforming itself partially into nationalism and socialism through its advocacy of political, social, and sometimes economic egalitarianism.

64 McManners, op. cit., 138.

65 Albert Mathiez, *La Théophilanthropie et le culte décadaire*, Paris, Félix Alcan, 1903, 23–5, 704–9.

66 Ronald Grimsley, *Rousseau and the Religious Quest*, Oxford, Clarendon Press, 1968, 138.

67 Leroy, op. cit., I, 205–7.

68 J. Christopher Herold, *The Mind of Napoleon*, New York, Columbia University Press, 1955, 105. Robert B. Holtman, *The Napoleonic Revolution*, Philadelphia, J. B. Lippincott, 1967, 125.

69 Reprinted in E. E. Y. Hales, *Revolution and Papacy 1769–1846*, London, Eyre & Spottiswoode, 1960, 297–8.

70 André Latreille, *L'Eglise catholique et la Révolution française*, Paris, Hachette, 1946–50, II, 36.

71 ibid., II, 34, 126–9, 139–40. Mellor, op. cit., 247.

72 Olwen Hufton, "The Reconstruction of a Church, 1796–1801," in G. Lewis and C. Lucas (eds), *Beyond the Terror. Essays in French Regional and Social History, 1794–1815*, Cambridge, Cambridge University Press, 1983, 52. Plongeron, *Conscience religieuse en révolution . . .*, 210.

73 Clark, op. cit., 250.

74 A. Latreille, E. Delaruelle, J.-R. Palanque, and R. Rémond, *Histoire du catholicisme en France*, Paris, Editions Spés, 1957–62, III, 216–17.

III PROPHECY OR ORDER: THE NINETEENTH-CENTURY CHURCH IN SEARCH OF A ROLE

1 Jeffrey B. Russell, *A History of Medieval Christianity. Prophecy and Order*, New York, Thomas Y. Crowell, 1968. Karl Marx, *The German Ideology* (ed. R. Pascal), New York, International Publishers, 1947, 199.
2 Emile Poulat, *Eglise contre bourgeoisie. Introduction au devenir du catholicisme actuel*, Tournai, Casterman, 1977, 63–79.
3 Theodore Zeldin. "The Conflicts of Moralities. Confession, Sin and Pleasure in the Nineteenth Century," in Theodore Zeldin (ed.), *Conflicts in French Society. Anticlericalism, Education and Morals in the Nineteenth Century*, London, George Allen and Unwin, 1970, 13–50. Theodore Zeldin, *France 1848–1945*, Oxford, Clarendon Press, 1973–7, II, 994.
4 Austin Gough, *Paris and Rome. The Gallican Church and the Ultramontane Campaign 1848–1853*, Oxford, Clarendon Press, 1986, 12.
5 ibid., 22–51.
6 Bernard Reardon, *Liberalism and Tradition. Aspects of Catholic Thought in Nineteenth-Century France*, Cambridge, Cambridge University Press, 1975, 63.
7 François Lebrun (ed.), *Histoire des catholiques en France du XVe siècle à nos jours*, Toulouse, Privat, 1980, 335ff.
8 Alec R. Vidler, *Prophecy and Papacy. A Study of Lamennais, the Church, and the Revolution*, New York, Charles Scribner's Sons, 1954, 44ff.
9 Article in *l'Avenir*, 16 October 1830, reprinted in Peter N. Stearns, *Priest and Revolutionary. Lamennais and the Dilemma of French Catholicism*, New York, Harper & Row, 1967, 169–71.
10 Article in *Revue des deux mondes*, 1 August 1834, quoted in Jean Lebrun, *Lamennais ou l'inquiétude de la liberté*, Paris, Fayard-Mame, 1981, 130–1.
11 "Mémoire adressé à Léon XII sur l'état de l'église en France," 1826–7, in *Correspondance générale de Félicité de Lamennais* (ed. Louis Le Guillou), Paris, Armand Colin, 1971, III, 279–80.
12 Louis Le Guillou, *L'Evolution de la pensée religieuse de Félicité Lamennais*, Paris, Armand Colin, 1966, 96–105.
13 Stearns, op. cit., 44–5. Vidler, op. cit., 128. Reardon, op. cit., 87–9.
14 Jean Lebrun, *Lamennais* . . ., 91.
15 Marie-Joseph Le Guillou, OP, "The Mennaisian Crisis," in Roger Aubert (ed.), *Progress and Decline in the History of Church Renewal*, New York, Paulist Press, 1967, 117.
16 Gaston Bordet, "Emmanuel d'Alzon et la crise mennaisienne 1828–1835," in Réné Rémond and Emile Poulat (eds), *Emmanuel d'Alzon dans la société et l'Eglise du XIXe siècle*, Paris, Le Centurion, 1982, 45–7, 61–4.
17 Le Guillou, *L'Evolution* . . ., 101–5.
18 "Mémoire adressé à Léon XII . . .," 283–4.
19 Lamennais to Vicomte Vilain, 7 October 1832, in *Correspondance générale* . . ., V, 187–8. Original italics have been removed.

20 Lamennais to Father Ventura, 25 January 1833, ibid., 293.
21 Lamennais to Count Rzewuski, 5 February 1833, ibid., 302–5.
22 Lamennais to Countess Senfft, 25 January 1833, ibid., 295. Lamennais, *Affaires de Rome*, Paris, Cailleux, 1836–7, 295–303.
23 Lamennais to Father Ventura, 25 January 1833, *Correspondance générale* . . ., 293.
24 Gough, op. cit., 60ff.
25 Lebrun (ed.), *Histoire des catholiques* . . ., 335ff.
26 Poulat, *Eglise contre bourgeoisie* . . ., 59.
27 It is interesting to note that the most intemperate champion of intransigent Catholicism in the entire nineteenth century, Louis Veuillot, still valued some connection with Lamennais in 1846 when his apostasy was completely unambiguous, and Veuillot demonstrated a most uncharacteristic charity in refusing to attack Lamennais as he was attacking other so-called liberal Catholics with glee. He actually stated that he preferred to pray for him! Jean Lebrun, *Lamennais* . . ., 251.
28 One hesitates to cite an apologist for the Vichy regime in support of anything, but a curious book first written in 1942, and reprinted in 1968, in seeking to claim that the murky National Revolution of Philippe Pétain owed much to the anti-individualistic thought of Lamennais, also contended that all the apparent contradictions and conflicts in Lamennais' thought and career could be resolved by considering him as basically *sociological*. For Claude Carcopino, Lamennais was neither a liberal nor a socialist, but a "Social Catholic." Since those who hoped that Vichy would be more than a makeshift accommodation to the German conqueror also entertained visions of a "third way" between capitalism and collectivism, they were, like Carcopino, at least well equipped for spying out signs of economic and social doctrines equally opposed to liberalism and socialism; they were thus better informed than many, when not blinded by wishful thinking, about the nature and history of Social Catholicism. Whatever Carcopino's original purposes in 1942, his evaluation of Lamennais is by no means devoid of merit. Claude Carcopino, *Les Doctrines sociales de Lamennais*, Geneva, Slatkine Reprints, 1968.
29 Jean-Baptiste Duroselle, *Les Débuts du catholicisme social en France (1822–1870)*, Paris, Presses Universitaires de France, 1951, 27–40. Bordet, op. cit., 43.
30 Stearns, op. cit., 48–68, 73–7, 94–5. Vidler, op. cit., 164. Pierre Thibault, *Savoir et pouvoir. Philosophie thomiste et politique cléricale au XIXe siècle*, Québec, Les Presses de l'Université de Laval, 1972, 26–7. Yvon Tranvouez, "Religion, politique et civilisation chrétienne: Lamennais en 1817. Etude sur le premier tome de l'*Essai sur l'Indifférence*," in J.-R. Derré *et al.* (eds.), *Civilisation chrétienne. Approche historique d'une idéologie, XVIIIe–XXe siècle*, Paris, Editions Beauchesne, 1975, 121–2, 134–5.
31 Poulat, *Une Eglise ébranlée. Changement, conflit et continuité de Pie XII à Jean-Paul II*, Tournai, Casterman, 1980, 290–1.

32 Tranvouez, op. cit., 135–41. Jean Lebrun, *Lamennais* . . ., 238–9. Stearns, op. cit., 107–8.
33 Lamennais to a Mexican correspondent, 12 March 1833, quoted in Vidler, op. cit., 222.
34 Adrien Dansette, *Histoire religieuse de la France contemporaine*, Paris, Flammarion, 1948–51, I, 353–62.
35 Duroselle, op. cit., 236.
36 ibid., 291–2.
37 Jean Lebrun, *Lamennais* . . ., 237–8. Louis Le Guillou, op. cit., 388ff.
38 Jean-Marie Mayeur, *Catholicisme social et démocratie chrétienne. Principes romains, expériences françaises*, Paris, Editions du Cerf, 1986, 267.
39 ibid.
40 Emile Poulat, *Modernistica*, Paris, Nouvelles Editions Latines, 1982, 33.
41 Thibault, op. cit., xiii–xiv, xvii–xviii. Poulat, *Eglise contre bourgeoisie . . ., passim*. Poulat, *Une Eglise ébranlée* . . ., 290–1.
42 Poulat, *Eglise contre bourgeoisie* . . ., 130, 200.
43 Gough, op. cit., 67–96, 203. Thibault, op. cit., xiii.
44 Gough, op. cit., 105–7.
45 Thomas A. Kselman, *Miracles and Prophecies in Nineteenth-Century France*, New Brunswick, New Jersey, Rutgers University Press, 1983, 90ff. Kselman also suggests that the growth and virulence of Catholic anti-Semitism in the last third of the nineteenth century was equally eschatological in origin, part of an offensive to accomplish the conversion of the Jews and thereby to precipitate the Second Coming: ibid., 138–9. Many French Catholics evidently had recourse to the Day of Judgement when all more mundane means of battling against Satan and his minions among their fellow citizens had failed. It is interesting in this connection to recall the anecdote about Napoleon I's reaction to the advent of the Day of Judgement. His uncle, Cardinal Fesch, told the rationalist but still residually superstitious emperor that tradition held that the restoration of the Jewish Sanhedrin would signal the end of the world. Napoleon thereupon promptly dismissed the Great Sanhedrin he had convened for organizing the Jews of the Empire! It had, in any case, already largely fulfilled most of his expectations.
46 Duroselle, op. cit., 420–2, 493–7. Pierre Pierrard, *L'Eglise et les ouvriers en France (1840–1940)*, Paris, Hachette, 1984, 179.
47 Quoted in Lebrun (ed.), *Histoire des catholiques* . . . 387.
48 Duroselle, op. cit., 701–2. Lebrun (ed.), *Histoire des catholiques* . . ., 355.
49 Pierrard, op. cit., 136. Poulat, *Eglise contre bourgeoisie* . . ., 121.
50 Pierrard, op. cit., 329. Duroselle, op. cit., 702.
51 Pierrard, op. cit., 152–66, 171. François-André Isambert, *Christianisme et classe ouvrière*, Tournai, Casterman, 1961, 117–18. Although Alexis de Tocqueville shared so much in social background and political outlook with Montalembert, the leading liberal Catholic in the anti-socialist movement, he was nevertheless convinced that "after Voltaire, the greatest enemy that the church has in France is Montalem-

bert," by which he meant to indicate the supposedly disastrous results of anti-working-class rhetoric on the reputation of the Church among the workers. Roger Magraw, *France 1815–1914: The Bourgeois Century*, New York, Oxford University Press, 1986, 139.

52 Pierrard, op. cit., 116–20. A. Latreille, E. Delaruelle, J.-R. Palanque, *et al.*, *Histoire du catholicisme en France*, Paris, Editions Spés, 1957–62, III, 367–8.

53 Emile Poulat, in François Bédarida and Jean Maitron (eds), *Christianisme et monde ouvrier*, Paris, Les Editions Ouvrières, 1975, 21.

54 Pierrard, op. cit., 141, 167–71.

55 Gérard Cholvy and Yves-Marie Hilaire, *Histoire religieuse de la France contemporaine*, Toulouse, Privat, 1985–8, I, 237–58. Isambert, op. cit., 140–2.

56 Jean Bruhat, in Bédarida and Maitron (eds), *Christianisme et monde ouvrier*, 106ff. Pierrard, op. cit., 120. Isambert, op. cit., 213.

57 Pierrard, op. cit., 496–7.

58 E. J. Hobsbawm, *Primitive Rebels. Studies in Archaic Forms of Social Movement in the 19th and 20th Centuries*, Manchester, Manchester University Press, 1959, 81. Hobsbawm was, it is true, speaking here of the Spanish Catholic Church and its relationship to the peasant masses, but his insight may also be applicable towards understanding the French Church's inability to speak to the working class as the workers developed an anti-bourgeois class consciousness.

59 B. Robert Kreiser, *Miracles, Convulsions, and Ecclesiastical Politics in Early Eighteenth-Century Paris*, Princeton, New Jersey, Princeton University Press, 1978, 396.

60 Pierrard, op. cit., 128ff. Isambert, op. cit., 148–51, 236–59. François Bédarida, in Bédarida and Maitron (eds), *Christianisme et monde ouvrier*, 19–20.

61 Edward Berenson, *Populist Religion and Left-Wing Politics in France, 1830–1852*, Princeton, New Jersey, Princeton University Press, 1984, 108ff., and *passim*.

62 Dominique Julia and Willem Frijhoff, "The French Priest in Modern Times," in Roger Aubert (ed.), *Sacralization and Secularization*, New York, Paulist Press, 1969, 157–8.

63 Ernst Troeltsch, *The Social Teaching of the Christian Churches*, London, George Allen and Unwin, 1931, I, 82–6.

64 "Affaires de Rome," in *Oeuvres complètes de F. de la Mennais*, Brussels, Société Belge de Librairie, 1839, II, 526.

65 "Essai sur l'indifférence en matière de religion," in ibid., I, 36.

66 Joseph N. Moody, *French Education Since Napoleon*, Syracuse, New York, Syracuse University Press, 1978, 52.

67 René Rémond, *L'Anti-cléricalisme en France de 1815 à nos jours*, Paris, Fayard, 1976, 124–6.

68 Joseph N. Moody, *The Church as Enemy. Anticlericalism in Nineteenth Century French Literature*, Washington, Corpus Books, 1968, 13.

69 Emile Poulat, in Bédarida and Maitron (eds), *Christianisme et monde ouvrier*, 17.

IV FRENCH CATHOLICS AND THE THIRD REPUBLIC: FROM DREYFUS TO PÉTAIN

1 François Lebrun (ed.), *Histoire des catholiques en France du xve siècle à nos jours*, Toulouse, Privat, 1980, 373–4.
2 Maurice Larkin, *Church and State after the Dreyfus Affair. The Separation Issue in France*, London, Macmillan, 1974, 50–1.
3 Emile Poulat, *Eglise contre bourgeoisie. Introduction au devenir du catholicisme actuel*, Tournai, Casterman, 1977, 175.
4 Margaret L. Anderson, *Windthorst. A Political Biography*, Oxford, Clarendon Press, 1981, 278–9, 321–2, 325ff., 400. Raymond H. Schmitt, "The Life and Work of Leo XIII," in Edward T. Gargan (ed.), *Leo XIII and the Modern World*, New York, Sheed & Ward, 1961, 24–31. S. William Halperin, "Leo XIII and the Roman Question," ibid., 116, 123–4.
5 Alexander Sedgwick, *The Ralliement in French Politics 1890–1898*, Cambridge, Harvard University Press, 1965, 4. Pierre Thibault, *Savoir et pouvoir. Philosophie thomiste et politique cléricale au xixe siècle*, Québec, Les Presses de l'Université de Laval, 1972, 165ff. See also Emile Poulat's introductory comments in ibid., ix–xix.
6 Larkin, op. cit., 206.
7 Michael Burns, *Rural Society and French Politics. Boulangism and the Dreyfus Affair 1886–1900*, Princeton, New Jersey, Princeton University Press, 1984, 121–64. Jean-Denis Bredin, *The Affair. The Case of Alfred Dreyfus*, New York, George Braziller, 1986, 515–45.
8 Pie Duployé, OP, *La Religion de Péguy*, Paris, Klincksieck, 1965, 51.
9 Ernst Nolte, *Three Faces of Fascism*, New York, Holt, Rinehart, and Winston, 1966, 54–7. Eugen Weber, *Action Française. Royalism and Reaction in Twentieth-Century France*, Stanford, Stanford University Press, 1962, 3–6, 16–17.
10 Weber, op. cit., 17.
11 A. Latreille, E. Delaruelle, J.-R. Palanque, *et al.*, *Histoire du catholicisme en France*, vol. III, Paris, Editions Spés, 1962, 495–6. René Rémond, *L'Anti-Cléricalisme en France de 1815 à nos jours*, Paris, Fayard, 1976, 200–3, 206.
12 Michael Sutton, *Nationalism, Positivism and Catholicism. The Politics of Charles Maurras and French Catholics, 1890–1914*, Cambridge, Cambridge University Press, 1982, 8, 260–1. H. R. Kedward, *The Dreyfus Affair*, London, Longmans, 1965, 72–3.
13 Jacob Katz, "Misreadings of Anti-Semitism," *Commentary*, vol. LXXVI, no. 1 (July 1983), 39–44.
14 Thomas A. Kselman, *Miracles and Prophecies in Nineteenth-Century France*, New Brunswick, New Jersey, Rutgers University Press, 1983, 135–9.
15 Pierre Pierrard, *Juifs et catholiques français*, Paris, Fayard, 1970, 18–35.
16 Jean-Marie Mayeur, "Les Congrès nationaux de la 'Démocratie chrétienne' à Lyon (1896–1897–1898)," *Revue d'histoire moderne et contemporaine*, vol. IX (July–September 1962), 203–6.
17 Stephen Wilson, *Ideology and Experience. Antisemitism in France at the*

Time of the Dreyfus Affair, Rutherford, New Jersey, Fairleigh Dickinson University Press, 1982, 736.

18 Stephen Wilson, op. cit., 519. Pierrard, op. cit., 220.

19 Nelly Wilson, *Bernard-Lazare. Antisemitism and the Problem of Jewish Identity in Late Nineteenth-Century France*, Cambridge, Cambridge University Press, 1978, 299.

20 Alexander Sedgwick, *The Ralliement* . . ., 157–9

21 Gérard Cholvy and Yves-Marie Hilaire are perhaps mistaken in thinking that the abolition of the Concordat eliminated one of the justifications for the Ralliement. It is true that the Separation encouraged the movement of the Action Française, but the association of Catholics with Maurras is not the story of the continued alienation of Catholics from the Republic but of their reconciliation with conservative republicans. The royalism of the Action Française, it will be seen below, was less important than its nationalism. (For the views of Cholvy and Hilaire, see their *Histoire religieuse de la France contemporaine*, vol. II, Toulouse, Privat, 1986, 119.)

22 Theodore Zeldin, *France 1848–1945*, Oxford, Oxford University Press, 1973–7, I, 697–8.

23 Sutton, op. cit., 7–8.

24 R. E. M. Irving, *Christian Democracy in France*, London, George Allen and Unwin, 1973, 36–40.

25 Oscar L. Arnal, *Ambivalent Alliance. The Catholic Church and the Action Française, 1899–1939*, Pittsburgh, University of Pittsburgh Press, 1985, 26.

26 J. M. Cameron, "Nuclear Catholicism," *The New York Review of Books*, vol. XXX, no. 20 (22 December 1983), 42.

27 Madeleine Barthélemy-Madaule, *Marc Sangnier 1873–1950*, Paris, Editions du Seuil, 1973, 167. Sutton, op. cit., 90.

28 Maurice Vaussard, *Histoire de la Démocratie chrétienne*, Paris, Editions du Seuil, 1956, 75. Jeanne Caron, *Le Sillon et la Démocratie chrétienne, 1894–1910*, Paris, Plon, 1967, 446. Latreille, *et al.*, III, 524.

29 Barthélemy-Madaule, op. cit., 196–7, 201–2.

30 René Rémond (ed.)., *Forces religieuses et attitudes politiques dans la France contemporaine*, Paris, Armand Colin, 1965, 14.

31 Larkin, op. cit., 191–206. Arnal, op. cit., 46–8.

32 Arnal, op. cit., 51–62.

33 Jean-Marie Mayeur, *L'Abbé Lemire, 1853–1928. Un Prêtre démocrate*, Tournai, Casterman, 1968, 53–5, 57, 65–6, 69–79, 180–210, 274–6, 607–10.

34 Arnal, op. cit., 53ff.

35 Mayeur, *L'Abbé Lemire*, 84–5.

36 Vaussard, op. cit., 79.

37 Zeev Sternhell, *La Droite révolutionnaire 1885–1914. Les origines françaises du fascisme*, Paris, Editions du Seuil, 1978, 207–16. Robert F. Byrnes, *Antisemitism in Modern France. The Prelude to the Dreyfus Affair*, New Brunswick, New Jersey, Rutgers University Press, 1950, 205, 298–304. Mayeur, "Les Congrès nationaux de la 'Démocratie chrétienne' . . .," 203–6. Adrien Dansette, *Histoire religieuse de la France*

contemporaine, Paris, Flammarion, 1951, II, 262. Maurice Montuclard, *Conscience religieuse et démocratie. La deuxième démocratie chrétienne en France, 1891–1902*, Paris, Editions du Seuil, 1965, 136. Marc Sangnier was one of the few pioneers of Christian democracy who was a Dreyfusard and completely clear of anti-Semitic appeals. Stephen Wilson, op. cit., 533.

38 Stephen Wilson, op. cit., 319ff., 737; and "Catholic Populism in France at the time of the Dreyfus Affair: the Union Nationale," *Journal of Contemporary History*, vol. X (1975), 667–705.

39 Eugen Weber, "Fascism(s) and Some Harbingers," *The Journal of Modern History*, vol. LIV, no. 4 (December 1982), 762. On the relationship of populism to anti-Semitism, see Margaret Canovan, *Populism*, London, Junction Books, 1981, 46–51; Norman Pollack, "The Myth of Populist Anti-Semitism," *The American Historical Review*, vol. LXVIII, no. 1 (October 1962), 76–80; John Lukacs, *The Last European War*, New York, Doubleday, 1976, 456–9; John W. Boyer, *Political Radicalism in Late Imperial Vienna. Origins of the Christian Social Movement 1848–1897*, Chicago, University of Chicago Press, 1981, 113–15, 122–3, 150ff. On the French forerunners of Christian democracy, see Montuclard, op. cit., 138; Emile Poulat, *Eglise contre bourgeoisie . . .*, 138–9; Mayeur, *L'Abbé Lemire . . .*, 181–210. See also Alfred Diamant, *Austrian Catholics and the First Republic. Democracy, Capitalism, and the Social Order, 1918–1934*, Princeton, New Jersey, Princeton University Press, 1960, 287; John T. Noonan, Jr, *The Scholastic Analysis of Usury*, Cambridge, Harvard University Press, 1957, 402–3; and Michael Novak, *The Spirit of Democratic Capitalism*, New York, Simon & Schuster, *passim*.

40 Jean-Marie Mayeur, *La Séparation de l'Eglise et de l'Etat*, Paris, Julliard, 1966, 99–100, 187ff.

41 Arnal, op. cit., 79–80; Sutton, op. cit., 98.

42 Sometimes the attacks were more than verbal, for its youthful auxiliaries, the Camelots du Roi, were often engaged in street brawls and the vicious use of personal violence. Here one thinks easily of Squadristi and Storm Troopers.

43 Sutton, op. cit., 108. Arnal, op. cit., 14, 81–2, 92ff. Weber, *Action Française . . .*, 530.

44 Sutton, op. cit., 26.

45 Pedro Descoqs, SJ, quoted in ibid., 108.

46 For Ernst Nolte, the Action Française was the earliest form of Fascism and shared with other Fascist movements a "resistance to transcendence," which is man's spiritual "freedom toward the infinite." Integral nationalism viewed man as deprived of any relationship to values higher or beyond the naturalistic needs of the community. Nolte, op. cit., 421, 429–34. Between Nolte and Sutton, on the one hand, who stress the modern and Fascistic aspects of Maurras' thought, and Weber, on the other hand, who emphasizes the purely verbal radicalism of the Action Française and its actual lack of activism, one can have difficulty deciding how seriously to take the affinities with Fascism. Certainly many of the supporters of the Action Française were oblivious to its Fascistic nature and viewed its

purposes as wholly traditional. Fascism, however, can profitably be viewed as the pursuit of traditional goals by means so radical that their achievement cannot really end up being traditional at all. Still, the appeal of Fascism can often seem wholly traditional – that is perhaps its greatest and most dangerous temptation for conservatives and Catholics. Thus, Weber may have missed something important in his conclusion that the Action Française had no viable ideology after all. See Weber, op. cit., 528–34.

47 Béla Menczer, *Catholic Political Thought 1789–1848*, Westminster, Maryland, The Newman Press, 1952, 26–7.

48 Sutton, op. cit., 109; Arnal, op cit., 14–15, 18.

49 Sutton, op. cit., 81–9.

50 Jacques Prévotat, "Remarques sur la notion de civilisation catholique dans la revue 'L'Action Française' (July 1899–March 1908)," in J.-R. Derré *et al.* (eds), *Civilisation chrétienne. Approche historique d'une ideologie, xviiie–xxe siècle*, Paris, Editions Beauchesne, 1975, 360, 365.

51 Sutton, op. cit., 93–4.

52 Arnal, op. cit., 81–2; Weber, *Action Française* . . ., 126–30.

53 Washington DC, The Catholic University of America Press, 1967. Paul is of course not the only historian with liberal proclivities generously to overestimate the importance of liberal sentiment in the French Church and in Rome. One of the most respected historians of French Catholicism in the modern period, René Rémond, has consistently overvalued the importance of liberal Catholics and underestimated the strength of intransigent Catholicism. The pro-Vichy sentiment of the French hierarchy, one would think, should long since have made such generous exaggerations untenable. Even about the Vichyite hierarchy Rémond is far too indulgent. See his "Le Catholicisme français pendant la Seconde Guerre mondiale," *Revue d'histore de l'Eglise de France*, vol. LXIV, no. 173 (July–December 1978), 208.

54 Arnal, op. cit., 92ff.

55 ibid., 154ff., 168–9. *The Papal Encyclicals 1903–1939* (ed. Claudia Carlen), Wilmington, North Carolina, McGrath Publishing Co., 1981, 430, paragraph 94.

56 Arnal, op. cit., 93, 112–13.

57 Lebrun (ed.), *Histoire des Catholiques en France* . . ., 417–18.

58 Arnal, op. cit., 94–6; Cholvy and Hilaire, op. cit., II, 285–8.

59 Arnal, op. cit., 98–102, 117. See also Adrien Dansette, *Destin du catholicisme français, 1926–1956*, Paris, Flammarion, 1957, 106.

60 ibid., 122–44.

61 Weber, *The Action Française* . . ., 220ff.

62 Eugen Weber believes with many other historians that the condemnation of the Action Française freed the Church of France and its various organizations from the reactionary influence of the Maurrasians. It is true, as he writes, that "the future lay with the champions of social Catholicism of one kind or another." *The Action Française* . . ., 255. Yet it is hard to see how this was the clear result of the condemnation of the Action Française. More likely, it was the moral extrava-

gances of the Vichy regime, very much the logical conclusion of the long influence of integral nationalism, which finally forced enough Catholics, priests and laity, to turn in a new direction, with, it should be stressed, little support from their bishops, archbishops, or cardinals.

63 Cholvy and Hilaire, op. cit., II, 306–7; Arnal, op. cit., 151–3.

64 Cholvy and Hilaire, op. cit., II, 308–9; Edward R. Tannenbaum, *The Action Française. Die-hard Reactionaries in Twentieth-Century France*, New York, John Wiley & Sons, 1962, 174.

65 Paul, op. cit., 172.

66 Arnal, op. cit., 169–70. *The Papal Encyclicals . . .*, 551–2, paragraphs 72–4.

67 Lebrun (ed.), *Histoire des Catholiques en France . . .*, 414, 420–1, 426, 460.

68 André Deroo, *L'Episcopat français dans la mêlée de son temps, 1930–1954*, Paris, Bonne Presse, 1955, 40–65. René Rémond, *Les Catholiques dans la France des années 30*, Paris, Editions Cana, 1979, 17–38. Adrien Dansette, op. cit., 115–16.

69 Emmanuel Mounier, *Oeuvres*, Paris, Editions du Seuil, 1961, IV, 24. The great Protestant theologian, Karl Barth, made much the same point about the susceptibility of Christians to authoritarian movements. See his *Against the Stream*, New York, Philosophical Library, 1954, 115, 127–46.

70 H. Stuart Hughes. *The Obstructed Path. French Social Thought in the Years of Desperation 1930–60*, New York, Harper & Row, 1966, 97. John Hellman, *Emmanuel Mounier and the New Catholic Left 1930–1950*, Toronto, University of Toronto Press, 1981, 258.

71 Dansette, op. cit., 123.

72 R. William Rauch, Jr, *Politics and Belief in Contemporary France, Emmanuel Mounier and Christian Democracy, 1932–1950*, The Hague, Martinus Nijhoff, 1972, 136.

73 ibid., 100–1.

74 Joseph Amato, *Mounier and Maritain: A French Catholic Understanding of the Modern World*, University, Alabama, The University of Alabama Press, 1975, 100, 123–4.

75 Rauch, op. cit., 120.

76 Emmanuel Mounier, "Confession pour nous autres chrétiens," *Esprit*, vol. I, no. 6 (March 1933), 893–6.

77 ibid., 880–1.

78 Hellman, op. cit., 182–4, 207ff. For a critical discussion of Mounier's relation to the Vichy regime and its National Revolution, see Zeev Sternhell, *Ni droite ni gauche. L'idéologie fasciste en France*, Paris, Editions du Seuil, 1983, 299–310.

79 Richard L. Rubenstein, *After Auschwitz. Radical Theology and Contemporary Judaism*, Indianapolis, Indiana, Bobbs-Merrill, 1966, especially 46–58.

80 Henri Amouroux, *La Grande histoire des Français sous l'occupation*, vol. II: *Quarante millions de pétainistes*, Paris, Robert Laffont, 1977, 276–8. In his study of Clermont-Ferrand during the Vichy period, John F. Sweets notes that a street formerly named for Emile Combes, the

architect of the Separation of Church and State, was renamed to commemorate a more acceptable personage. Thus Vichy politicians knew how cheaply they could purchase clerical support. *Choices in Vichy France. The French Under Nazi Occupation*, New York, Oxford University Press, 1986, 30–1.

81 Amouroux, *Quarante millions de pétainistes*, 282–306.

82 Georges Montaron, *Quoi qu'il en coûte*, Paris, Stock, 1975, 53.

83 René Rémond, "Le Catholicisme français pendant la Seconde Guerre mondiale," 208.

84 Michael R. Marrus and Robert O. Paxton, *Vichy France and the Jews*, New York, Basic Books, 1981.

85 Jacques Maritain, "Religion and Politics in France," *Foreign Affairs*, vol. XX, no. 2 (January 1942), 277.

86 Marrus and Paxton, op. cit., 210.

87 ibid., 203–7.

88 Henri Amouroux, op. cit., vol. V: *Les Passions et les haines*, Paris, Editions Robert Laffont, 1981, 314–16. Marrus and Paxton, op. cit., 52.

89 Maurras' ideals had so deeply penetrated all rightist thought that by the time of the Vichy regime one could be fully influenced by them without any direct association with the Action Française. Weber, *Action Française* . . ., 201, 443.

90 Amouroux, *Les Passions et les haines*, 324–39; Marrus and Paxton, op. cit., 203, 271–8. Cardinal Liénart's silence on the deportations and on some other important questions earned him enough suspicion to lead some Catholic Resisters after the Liberation to seek to have him deposed, along with Cardinals Suhard and Gerlier. This attempt failed. Peter Hebblethwaite, *Pope John XXIII. Shepherd of the Modern World*, Garden City, New York, Doubleday, 1985, 211.

91 Aline Coutrot, in René Rémond (ed.), *Forces religieuses* . . ., 139.

92 Pierrard, *Juifs et catholiques français*, 291

93 Hannah Arendt, *The Origins of Totalitarianism*, New York, Meridian Books, 1958, 93.

94 According to Jacques Duquesne, "Hearts responded better than minds." *Les Catholiques français sous l'occupation*, Paris, Grasset, 1966, 267.

95 Amouroux, *Les Passions et les haines*, 130–6, 340–1.

96 Duquesne, op. cit., 57, 356–64. Rauch, op. cit., 233. Perhaps only a mind influenced by the ideology of the Action Française could conceive of such a cruel revenge.

97 Rauch, ibid., 235.

98 Arnal, op. cit., 180.

99 *Dynamics of Counterrevolution in Europe, 1870–1956. An Analytic Framework*, New York, Harper & Row, 1971, 49.

100 Ferdinand Fabre, *L'Abbé Tigrane. Candidat à la papauté*, Paris, Bibliothèque Charpentier, 1891, 245.

V THE CHURCH IN CONTEMPORARY FRANCE

1 See Henri Michel, *Les Courants de pensée de la Résistance*, Paris, Presses Universitaires de France, 1962, 766–75.

2 Georges Suffert, *Les Catholiques et la gauche*, Paris, Maspero, 1960, 10–12.

3 Paul Clay Sorum, *Intellectuals and Decolonization in France*, Chapel Hill, North Carolina, University of North Carolina Press, 1977, 23, 52. Françoise Kempf, "Les Catholiques français," in Marcel Merle (ed.), *Les Eglises chrétiennes et la décolonisation*, Paris, Armand Colin, 1967, 155.

4 See Irwin M. Wall, *French Communism in the Era of Stalin. The Quest for Unity and Integration, 1945–1962*, Westport, Connecticut, Greenwood Press, 1983, 188–98; and Tony Smith, *The French Stake in Algeria, 1945–1962*, Ithaca, New York, Cornell University Press, 1978, 76–7.

5 François Mauriac, *L'Imitation des bourreaux de Jésus Christ*, and *Présentation des bloc-notes sur la torture* (eds Jean Lacouture and Alain de La Morandais), Paris, Desclée de Brouwer, 1984, 58–9, and *passim*. Kempf, op. cit., 166. See also Jean Lacouture, *François Mauriac*, Paris, Editions du Seuil, 1980, 446–92.

6 Mauriac, op. cit., 51ff.

7 ibid., 88

8 Pierre Houart, *L'Attitude de l'Eglise dans la guerre d'Algérie, 1954–1960*, Brussels, Le Livre Africain, 1960, 20–1, 29–37. Kempf, op. cit., 173. Georges Bidault, *Resistance, the Political Autobiography of Georges Bidault*, New York, Praeger, 1965, 251–61.

9 Gérard Cholvy, Yves-Marie Hilaire, *et al.*, *Histoire religieuse de la France contemporaine*, vol. III, *1930–1988*, Toulouse, Privat, 1988, 243–4.

10 Mauriac, op. cit., 87, 104–5.

11 Sorum, op. cit., 116, and *passim*.

12 Suffert, op. cit., 12.

13 Emile Poulat, *Le Catholicisme sous observation, du modernisme à aujourd'hui. Entretiens avec Guy Lafon*, Paris, Le Centurion, 1983, 114–15.

14 Emile Poulat, *Naissance des prêtres-ouvriers*, Tournai, Casterman, 1965, 185, 207–8.

15 ibid., 234–6.

16 John Petrie (ed.), *The Worker-Priests. A Collective Documentation*, London, Routledge and Kegan Paul, 1956, 99–108. Pierre Pierrard, *Le Prêtre français*, Paris, Bloud & Gay, 1969, 170–1. Poulat, *Naissance* . . ., 407–8.

17 Poulat, *Naissance* . . ., 408–9, 494ff, 523.

18 Cholvy and Hilaire, op. cit., III, 233. Suffert, op. cit., 64–5. Poulat, op. cit., 501–10. The "Green Paper" drawn up by worker-priests for Cardinal Feltin in October 1953, in response to the Papal Nuncio's action against the Mission de France, certainly demonstrated that a number of worker-priests had become convinced that as long as the Church supported capitalism and a bourgeois social order, they had no choice but to cooperate with the communists. This in turn made Vatican officials even more certain that the separation between clergy

and laity was a necessary one, that the priest must remain a man "set apart." Petrie (ed.), *The Worker-Priests . . .*, 147–70.

19 Adrien Dansette, *Destin du catholicisme français 1926–1956*, Paris, Flammarion, 1957, 299–300.

20 Jacques Duquesne, *Les Prêtres*, Paris, Grasset, 1965, 232.

21 See above in Chapter IV, pp. 123–34.

22 Paul-Marie de la Gorce, *L'Après-Guerre, 1944–52*, Paris, Bernard Grasset, 1978, 32–3, 444ff. Roger Mehl, *Le Catholicisme français dans la société actuelle*, Paris, Le Centurion, 1977, 156. François Mauriac wrote concerning MRP colonial policy: "The failure of Christian Democracy has equalled the failure of integral nationalism." See Jean-Marie Domenach and Robert de Montvalon, *The Catholic Avant-Garde. French Catholicism Since World War II*, New York, Holt, Rinehart, and Winston, 1967, 188. See also William Bosworth, *Catholicism and Crisis in Modern France. French Catholic Groups at the Threshold of the Fifth Republic*, Princeton, New Jersey, Princeton University Press, 1962, 245–6.

23 André Mandouze in 1948, quoted in Jean-Marie Domenach and Robert de Montvalon, op. cit., 167.

24 ibid., 169–72. François Lebrun (ed.), *Histoire des Catholiques en France du xve siècle à nos jours*, Toulouse, Privat, 1980, 475–8. André Latreille, E. Delaruelle, J.-R. Palanque, *et al.*, *Histoire du catholicisme en France*, Paris, Editions Spés, 1962, III, 636–9. La Gorce, op. cit., 446ff. René Pucheu, in "Les Militants d'origine chrétienne," *Esprit*, no. 4–5 (April–May 1977), 41.

25 John Hellman, *Emmanuel Mounier and the New Catholic Left, 1930–1950*, Toronto, University of Toronto Press, 1981, 212, 252, 256–9. An important study of French university students in the early 1960s found that while religion had little to do with the differences between them, ideological or philosophical commitments were linked to religion. 43 per cent of Catholic students who identified with a school of thought named personalism, while only 9 per cent chose Marxism and 48 per cent existentialism. Of non-Catholic students, on the other hand, only 7 per cent named personalism, with 53 per cent claiming Marxism and 40 per cent existentialism as their major commitment. It would appear that personalism was among the students the Catholic "answer" to Marxism. Pierre Bourdieu and Jean-Claude Passeron, *The Inheritors. French Students and their Relation to Culture*, Chicago, University of Chicago Press, 1979, 9.

26 Hellman, op. cit., 207. Bosworth, op. cit., 234ff.

27 Hellman, op. cit., 236. R. William Rauch, Jr, *Politics and Belief in Contemporary France. Emmanuel Mounier and Christian Democracy, 1932–1950*, The Hague, Martinus Nijhoff, 1972, 255, 277–8.

28 Hellman, op. cit., 208–9, 243–4.

29 Rauch, op. cit., 256–70.

30 Hellman, op. cit., 228. Rauch, op. cit., 289ff.

31 Pucheu, op. cit., 25–6.

32 30 April 1957, cited in Cholvy, Hilaire *et al.*, op. cit., III, 255.

33 Mehl, op. cit., 113.

34 John Ardagh, *The New France. A Society in Transition 1945–1977*, London, Penguin Books, 3rd edn, 1977, 577.

35 Jacques Sommet, SJ, "Confrontations avec le marxisme," in Centre catholiques des intellectuels français, *Réflexion chrétienne et monde moderne 1945–1965*, n.s. no. 54, Paris, Desclée de Brouwer, 1966, 115. For a general discussion of Catholic–Marxist affinities and antagonisms, see Norman Ravitch, "Catholics and the Marxist Temptation," *The World & I*, vol. II, no. 9 (September 1987), 675–82. For Jean-Marie Domenach it is important to observe that Catholics and Marxists share the presence of a well-developed theoretical foundation for their social activism; for this reason those who, for example, volunteer to do social work in France are almost always either Catholics or Marxists. Ardagh, *The New France . . .*, 580.

36 Assemblée plénière de l'Episcopat français, Lourdes, 1972, 'Pour une Pratique chrétienne de la Politique," in Mgr Gabriel Matagrin, *Politique, Eglise et Foi*, Paris, Editions du Centurion, 1972, 88–9. It was in the ranks of the organizations of Catholic Action among workers and peasants, the JOC and the JAC, that the myths of Catholic social thought about class collaboration were first seen to be erroneous. It became clear that social and economic antagonisms were as strong among Catholic workers and peasants as among non-Catholics. Danièle Hervieu-Léger, *Vers un nouveau christianisme? Introduction à la sociologie du christianisme occidental*, Paris, Editions du Cerf, 1986, 316–17.

37 ibid., 90ff. Also cited in Mehl, op cit., 161.

38 "Le Marxisme, l'homme et la foi chrétienne," Déclaration du Conseil permanent de l'épiscopat, in *Cahiers de l'Actualité religieuse*, no. 146 (15 September 1977), 5–24. See also Arthur F. McGovern, SJ, *Marxism: An American Christian Perspective*, Maryknoll, New York, Orbis Books, 1980, 97–122.

39 Maurice Druon, in *Le Monde*, 7 August 1971, cited by Robert Solé, *Les Chrétiens en France*, Paris, Presses Universitaires de France, 1972, 32–3. See also Alain Woodrow, *L'Eglise déchirée*, Paris, Editions Ramsay, 1978, 56–8, 107.

40 Pierre de Boisdeffre, *La Foi des anciens jours . . . et celle des temps nouveaux*, Paris, Fayard, 1977, 153ff. Etienne Fouilloux, in "Les Militants d'origine chrétienne," *Esprit*, no. 4–5 (April–May 1977), 47.

41 Fouilloux, op. cit., 57.

42 Woodrow, op. cit., 154–9. Mehl, op. cit., 161.

43 Mehl, op. cit., 164–5.

44 Hervieu-Léger, op. cit., 320ff.

45 Jean-Marie Domenach, "Le Spirituel et le politique," *Esprit*, vol. XXXIX, no. 408 (November 1971), 781–2.

46 Hervieu-Léger, op. cit., 61.

47 See S. S. Acquaviva, *The Decline of the Sacred in Industrial Society*, Oxford, Basil Blackwell, 1979, 162–202.

48 F. Lebrun (ed.), *Histoire des catholiques en France . . .*, 488–9.

49 François A. Isambert, "Les Ouvriers et l'Eglise catholique," *Revue française de sociologie*, vol. XV, no. 4 (October–December 1974), 539.

Catholicism diffuses a moralistic ideology typical of the middle classes. It stresses social advancement and respectability which only attract workers who are already alienated from working-class culture, workers who have psychologically already entered the lower middle class. Jules Gritti and André Rousseau, *Trois enquêtes sur les catholiques*, Paris, Chalet, 1977, 125.

50 Jacques Capdevielle, *et al.*, *France de gauche, vote à droite*, Paris, Presses de la Fondation nationale des Sciences politiques, 1981, 157, 314.

51 Gérard Cholvy, *et al.*, op. cit., III, 324–6. Julien Potel, *Les Prêtres séculiers en France. Evolution de 1965 à 1975*, Paris, Le Centurion, 1977, 35, 49. Emmanuel Todd, *La Nouvelle France*, Paris, Editions du Seuil, 1988, 238.

52 Potel, op. cit., 69–70. Rousseau, op. cit., 499–502.

53 Jean-Marie Mayeur, *Catholicisme social et démocratie chrétienne. Principes romains, expériences françaises*, Paris, Editions du Cerf, 1986, 217–21.

54 Guy Michelat and Michel Simon, *Classe, religion et comportement politique*, Paris, Presses de la Fondation nationale des Sciences politiques, 1977, 366–406, 464.

55 Bernard Gouley, *Les Catholiques français aujourd'hui. Survol d'un peuple*, Paris, Fayard, 1977, 107–8. Mehl, op. cit., 168–73.

56 Woodrow, op. cit., 159.

57 Gouley, op. cit., 228. Michel de Certeau and Jean-Marie Domenach, *Le Christianisme éclaté*, Paris, Editions du Seuil, 1974, 10–11.

58 Gouley, op. cit., 226–7.

59 Brigitte Vassort-Rousset, *Les Evêques de France en politique*, Paris, Editions du Cerf, 1986, 124–9.

60 Solé, op. cit., 32. For a somewhat different division in a 1972 poll of possible clerical activities in the public sphere, but one which also disapproved of the clergy's involvement directly in politics, see Mehl, op. cit., 214–15. See also F. A. Isambert, "Les Indicateurs d'intégration et de marginalisation: catholicisme," in *Eglises et groupes religieux dans la société française. Intégration ou marginalisation*, Strasbourg, Cerdic-Publications, 1977, 82–4.

61 Jacques Sutter, *La Vie religieuse des Français à travers les sondages d'opinion (1944–1976)*, Paris, CNRS, 1984, II, 674, 947.

62 *France in the 1980's*, London, Penguin Books, 1982, 452.

63 Solé, op. cit., 35. The million-strong demonstration in April 1984, at Versailles against the Socialist government's attempt to nationalize the Catholic school system convinced the Left finally that anti-clericalism was anachronistic and could only play into the hands of the Right. Catholics, whether practicing or not, now constituted too powerful a clientele for the Left to offend.

64 Cholvy *et al.*, op. cit., III, 333–5. Rousseau, op. cit., 504. Isambert, "Les Indicateurs . . .," 78. Gouley, op. cit., 385–7. For more discussion of Mgr Lefebvre see Woodrow, op. cit., 69ff.; and Claude-François Jullien, "Voyage chez les intégristes français. L'Extrême-Droite de Dieu," *Le Nouvel Observateur*, no. 1,238 (29 July–4 August 1988), 24–30.

65 Yves Lambert, *Dieu change en Bretagne. La religion à Limerzel de 1900 à nos jours*, Paris, Editions du Cerf, 1985, 233. Isambert, "Les Indicateurs . . .," 76.
66 Rousseau, op. cit., 503–5.
67 Lambert, op. cit., 252–4.
68 Cholvy, *et al.*, III, 320–1.
69 Lambert, op. cit., 253–4.
70 Gouley, op. cit., 105–6. Sutter, op. cit., 709–10.
71 Olivier de Dinechin (ed.), *En marge, les chrétiens? Points de vue sur la marginalisation des catholiques en France*, Paris, Editions du Centurion, 1979, 57.
72 Hervieu-Léger, op. cit., 99–100, 319.
73 Gouley, op. cit., 97, 124. François-André Isambert, *Le Sens du sacré. Fête et religion populaire*, Paris, Editions de Minuit, 1982, 97–9.
74 Woodrow, op. cit., 188ff. Gouley, op. cit., 385–7.
75 Rousseau, op. cit., 505.
76 Cholvy, *et al.*, III, 306. François Houtart and André Rousseau, *The Church and Revolution*, Maryknoll, New York, Orbis Books, 1971, 286–95.
77 Houtart and Rousseau, ibid., 313.

AFTERWORD

1 Peter L. Berger, *The Sacred Canopy. Elements of a Sociological Theory of Religion*, Garden City, New York, Doubleday, 1967, 133–4.
2 Herbert Luethy, *France Against Herself*, New York, Praeger, 1955, 34–5.
3 Berger, op. cit., 133–4.
4 Adrien Dansette, *Destin du catholicisme français 1926–1956*, Paris, Flammarion, 1957, 76.
5 Alain Besançon, "Après le voyage du Pape," *L'Express*, 17 October 1986, 17.

Bibliography

Abercrombie, Nigel, *The Origins of Jansenism*, Oxford, Clarendon Press, 1936.

Acquaviva, S. S., *The Decline of the Sacred in Industrial Sociey*, Oxford, Basil Blackwell, 1979.

Adam, Antoine, *Du mysticisme à la révolte. Les Jansénistes du XVIIe siècle*, Paris, Fayard, 1968.

Allen, J. W., *A History of Political Thought in the Sixteenth Century*, London, Methuen, 1928.

Amato, Joseph, *Mounier and Maritain: A French Catholic Understanding of the Modern World*, University, Alabama, The University of Alabama Press, 1975.

Amouroux, Henri, *La grande histoire des Français sous l'occupation*, Paris, Robert Laffont, 1976–85, 7 volumes.

Ardagh, John, *The New France. A Society in Transition 1945–1977*, London, Penguin Books, 3rd edn, 1977.

Ardagh, John, *France in the 1980's*, London, Penguin Books, 1982.

Armogathe, J.-R., *Le Quiétisme*, Paris, Presses Universitaires de France, 1973.

Arnal, Oscar L., *Ambivalent Alliance. The Catholic Church and the Action Française, 1899–1939*, Pittsburgh, University of Pittsburgh Press, 1985.

Aubert, Roger (ed.), *Progress and Decline in the History of Church Renewal*, New York, Paulist Press, 1967.

Aubert, Roger (ed.), *Sacralization and Secularization*, New York, Paulist Press, 1969.

Barthélemy-Madaule, Madeleine, *Marc Sangnier 1873–1950*, Paris, Editions du Seuil, 1973.

Baumgartner, Frederic J., *Radical Reactionaries: the Political Thought of the French Catholic League*, Geneva, Librairie Droz, 1975.

Baumgartner, Frederic J., *Change and Continuity in the French Episcopate. The Bishops and the Wars of Religion 1547–1610*, Durham, North Carolina, Duke University Press, 1986.

Bédarida, François and Maitron, Jean (eds), *Christianisme et monde ouvrier*, Paris, Les Editions Ouvrières, 1975.

de la Bedoyere, Michael, *The Archbishop and the Lady. The Story of Fénelon and Madame Guyon*, London, Collins, 1956.

Berenson, Edward, *Populist Religion and Left-Wing Politics in France, 1830–1852*, Princeton, New Jersey, Princeton University Press, 1984.

Bien, David D., *The Calas Affair. Persecution, Toleration, and Heresy in Eighteenth-Century Toulouse*, Princeton, New Jersey, Princeton University Press, 1960.

Blet, Pierre, *Le Clergé de France et la monarchie*, Rome, Librairie Editrice de l'Université Grégorienne, 1959, 2 volumes.

Blet, Pierre, *Les Assemblées du clergé et Louis XIV, de 1670 à 1693*, Rome, Universita Gregoriana Editrice, 1972.

de Boisdeffre, Pierre, *La Foi des anciens jours . . . et celle des temps nouveaux*, Paris, Fayard, 1977.

Bossy, John, *Christianity in the West 1400–1700*, Oxford, Oxford University Press, 1985.

Bosworth, William, *Catholicism and Crisis in Modern France. French Catholic Groups at the Threshold of the Fifth Republic*, Princeton, New Jersey, Princeton University Press, 1962.

Bourdieu, Pierre and Passeron, Jean-Claude, *The Inheritors. French Students and their Relation to Culture*, Chicago, University of Chicago Press, 1979.

Bowman, Frank, *Le Christ romantique*, Geneva, Droz, 1973.

Bredin, Jean-Denis, *The Affair. The Case of Alfred Dreyfus*, New York, George Braziller, 1986.

Bressolette, Claude, *L'Abbé Maret*, Paris, Beauchesne, 1977.

Brockliss, L. W. B., *French Higher Education in the Seventeenth and Eighteenth Centuries: A Cultural History*, Oxford, Clarendon Press, 1987.

Broderick, SJ, James, *Robert Bellarmine. Saint and Scholar*, Westminster, Maryland, The Newman Press, 1961.

de Broglie, Abbé A.-T.-P., *Le Présent et l'avenir du catholicisme en France*, Paris, Librairie Plon, 1892.

Brown, Marvin Luther, *Louis Veuillot. French Ultramontane Catholic Journalist and Layman*, Durham, North Carolina, Moore Publishing Co., 1977.

Brugerette, J., *Le Prêtre français et la société contemporaine*, Paris, P. Lethielleux, 1933–8, 3 volumes.

Burns, Michael, *Rural Society and French Politics. Boulangism and the Dreyfus Affair 1886–1900*, Princeton, New Jersey, Princeton University Press, 1984.

Byrnes, Robert F., *Antisemitism in Modern France. The Prelude to the Dreyfus Affair*, New Brunswick, New Jersey, Rutgers University Press, 1950.

Cameron, J. M., "Nuclear Catholicism," *The New York Review of Books*, vol. XXX, no. 20 (22 December 1983), 38–42.

Capdevielle, Jacques *et al.*, *France de gauche, vote à droite*, Paris, Presses de la Fondation nationale des Sciences politiques, 1981.

Carcopino, Claude, *Les Doctrines sociales de Lamennais*, Geneva, Slatkine Reprints, 1968.

Caron, Jeanne, *Le Sillon et la démocratie chrétienne, 1894–1910*, Paris, Plon, 1967.

de Certeau, Michel and Domenach, Jean-Marie, *Le Christianisme éclaté*, Paris, Editions du Seuil, 1974.

Chadwick, Owen, *The Popes and European Revolution*, Oxford, Clarendon Press, 1981.

Cholvy, Gérard and Hilaire, Yves-Marie *et al.*, *Histoire religieuse de la France contemporaine*, Toulouse, Privat, 1985–8, 3 volumes.

Church, William F., *Constitutional Thought in Sixteenth-Century France. A Study in the Evolution of Ideas*, Cambridge, Harvard University Press, 1941.

Church, William F., *Richelieu and Reason of State*, Princeton, New Jersey, Princeton University Press, 1972.

Cognet, Louis, *Crépuscule des mystiques*, Tournai, Desclée, 1958.

Comte, Bernard, "Emmanuel Mounier devant Vichy et la Révolution nationale," *Revue d'histoire de l'Eglise de France*, vol. LXXI, no. 187 (July–December 1985), 253–79.

Correspondance générale de Félicité de Lamennais (ed. Louis Le Guillou), Paris, Armand Colin, 1971–81, 9 volumes.

Curtis, Michael, *Three Against the Third Republic, Sorel, Barrès, and Maurras*, Princeton, New Jersey, Princeton University Press, 1959.

Dakin, Douglas, *Turgot and the Ancien Regime in France*, London, Methuen, 1939.

Dansette, Adrien, *Histoire religieuse de la France contemporaine*, Paris, Flammarion, 1948–51, 2 volumes.

Dansette, Adrien, *Destin du catholicisme français 1926–1956*, Paris, Flammarion, 1957.

Delumeau, Jean, *Le Catholicisme entre Luther et Voltaire*, Paris, Presses Universitaires de France, 1971.

Delumeau, Jean, *Un Chemin d'histoire. Chrétienté et christianisation*, Paris, Fayard, 1981.

Derré, J. R. *et al.*, *Civilisation chrétienne. Approche historique d'une idéologie, xviiie–xxe siècle*, Paris, Editions Beauchesne, 1975.

Deroo, André, *L'Episcopat français dans la mêlée de son temps, 1930–1954*, Paris, Bonne Presse, 1955.

de Dinechin, Olivier (ed.), *En Marge, Les Chrétiens? Points de vue sur la marginalisation des catholiques en France*, Paris, Editions du Centurion, 1979.

Doering, Bernard E., *Jacques Maritain and the French Catholic Intellectuals*, Southbend, Indiana, University of Notre Dame Press, 1983.

Domenach, Jean-Marie, "Le Spirituel et le politique," *Esprit*, vol. XXXIX, no. 408 (November 1971), 781–92.

Domenach, Jean-Marie and de Montvalon, Robert, *The Catholic Avant-Garde. French Catholicism Since World War II*, New York, Holt, Rinehart, and Winston, 1967.

Dreyfus, François-Georges, *Des Evêques contre le pape*, Paris, Bernard Grasset, 1985.

Droulers, P., *Action pastorale et problèmes sociaux sous la monarchie de Juillet*, Paris, J. Vrin, 1954.

Duployé, OP, Pie, *La Religion de Péguy*, Paris, Klincksieck, 1965.

Duquesne, Jacques, *Les Prêtres*, Paris, Grasset, 1965.

Duquesne, Jacques, *Les Catholiques français sous l'occupation*, Paris, Grasset, 1966.

Duroselle, Jean-Baptiste, *Les Débuts du catholicisme social en France (1822–1870)*, Paris, Presses Universitaires de France, 1951.

Faguet, Emile, *L'Anticléricalisme*, Paris, Société Française d'Imprimerie et de Librairie, 1906.

Fanfani, Amintore, *Catholicism, Protestantism and Capitalism*, New York, Sheed and Ward, 1955.

Gabbert, M. A., "Bishop *avant tout*. Sibour's Betrayal of the Republic," *The Catholic Historical Review*, vol. LXIV (1978), 337–56.

Gargan, Edward T. (ed.), *Leo XIII and the Modern World*, New York, Sheed and Ward, 1961.

Gay, Francisque, *Les Démocrates d'inspiration chrétienne à l'épreuve du pouvoir*, Paris, Bloud & Gay, 1951.

Gay, Peter, *The Enlightenment. An Interpretation*, London, Weidenfeld and Nicolson, 1966–9, 2 volumes.

Giesey, Ralph E., *The Juristic Basis of Dynastic Right to the French Throne*, *Transactions of the American Philosophical Society*, ns, vol. LI, pt 5, 1961.

Golden, Richard M., *The Godly Rebellion. Parisian Curés and the Religious Fronde, 1652–1662*, Chapel Hill, North Carolina, University of North Carolina Press, 1981.

Goldmann, Lucien, *Le Dieu caché. Etudes sur la vision tragique dans les penseés de Pascal et dans le theâtre de Racine*, Paris, Gallimard, 1955.

Goldmann, Lucien, *The Philosophy of the Enlightenment. The Christian Burgess and the Enlightenment*, London, Routledge and Kegan Paul, 1973.

de la Gorce, Paul-Marie, *L'Après-Guerre, 1944–1952*, Paris, Bernard Grasset, 1978.

Gough, Austin, *Paris and Rome. The Gallican Church and the Ultramontane Campaign 1848–1853*, Oxford, Clarendon Press, 1986.

Gouley, Bernard, *Les Catholiques français aujourd'hui. Survol d'un peuple*, Paris, Fayard, 1977.

Goyau, G., *Histoire religieuse de la France*, Paris, Librairie Plon, 1922.

de Gramont, Sanche, *Epitaph for Kings*, New York, G. P. Putnam's Sons, 1967.

Griffiths, Richard, *The Reactionary Revolution. The Catholic Revival in French Literature 1870–1914*, New York, Frederick Ungar, 1965.

Grimsley, Ronald, *Rousseau and the Religious Quest*, Oxford, Clarendon Press, 1968.

Gritti, Jules and Rousseau, André, *Trois enquêtes sur les catholiques*, Paris, Chalet, 1977.

Groethuysen, Bernard, *The Bourgeois. Catholicism vs. Capitalism in Eighteenth-Century France*, London, Barrie & Rockliff, 1968.

Hales, E. E. Y., *Revolution and Papacy 1769–1846*, London, Eyre & Spottiswoode, 1960.

Hellman, John, *Emmanuel Mounier and the New Catholic Left 1930–1950*, Toronto, University of Toronto Press, 1981.

Hervieu-Léger, Danièle, *Vers un nouveau christianisme? Introduction à la sociologie du christianisme occidental*, Paris, Editions du Cerf, 1986.

Hoffman, Philip T., *Church and Community in the Diocese of Lyon 1500–1789*, New Haven, Connecticut, Yale University Press, 1984.

Houart, Pierre, *L'Attitude de l'Eglise dans la guerre d'Algérie, 1954–1960*, Brussels, Le Livre Africain, 1960.

Houtart, François and Rousseau, André, *The Church and Revolution*, Maryknoll, New York, Orbis Books, 1971.

Hufton, Olwen, "The Reconstruction of a Church, 1796–1801," in G. Lewis and C. Lucas (eds), *Beyond the Terror. Essays in French Regional and Social History, 1794–1815*, Cambridge, Cambridge University Press, 1983.

Hughes, H. Stuart, *The Obstructed Path. French Social Thought in the Years of Desperation 1930–1960*, New York, Harper & Row, 1966.

Hutt, M. G., "The Curés and the Third Estate: the Ideas of Reform in the Pamphlets of the French Lower Clergy in the Period 1787–1789," *The Journal of Ecclesiastical History*, vol. VIII, no. 1 (April 1957), 74–92.

Hyman, Paula, *From Dreyfus to Vichy. The Remaking of French Jewry 1906–1939*, New York, Columbia University Press, 1979.

Irving, R. E. M., *Christian Democracy in France*, London, George Allen & Unwin, 1973.

Isambert, François-André, *Christianisme et classe ouvrière*, Tournai, Casterman, 1961.

Isambert, François-André, "Les Ouvriers et l'Eglise catholique," *Revue française de sociologie*, vol. XV, no. 4 (October–December 1974), 529–51.

Isambert, François-André, "Les Indicateurs d'intégration et de marginalisation: catholicisme," in *Eglises et groupes religieux dans la société française. Intégration ou marginalisation*, Strasbourg, Cerdic-Publications, 1977.

Isambert, François-André, *Le Sens du sacré. Fête et religion populaire*, Paris, Editions du Minuit, 1982.

Jansen, P., *Arnaud d'Andilly, Défenseur de Port-Royal (1654–1659). Sa correspondance inédite avec la cour conservée dans les archives du Ministère des Affaires Etrangères*, Paris, J. Vrin, 1973.

Jedin, H. and Dolan, J. (eds), *History of the Church*, New York, Crossroads, 1981.

Jullien, Claude-François, "Voyage chez les intégristes français. L'Extrême Droite de Dieu," *Le Nouvel Observateur*, no. 1,238 (29 July–4 August 1988), 24–30.

Kamen, Henry, *The Rise of Toleration*, New York, World University Library, 1967.

Kates, Gary, *The Cercle Social, the Girondins, and the French Revolution*, Princeton, New Jersey, Princeton University Press, 1985.

Kedward, H. R., *The Dreyfus Affair*, London, Longmans, 1965.

Knox, Ronald, *Enthusiasm. A Chapter in the History of Religion*, New York, Galaxy, 1961.

Kolakowski, Leszek, *Chrétiens sans Eglise. La conscience religieuse au XVIIe siècle*, Paris, Gallimard, 1969.

Kreiser, B. Robert, *Miracles, Convulsions, and Ecclesiastical Politics in Early Eighteenth-Century Paris*, Princeton, New Jersey, Princeton University Press, 1978.

Kselman, Thomas A., *Miracles and Prophecies in Nineteenth-Century France*, New Brunswick, New Jersey, Rutgers University Press, 1983.

Kurtz, L. R., *The Politics of Heresy. The Modernist Crisis in Roman Catholicism*, Berkeley, California, University of California Press, 1986.

Labrousse, Elisabeth, *"Une Foi, une loi, un roi?" Essai sur la révocation de l'Edit de Nantes*, Geneva, Labor et Fides, 1985.

Lacouture, Jean, *François Mauriac*, Paris, Editions du Seuil, 1980.

Lambert, Yves, *Dieu change en Bretagne. La religion à Limerzel de 1900 à nos jours*, Paris, Editions du Cerf, 1985.

Lamennais, Félicité, *Affaires de Rome*, Paris, Cailleux, 1836–7.

Larkin, Maurice, *Church and State after the Dreyfus Affair. The Separation Issue in France*, London, Macmillan, 1974.

Latreille, André, *L'Eglise catholique et la Révolution française*, Paris, Hachette, 1946–50, 2 volumes.

Latreille, André, *De Gaulle, la Libération et l'Eglise catholique*, Paris, Editions du Cerf, 1978.

Latreille, A., Delaruelle, E., Palanque, J.-R., and Rémond, R., *Histoire du catholicisme en France*, Paris, Editions Spés, 1957–62, 3 volumes.

Lebrun, François, (ed.), *Histoire des catholiques en France du XVème siècle à nos jours*, Paris, Privat, 1980.

Lebrun, Jean, *Lamennais ou l'inquiétude de la liberté*, Paris, Fayard-Mame, 1981.

Lecler, Joseph, "Le Roi de France 'Fils ainé de l'Eglise,'" *Etudes*, vol. CCXIV (5 and 20 January 1933), 21–36, 170–89.

Lecler, Joseph, *Histoire de la tolérance au siècle de la Réforme*, Paris, Aubier, 1955, 2 volumes.

Le Guillou, Louis, *L'Evolution de la pensée religieuse de Félicité Lamennais*, Paris, Armand Colin, 1966.

"Le Marxisme, l'homme et la foi chrétienne," Déclaration du Conseil permanent de l'épiscopat, in *Cahiers de l'actualité religieuse*, no. 146 (15 September 1977), 5–24.

Léonard, Emile, *Histoire générale du protestantisme*, Paris, Presses Universitaires de France, 1961–4, 3 volumes.

Leroy, Maxime, *Histoire des idées sociales en France*, Paris, Gallimard, 1946–54, 3 volumes.

"Les Militants d'origine chrétienne," *Esprit*, no. 4–5 (April–May 1977), whole issue.

McGovern, SJ, Arthur F., *Marxism: An American Christian Perspective*, Maryknoll, New York, Orbis Books, 1980.

McManners, John, *The French Revolution and the Church*, New York, Harper & Row, 1969.

McManners, John, *Death and the Enlightenment*, Oxford, Oxford University Press, 1981.

Mandrou, R. *et al.*, (eds), *Histoire des protestants en France*, Paris, Privat, 1977.

Maritain, Jacques, "Religion and Politics in France," *Foreign Affairs*, vol. XX, no. 2 (January 1942), 266–81.

Marrus, Michael R. and Paxton, Robert O., *Vichy France and the Jews*, New York, Basic Books, 1981.

Martimort, Aimé-Georges, *Le Gallicanisme de Bossuet*, Paris, Editions du Cerf, 1953.

Martin, Victor, *Le Gallicanisme et la réforme catholique*, Geneva, Slatkine Reprints, 1975.

Matagrin, Mgr Gabriel, *Politique, Eglise et foi*, Paris, Editions du Centurion, 1972.

Mathiez, Albert, *La Théophilanthropie et le culte décadaire*, Paris, Félix Alcan, 1903.

Mauriac, François, *L'Imitation des bourreaux de Jésus Christ* and *Présentation des bloc-notes sur la torture* (eds Jean Lacouture and Alain de La Morandais), Paris, Desclée de Brouwer, 1984.

Mauzi, Robert, *L'Idée du bonheur dans la littérature et la pensée françaises au XVIIIe siècle*, Paris, Armand Colin, 1969.

May, Anita Rasi, "Is 'Les Deux France' a Valid Framework for Interpreting the Nineteenth-Century Church? The French Episcopate as a Case Study," *The Catholic Historical Review*, vol. LXXIII, no. 4 (October 1987), 541–61.

Mayeur, Jean-Marie, "Les Congrès Nationaux de la 'Démocratie chrétienne' à Lyon (1896–1897–1898)," *Revue d'histoire moderne et contemporaine*, vol. IX (July–September 1962), 171–206.

Mayeur, Jean-Marie, *La Séparation de l'Eglise et de l'Etat*, Paris, Julliard, 1966.

Mayeur, Jean-Marie, *L'Abbé Lemire, 1853–1928. Un Prêtre démocrate*, Tournai, Casterman, 1968.

Mayeur, Jean-Marie, *Catholicisme social et démocratie chrétienne. Principes romains, expériences françaises*, Paris, Editions du Cerf, 1986.

Mehl, Roger, *Le Catholicisme français dans la société actuelle*, Paris, Le Centurion, 1977.

Mellor, Alec, *Histoire de l'anticléricalisme français*, Tours, Mame, 1966.

Menczer, Béla, *Catholic Political Thought 1789–1848*, Westminster, Maryland, The Newman Press, 1952.

Merle, Marcel (ed.), *Les Eglisès chrétiennes et la décolonisation*, Paris, Armand Colin, 1967.

Merrick, Jeffrey, "Conscience and Citizenship in Eighteenth-Century France," *Eighteenth-Century Studies*, vol. XXI, no. 1 (Fall 1987), 48–70.

Merrick, Jeffrey, *The Desacralization of the French Monarchy in the Eighteenth Century*, Baton Rouge, Louisiana, Louisiana State University Press, 1990.

Michel, Henri, *Les Courants de pensée de la Résistance*, Paris, Presses Universitaires de France, 1962.

Michelat, Guy and Simon, Michel, *Classe, religion et comportement politique*, Paris, Presses de la Fondation nationale des Sciences politiques, 1977.

Minier, Marc, *L'Episcopat français du Ralliement à Vatican II*, Padua, CEDAM, 1982.

Mitchell, Allan, *Victors and Vanquished. The German Influence on Army and Church in France after 1870*, Chapel Hill, North Carolina, University of North Carolina Press, 1984.

Molnar, Thomas, *Bernanos. His Political Thought and Prophecy*, New York, Sheed & Ward, 1960.

de Montalembert, Charles, *Les Intérêts catholiques au XIXe siècle*, Paris, Jacques Lecoffre, 1852.

Montaron, Georges, *Quoi qu'il en coûte*, Paris, Stock, 1975.

Montuclard, Maurice, *Conscience religieuse et démocratie. La deuxième démocratie chrétienne en France, 1891–1902*, Paris, Editions du Seuil, 1965.

Moody, Joseph N., *The Church as Enemy. Anticlericalism in Nineteenth Century French Literature*, Washington, Corpus Books, 1968.

Moody, Joseph N., *French Education Since Napoleon*, Syracuse, New York, Syracuse University Press, 1978.

Moon, Parker T., *The Labor Problem and the Social Catholic Movement in France*, New York, Macmillan, 1921.

Mornet, Daniel, *Les Origines intellectuelles de la Révolution française*, Paris, Armand Colin, 6th edn, 1967.

Mounier, Emmanuel, "Confession pour nous autres chrétiens," *Esprit*, vol. I, no. 6 (March 1933), 873–96.

Mounier, Emmanuel, *Oeuvres*, Paris, Editions du Seuil, 1961, 4 volumes.

Mousnier, Roland, *The Assassination of Henry IV. The Tyrannicide Problem and the Consolidation of the French Absolute Monarchy in the Early Seventeenth Century*, New York, Scribner's, 1973.

Mousnier, Roland, *Les Institutions de France sous la monarchie absolue, 1598–1789*, Paris, Presses Universitaires de France, 1974–80, 2 volumes.

Murray, SJ, John Courtney, "St. Robert Bellarmine on the Indirect Power," *Theological Studies*, vol. IX, no. 4 (December 1948), 491–535.

Necheles, Ruth F., "The Curés in the Estates General of 1789," *The Journal of Modern History*, vol. XLVI, no. 3 (September 1974), 425–44.

Nolte, Ernst, *Three Faces of Fascism*, New York, Holt, Rinehart, and Winston, 1966.

Oeuvres complètes de F. de la Mennais, Brussels, Société Belge de Librairie, 1839, 2 volumes.

Oeuvres de Turgot (ed. Gustave Schelle), Paris, Librairie Félix Alcan, 1913–23, 5 volumes.

Orcibal, Jean, *Jean Duvergier de Hauranne, Abbé de Saint-Cyran et son temps (1581–1638)*, Paris, J. Vrin, 1947.

Orcibal, Jean, *Louis XIV et les protestants*, Paris, J. Vrin, 1951.

Orcibal, Jean, "Louis XIV and the Edict of Nantes," in R. Hatton (ed.), *Louis XIV and Absolutism*, London, Macmillan, 1976.

Palmer, Robert R., *Catholics and Unbelievers in Eighteenth-Century France*, Princeton, New Jersey, Princeton University Press, 1939.

The Papal Encyclicals 1903–1939 (ed. Claudia Carlen), Wilmington, North Carolina, McGrath Publishing Co., 1981.

Paul, Harry W., *The Second Ralliement. The Rapprochement between Church and State in France in the Twentieth Century*, Washington, DC, The Catholic University of America Press, 1967.

Pernoud, Régine, *Histoire de la bourgeoisie en France*, vol. II: *Les Temps Modernes*, Paris, Editions du Seuil, 1962.

Pickles, Dorothy, *Algeria and France. From Colonialism to Cooperation*, New York, Frederick A. Praeger, 1963.

Pierrard, Pierre, *Le Prêtre français*, Paris, Bloud & Gay, 1969.

Pierrard, Pierre, *Juifs et catholiques français*, Paris, Fayard, 1970.

Pierrard, Pierre, *L'Eglise et les ouvriers en France (1840–1940)*, Paris, Hachette, 1984.

Pilastre, E., *La Religion au temps du duc de Saint-Simon, d'après ses écrits*, Paris, Félix Alcan, 1909.

Plongeron, Bernard, *Conscience religieuse en révolution. Regards sur l'historiographie de la Révolution française*, Paris, A. & J. Picard, 1969.

Plongeron, Bernard, "Recherches sur 'l'Aufklärung' catholique en Europe occidentale (1770–1830)," *Revue d'histoire moderne et contemporaine*, vol. XVI (October–December 1969), 555–605.

Plongeron, Bernard, *Théologie et politique au siècle des lumières (1770–1820)*, Geneva, Droz, 1973.

Plongeron, Bernard, "Permanence d'une idéologie de 'civilisation chrétienne' dans le clergé constitutionnel," *Studies in Eighteenth-Century Culture*, vol. VII (1978), 263–87.

Poland, Burdette C., *French Protestantism and the French Revolution. A Study in Church and State, Thought and Religion, 1685–1815*, Princeton, New Jersey, Princeton University Press, 1957.

Pomeau, René, *La Religion de Voltaire*, Paris, Librairie Nizet, new edn, 1969.

Potel, Julien, *Les Prêtres séculiers en France, evolution de 1965 à 1975*, Paris, Le Centurion, 1977.

Poulat, Emile, *Naissance des prêtres-ouvriers*, Tournai, Casterman, 1965.

Poulat, Emile, *Eglise contre bourgeoisie. Introduction au devenir du catholicisme actuel*, Tournai, Casterman, 1977.

Poulat, Emile, *Une Eglise ébranlée. Changement, conflit et continuité de Pie XII à Jean-Paul II*, Tournai, Casterman, 1980.

Poulat, Emile, *Modernistica*, Paris, Nouvelles Editions Latines, 1982.

Poulat, Emile, *Le Catholicisme sous observation, du modernisme à aujourd'hui. Entretiens avec Guy Lafon*, Paris, Le Centurion, 1983.

Prévotat, Jacques, "L'Antisémitisme de l'Action Française: quelques repères," in V. Nikiprowetzky (ed.), *De l'Anti-judaïsme antique à l'antisémitisme contemporain*, Lille, Presses Universitaires de Lille, 1979, 247–75.

Quéniart, Jean, *Les Hommes, l'Eglise et Dieu dans la France du XVIIIe siècle*, Paris, Hachette, 1978.

Rauch, Jr, R. William, *Politics and Belief in Contemporary France. Emmanuel Mounier and Christian Democracy, 1932–1950*, The Hague, Martinus Nijhoff, 1972.

Ravitch, Norman, *Sword and Mitre. Government and Episcopate in France and England in the Age of Aristocracy*, The Hague, Mouton, 1966.

Ravitch, Norman, "Liberalism, Catholicism, and the Abbé Grégoire," *Church History*, vol. XXXVI (December 1967), 419–39.

Ravitch, Norman, "The Abbé Fauchet: Romantic Religion During the French Revolution," *Journal of the American Academy of Religion*, vol. XLII, no. 2 (June, 1974), 247–62.

Ravitch, Norman, "Catholicism in Crisis: the Impact of the French Revolution on the Thought of the Abbé Adrien Lamourette," *Cahiers internationaux d'histoire économique et sociale*, vol. IX (1978), 354–85.

Ravitch, Norman, "Catholics and the Marxist Temptation," *The World & I*, vol. II, no. 9 (September 1987), 675–82.

Reardon, Bernard, *Liberalism and Tradition. Aspects of Catholic Thought in Nineteenth-Century France*, Cambridge, Cambridge University Press, 1975.

Reardon, Bernard, *Religion in the Age of Romanticism. Studies in Early Nineteenth-Century Thought*, Cambridge, Cambridge University Press, 1985.

Rémond, René (ed.), *Forces religieuses et attitudes politiques dans la France contemporaine*, Paris, Armand Colin, 1965.

Rémond, René, *L'Anti-cléricalisme en France de 1815 à nos jours*, Paris, Fayard, 1976.

Rémond, René, "Le Catholicisme français pendant la Seconde Guerre mondiale," *Revue d'histoire de l'Eglise de France*, vol. LXIV, no. 173 (July–December 1978), 203–13.

Rémond, René, *Les Catholiques dans la France des années 30*, Paris, Editions Cana, 1979.

Rémond, René and Poulat, Emile (eds), *Emmanuel d'Alzon dans la société et l'Eglise du XIXe siècle*, Paris, Le Centurion, 1982.

Richard, Michel, *La Vie quotidienne des protestants sous l'ancien régime*, Paris, Hachette, 1966.

Rothkrug, Lionel, *Opposition to Louis XIV. The Political and Social Origins of the French Enlightenment*, Princeton, New Jersey, Princeton University Press, 1965.

Rothkrug, Lionel, "Religious Practices and Collective Perceptions. Hidden Homologies in the Renaissance and Reformation," *Historical Reflections/Réflexions historiques*, vol. VII, no. 1 (spring 1980), whole issue.

Rousseau. Religious Writings (ed. Ronald Grimsley), Oxford, Clarendon Press, 1970.

Sage, Pierre, *Le 'bon prêtre' dans la littérature française*, Geneva, Droz, 1951.

Sainte-Beuve, Charles Augustin, *Port-Royal*, Paris, Gallimard, 1952–5, 3 volumes.

Salmon, J. H. M., *Society in Crisis. France in the Sixteenth Century*, London, Ernest Benn, 1975.

Sedgwick, Alexander, *The Ralliement in French Politics 1890–1898*, Cambridge, Massachusetts, Harvard University Press, 1965.

Sedgwick, Alexander, *Jansenism in Seventeenth-Century France. Voices from the Wilderness*, Charlottesville, Virginia, University Press of Virginia, 1977.

Serant, Paul, *Les Dissidents de l'Action Française*, Paris, Copernic, 1978.

de Seysell, Claude, *The Monarchy of France* (ed. Donald R. Kelley), New Haven, Connecticut, Yale University Press, 1981.

Simon, Yves R., *The Road to Vichy 1918–1938*, New York, Sheed & Ward, 1942.

Solé, Robert, *Les Chrétiens en France*, Paris, Presses Universitaires de France, 1972.

Sommet, SJ, Jacques, "Confrontations avec le marxisme," *Réflexion chrétienne et monde moderne 1945–1965*, Paris, Desclée de Brouwer, 1966, 103–20.

Sorum, Paul Clay, *Intellectuals and Decolonization in France*, Chapel Hill, North Carolina, University of North Carolina Press, 1977.

Spencer, Philip, *Politics of Belief in Nineteenth-Century France. Lacordaire, Michon, Veuillot*, London, Faber and Faber, 1954.

Stankiewicz, W. J., *Politics and Religion in Seventeenth-Century France*, Berkeley, California, University of California Press, 1960.

Stearns, Peter N., *Priest and Revolutionary. Lamennais and the Dilemma of French Catholicism*, New York, Harper & Row, 1967.

Sternhell, Zeev, *La Droite révolutionnaire 1885–1914. Les origines françaises du fascisme*, Paris, Editions du Seuil, 1978.

Sternhell, Zeev, *Ni droite ni gauche. L'idéologie fasciste en France*, Paris, Editions du Seuil, 1983.

Suffert, Georges, *Les Catholiques et la gauche*, Paris, Maspero, 1960.

Sutter, Jacques, *La Vie religieuse des Français à travers les sondages d'opinion (1944–1976)*, Paris, CNRS, 1984, 2 volumes.

Sutton, Michael, *Nationalism, Positivism and Catholicism. The Politics of Charles Maurras and French Catholics, 1890–1914*, Cambridge, Cambridge University Press, 1982.

Sweets, John F., *Choices in Vichy France. The French Under Nazi Occupation*, New York, Oxford University Press, 1986.

Tackett, Timothy, *Religion, Revolution, and Regional Culture in Eighteenth-Century France. The Ecclesiastical Oath of 1791*, Princeton, New Jersey, Princeton University Press, 1986.

Tannenbaum, Edward R., *The Action Française. Die-hard Reactionaries in Twentieth-Century France*, New York, John Wiley & Sons, 1962.

Taveneaux, René, *Jansénisme et politique*, Paris, Armand Colin, 1965.

Thibault, Pierre, *Savoir et pouvoir. Philosophie thomiste et politique cléricale au XIXe siècle*, Québec, Les Presses de L'Université de Laval, 1972.

Todd, Emmanuel, *La Nouvelle France*, Paris, Editions du Seuil, 1988.

Troeltsch, Ernst, *The Social Teachings of the Christian Churches*, London, George Allen and Unwin, 1931, 2 volumes

Van Kley, Dale, *The Jansenists and the Expulsion of the Jesuits from France, 1757–1765*, New Haven, Connecticut, Yale University Press, 1975.

Van Kley, Dale, "Church and State, and the Ideological Origins of the French Revolution: the Debate over the General Assembly of the Gallican Clergy in 1765," *The Journal of Modern History*, vol. LI, no. 4 (December 1979), 629–66.

Van Kley, Dale, *The Damiens Affair and the Unraveling of the Ancien Regime, 1750–1770*, Princeton, New Jersey, Princeton University Press, 1984.

Vassort-Rousset, Brigitte, *Les Evêques de France en politique*, Paris, Editions du Cerf, 1986.

Vaussard, Maurice, *Histoire de la démocratie chrétienne*, Paris, Editions du Seuil, 1956.

Vidler, Alec R., *Prophecy and Papacy. A Study of Lamennais, the Church, and the Revolution*, New York, Charles Scribner's Sons, 1954.

Voltaire, *Le Siècle de Louis XIV*, in *Oeuvres historiques*, Paris, Gallimard, 1957.

Vovelle, Michel, *Religion et révolution. La déchristianisation de l'an II*, Paris, Hachette, 1976.

Wade, Ira O., *The Intellectual Development of Voltaire*, Princeton, New Jersey, Princeton University Press, 1969.

Wall, Irwin M., *French Communism in the Era of Stalin. The Quest for Unity and Integration, 1945–1962*, Westport, Connecticut, Greenwood Press, 1983.

Weber, Eugen, *Action Française. Royalism and Reaction in Twentieth-Century France*, Stanford, Stanford University Press, 1962.

Weber, Eugen, "Fascism(s) and Some Harbingers," *The Journal of Modern History*, vol. LIV, no. 4 (December 1982), 746–65.

Weill, G., *Histoire du catholicisme libéral en France, 1828–1908*, Paris, Félix Alcan, 1909.

Williams, William H., "Voltaire and the Utility of the Lower Clergy," *Studies on Voltaire and the Eighteenth Century*, vol. LVIII (1967), 1869–91.

Wilson, Nelly, *Bernard-Lazare, Antisemitism and the Problem of Jewish Identity in Late Nineteenth-Century France*, Cambridge, Cambridge University Press, 1978.

Wilson, Stephen, *Ideology and Experience. Antisemitism in France at the Time of the Dreyfus Affair*, Rutherford, New Jersey, Fairleigh Dickinson University Press, 1982.

Winock, Michel, *Histoire politique de la revue 'Esprit' 1930–1950*, Paris, Editions du Seuil, 1975.

Woodrow, Alain, *L'Eglise déchirée*, Paris, Editions Ramsay, 1978.

Worker-Priests. A Collective Documentation, The (ed. John Petrie), London, Routledge and Kegan Paul, 1956.

Yardeni, Myriam, *La Conscience nationale en France pendant les guerres de religion (1559–1598)*, Louvain and Paris, Nauwelaerts, 1971.

Zeldin, Theodore (ed.), *Conflicts in French Society. Anticlericalism, Education and Morals in the Nineteenth Century*, London, George Allen and Unwin, 1970.

Zeldin, Theodore, *France 1848–1945*, Oxford, Clarendon Press, 1973–7, 2 volumes.

Index